*This book is dedicated to those who love food
and all the social rituals that surround it.*

The Best of
Annabel Langbein
Great Food for Busy Lives

AUTHOR
Annabel Langbein

PHOTOGRAPHY
Kieran Scott

KÖNEMANN

An Annabel Langbein book

By the same author
Annabel Langbein's Cookbook
Outdoors Cookbook
Smart Food For Busy People
Brilliant Budget Dining
More Taste Than Time
With Fork & Spoon

Published by The Culinary Institute Press

Design: Grace Design
Food Styling: Annabel Langbein
Editor: Louise Callan
Typesetting and Production: The Culinary Institute Press, Natalie Keys

The Culinary Insitute Press is the imprint of
The Culinary Institute of New Zealand Ltd.
PO Box 99068
Auckland
New Zealand

Production: Ursula Schümer
Printing and binding: Sing Cheong Printing Co. Ltd., Hong Kong
Printed in Hong Kong, China

ISBN 3-8290-3346-X

10 9 8 7 6 5 4 3 2 1

Contents

Introduction

When I first began cooking more than twenty years ago, I never imagined there would come a time when I might worry about what I was eating. Yet currently the world's food supply is at great risk. Our natural genetic base is fast disappearing into the hands of large conglomerates; while more and more natural varieties and species are being lost each year, we are being overwhelmed by genetically engineered foods with insufficient history to let us ascertain their long term effects on our bodies. Additionally, we face the growing issue of food safety – the proliferation of diseases such as BSE and *E.coli* which are the result of unnatural and unsustainable food production practices. Increasingly, irradiation is being used as a Band-aid to keep pathogens at bay, killing the life-giving properties of food as well as the toxins. I am also alarmed by the way our present society appears to be abandoning the skills and knowledge of the kitchen in favour of fast food takeouts and heavily processed foods. Convenience does have a useful place but it does not have to take over our lives, reducing meals to hurried snacks eaten in the car. The ritual of sitting together to share a daily meal was established as a means to nourish both the senses and the spirit; food is one of our greatest sensual pleasures. I was lucky to grow up in a household where food fresh from the garden marked the seasons and home-cooked meals were a pleasurable ritual that punctuated our daily lives. I do not believe it is too late to make a stand for real food – food which has been grown in a sustainable fashion by people who care and which does not use chemicals or processes which have long term negative effects on our fragile environment. Since the dawn of time, nature has provided us with extraordinary resources. It seems only right that we take a little care to choose and prepare our food, and then make the time to enjoy it. I hope this book will show you how easy it is to eat really well with very little effort.

Annabel Langbein

Starting Out

INGREDIENTS DIFFER FROM PLACE TO PLACE, STOVES DIFFER FROM KITCHEN TO KITCHEN, POTS AND PANS DIFFER DEPENDING ON THEIR CONSTRUCTION. ALL IN ALL, COOKING IS AN INEXACT BUSINESS AND EVEN THE BEST COOKS MAKE MISTAKES. BEING COMFORTABLE IN THE KITCHEN IS ABOUT BEING FAMILIAR WITH INGREDIENTS AND YOUR EQUIPMENT. WHEREVER POSSIBLE, SEEK OUT THE BEST QUALITY, AS THIS GIVES YOU AN ADVANTAGE FROM THE START. MAKE A COMMITMENT TO SUSTAINABLE AGRICULTURE AND BUY LOCAL ORGANICALLY GROWN FOOD WHENEVER YOU CAN.

Shopping

Always choose what looks really fresh, don't just shop for what is on your list. Buy in-season produce and wherever possible choose organically-grown food that is cultivated locally.

Timing

The most asked questions at my classes are always about timing – how to get everything on the table at the same time and looking terrific. When planning a meal you need to take into account all the components and create a work plan. Make a list of what has to be done and when. Wherever possible prepare and cook ahead so that the cooking you need to do at the last minute is reduced to a minimum.

Using a Recipe

Unless you are a very experienced cook you need to read recipes thoroughly before you start. Read the recipe aloud to yourself if need be, so you can follow the process and know where you are heading. I have tried to include as many helpful hints as possible along the way but, baking aside, cooking is not an exact business. The most important element you can bring to it is confidence, and the more you cook the easier it gets to make judgements about weights and measures, and food and flavour combinations.

Taste Your Food

Always taste food as you go and don't be afraid to add or change ingredients to suit your palate. Follow a recipe exactly, or you may prefer to give food your own individual stamp and treat the recipe much more as a guide.

Avoid Apologies

People are enormously grateful for the mere fact that you have gone to the effort to cook for them, so you don't need to start apologising...that the beans are over-cooked, the sauce is a little bit thicker and the pudding is dry. The power of suggestion is huge. Tell them the meal is tough and they will agree.

Setting the Table

Take a little time before friends or guests arrive to set an inviting table. Fresh flowers, clean shiny cutlery and glasses, and laundered napkins are little things, but they clearly say "I care". Food usually looks better on plain plates rather than brightly coloured ones. If the dinner is hot, then hot serving dishes and plates help keep it that way. Lighting sets the mood, so candles and indirect light provide a much more relaxing environment than a bright overhead light.

Symbol ✪

This symbol is used throughout the book to indicate a recipe that can be found in another place. Check the index for the page number.

The Essentials

Baking paper: This is extremely useful for saving on cleaning up time. Use it to line baking dishes before cooking chicken, meats and seafood, as well as for cakes and other baked items.

Blender: One piece of equipment that you'll really get mileage out of is a blender. Ultimately useful for puréeing sauces, soups, chopping up herbs and making pestos and dressings. A hand held immersion blender can be used directly in the cooking pot.

Bottle-opener: Get a good one and buy a wine sealer as well so you can use left-over wine.

Cake tins: Non-stick cake tins save hassle. Include a springform loose-bottomed cake tin to make turning out cakes easy.

Can-opener: The 20th century's key addition to the drawer of essential utensils. Wash well after use.

Casserole dish: Preferably one that can be used on top of the stove as well as in the oven.

Cheese grater: A hand held grater is ideal for fine shreds of parmesan cheese or carrot.

Chopping boards: Wood's antiseptic properties seem to keep bacteria at bay. Always wash well after use, especially after chopping raw meats, fish and poultry. Never chop vegetables or fruit on a board that has just been used for raw meat, fish or poultry, and never chop cooked meat on a board that has not been cleaned.

Chopsticks: Useful also for stirring pasta and noodles in the pot.

Citrus zester: This small hand held tool efficiently removes thin strips of citrus rinds without the bitter pith. Good also for scoring cucumbers.

Colander or sieve: Essential for draining pasta, rinsing and washing vegetables. The finer holes of a sieve are required for rice.

Corkscrew: Buy a good one. There's nothing worse than having to resort to pushing the cork into the bottle.

Ginger grater: A small ceramic grater that produces a fine paste of ginger with a couple of rubs across its nobbly surface. Available from Asian food stores.

Knives: Good knives are the cook's greatest ally. A sharp knife with good balance makes fast work of menial tasks. Invest in quality knives – one really good knife is far better than a set that looks good, but really doesn't do the job. First up, a 20-25cm chef's knife, next a thin bladed filleting knife and also a small paring knife. Store on a wall magnet or in a knife block where they won't get damaged and lose their edge. Find out from your local butcher when you can bring them to be sharpened, and get them sharpened about every 6 weeks.

Measuring cups and spoons: Imperative for baking and useful for everyday cooking until you get used to judging amounts by eye.

Mixing bowls: Have a selection, preferably ones which can also be used in the microwave.

Mortar and pestle: A bowl and pounding stick used to crush and grind. The ceramic ones are best as they don't absorb flavours. Crushing spices really brings out their flavours.

Olive and cherry pitter: A handy gadget to remove stones, if you happen to like olives and cherries.

Pepper grinder: Try before you buy as the quality varies tremendously.

Potato masher: The old fashioned wire coil variety delivers the best mash.

Pots and pans: Thin bottomed pots burn, pit and buckle which makes it nigh impossible to cook anything successfully. Heavy bottomed pots take longer to heat but carry their heat evenly. Aluminium pots can impart an off taste and acid foods actually strip the surface. It is especially important therefore never to marinate foods in an aluminium or tin pot. Buy the best pots you can afford. The following is an ideal basic set of pots and pans rather than an absolute basic: 1 extra large pot (for stocks, big soups, preserves and party fare), 1 large wok for stir-fries and quick pan dinners, 2 medium to large pots, 1-2 small pots, 1 heavy fry-pan that can double as an oven dish, and a small chef's omelette pan (available cheaply from chef's supply stores). Inexpensive bamboo steamers can be fitted on top of a pot and are found at Chinese food stores.

Pressure cooker: This is a great machine – ideal for speedily cooking tough meat cuts and pulses. If you like comfort food but never eat it because it takes too long to cook, buy a pressure cooker.

Salad spinner: Salad greens which have been washed and dried last for over a week in the fridge in an airtight container or plastic bag. If they are wet, they don't.

Scissors: Buy a heavy-duty kitchen pair for cutting up poultry, as well as baking paper.

Serving platters: Food always looks good on large flat white platters. Available inexpensively at Chinese grocers.

Spatulas and spoons: Get a flat metal spatula for turning foods, wooden spoons for stirring sauces (don't leave them in the pot while food cooks) and a large spoon to transfer food from pot to platter.

Splatter shield: This fine meshed cover lets frying food cook crisp and stops the splatter.

Timer: If your oven does not have one, buy a timer. Free your mind of worrisome thoughts like "When did I put that fillet of beef on"

Tongs: Who needs asbestos fingers. Get two or three sets.

Vegetable peeler: Keep two on hand – it's very boring when they break.

Wall magnet: This is the best way to store sharp knives. Tilt the blade away from the cutting edge to lift off magnet so as not to dull the edge.

Ovens

When you want to eat quickly, your heat sources need to deliver intense, fast heat. Gas gives the quickest heat and greatest control for stove top cooking. Ovens vary tremendously in their heating power. A fan forced oven heats up more quickly and tends to cook food more evenly than a conventional oven. Fan forced ovens deliver about 10-15% more heat than conventional ovens, so reduce cooking times by about 10%.

Freezer

It's easy for your freezer to end up being a cemetery for leftovers and forgotten 'specials'. Nothing freezes indefinitely and the more you open and shut the freezer, the greater the temperature fluctuations which cause deterioration in frozen foods. Throw out any foods which have 'freezer burn', have thawed partially, where ice has collected in their packet, or where they have been in the freezer longer than the time recommended by the manufacturer. As a guide, seafood will keep 1-2 months, poultry and pork up to 3 months, while lamb and beef keep much longer, as their fat does not break down like that of other foods.

Measures Used in This Book

- A standard metric cup equals 250mls
- 1 tbsp equals 15mls
- 1 tsp equals 5mls

If you do not have a metric measuring cup, use the same cup to measure with throughout the recipe.

Menu Planning

The best place to head before you start planning a menu is a market where you can see what is in season and is freshest. You don't need to choose expensive ingredients to create a wonderful meal, but you do need the best quality. In winter people prefer heartier foods, while in summer our preference is for lighter tastes. In terms of the meal, every course does not have to be a star – you can choose to put your energy into the main course and use fresh or store bought ingredients to start and end with (for example oysters, mussels and sushi to start and fresh fruits or a bought cake for dessert). In designing a meal, try and create a harmony of flavours, a good combination of textures and colours and a balance of heavy and light dishes. For instance, don't follow a creamy pasta sauce with a custard pudding, or a rich casserole with a baked pudding. At the end of a meal your guests should feel satisfied, not uncomfortable. Choose wines to match your meal that will compliment the flavours of the food. No rules apply – red wines sometimes go well with white meats and vice versa. In general, the bigger the flavours of a dish, the fuller the wine that will suit. Serve white wines lightly chilled and red wines at room temperature.

Pantry Power

HAVING A WELL-ORGANISED PANTRY OF LONG-LIFE DRY GOODS, SPICES, SEASONINGS, CANS AND
BASIC STAPLES LIKE RICE AND PASTA IS THE KEY TO SUCCESS IN MAKING GOOD FOOD FAST.
STOCKING YOUR CUPBOARD IN DIFFERENT ETHNIC STYLES, EG MEDITERRANEAN, ASIAN AND
MEXICAN, ALLOWS YOU TO CREATE DELICIOUS AND VARIED MEALS WITH LITTLE FORETHOUGHT.

Oils

Pure olive – cooking and frying; **Virgin and extra virgin olive** – salads, cold uses, dressing pasta, cooking vegetables; **Canola, Corn or Safflower** – flavourless, for Asian cooking and dressings; **Sesame** – hot and cold uses.

Vinegars

Red and white wine – wine-based sauces and mustard dressings; **Balsamic** – sweet aged vinegar, ideal for bitter greens, tomatoes or strawberries, and to finish casseroles and sauces; **Rice** – slightly sweet, aromatic vinegar, ideal for cooking and cold uses; **Flavoured, eg tarragon, raspberry** – use in sauces and dressings; **Chinese Black Vinegar** – use like balsamic vinegar in sauces.

Fresh Aromatics

Fresh ginger, garlic, spring onions and lemons, lemongrass, fresh lime and lemon leaves.

Flavour Pastes and Boosters

Seaweed, wasabi, tamarind, peanut butter, tahini, olives and capers. Miso, green curry paste, tomato paste, anchovies, pestos and olive pastes need to be refrigerated once opened.

Spices and Herbs

Buy spices regularly and keep sealed for freshness. Discard those which don't have any aroma when you open them. Freeze soft herbs puréed with a little oil or made into pesto, eg basil, coriander, parsley. Freeze woody herbs on the branch, eg thyme, etc. Purchase whole spices and toast and grind for more flavour, eg cumin and coriander seeds, etc. Spices such as fennel seeds, cardamoms, star anise, wasabi and saffron are a fast track to exotic flavours. Make up spice mixes, eg Cajun spice mix, or Moroccan spice mix, for easy anytime use.

Sauces

Soy, hoisin, black bean, oyster, fish, chilli (Thai brands), taco, hot pepper or Tabasco and bottled pasta sauce.

Dry Goods

Dried mushrooms, peanuts, cashews, pistachios, walnuts, sesame seeds (store nuts in fridge or freezer), Japanese short grain rice, Thai long grain rice, eg basmati or jasmine, brown rice, risotto rice, noodles, cornflour, rice flour, packaged stocks, semolina, polenta, tortillas, tacos.

Useful Cans

Tomatoes in juice, baby corn, straw and other canned mushrooms, water chestnuts, artichokes, beans and chickpeas, tuna, anchovies and smoked oysters or mussels.

Desserts

Meringues, brandy snaps, lady finger biscuits, biscotti, passionfruit pulp, apricot jam, pure vanilla essence, and canned fruit – apple slices, lychees, mandarins, mangoes.

Convenience Foods

If you have little time and the money and access to good convenience foods, buy them. There are some terrific products available now that take a lot of the time and effort out of home cooking. Fresh, vacuum packed, chilled stocks need to be kept in the fridge or frozen, but are infinitely preferable to stock powders.

Useful Freezer Supplies

Bacon, chicken livers, fresh parmesan cheese, frozen berries, frozen spinach, passionfruit pulp, pastry and filo pastry, smoked salmon, meat and fish stocks.

Fridge Fixings

WHEN YOU ARE TIRED AND HUNGRY, IT'S VIRTUALLY IMPOSSIBLE TO FEEL CREATIVE. YOU JUST WANT TO EAT RIGHT NOW, WITHOUT HAVING TO THINK ABOUT HOW OR WHAT. TAKING A LITTLE TIME EACH WEEK TO PREPARE FLAVOUR BASES SUCH AS TASTY PESTOS AND ENTICING DRESSINGS GREATLY STREAMLINES THE COOKING PROCESS AND HAS A DRAMATIC EFFECT ON THE RESULTS.

Roasted Garlic

Place peeled garlic cloves in an oven dish, pour over about $\frac{1}{2}$ cup olive oil and bake at 150°C for 35-45 minutes until tender. Store in the fridge. This garlic will be buttery and soft with a mild, sweet, nutty flavour that is a great addition to risottos and casseroles and as a spread for bruschetta and crostini.

Prepared Ginger

Store fresh whole pieces of ginger in the fridge wrapped in paper, or peel fresh ginger and store in sherry, vinegar or white wine.

Tapenade

Purée together 1 cup stoned Calamata olives, 1 tbsp crushed garlic, 4-6 anchovy fillets and 2 tbsp capers. Store in the fridge. Use in pastas, as a topping for steaks, mix into stuffings and fillings, and add as a flavour boost to casseroles.

Pesto

Delicious pestos can be made with a variety of fresh soft herbs. Simply blend the herbs with olive oil, garlic and other flavourings, eg parmesan, nuts, sun-dried tomatoes, etc.

Basil Pesto

Into a food processor place about 2 packed cups of basil leaves, 2 large cloves garlic, peeled and sliced, $\frac{3}{4}$ cup good quality olive oil, $\frac{1}{4}$ cup parmesan cheese, salt and pepper to taste, and $\frac{1}{4}$ cup toasted pinenuts or walnuts (optional). Purée until they form a smooth paste. Store in the fridge or freeze in small containers.

Winter Pesto

Into a food processor place a large bunch each of parsley and mint without stalks, 2-3 cloves garlic, $\frac{1}{4}$ cup freshly grated parmesan cheese, $\frac{1}{4}$ cup fresh shelled walnuts, $\frac{1}{2}$ cup olive oil and a pinch each of salt and pepper. Purée until smooth, adjusting the quantity of oil until it becomes a smooth soft paste. Makes about 1 cup. Mix will keep in the fridge for about 2 weeks. Spicy greens such as rocket or watercress can be used in place of parsley.

Asian Pesto

Use landcress or watercress to make this indispensable pesto. Boiling water fixes the colour of the herbs and prevents them from oxidising.
Wash a big bunch of cress and a whole coriander plant and remove and discard tough stems. Place in a heat-proof bowl and pour over boiling water to cover. Drain at once. Place in a blender with 2 cloves garlic, peeled, 2 small chillies, stems and seeds removed, $\frac{1}{4}$ cup roasted peanuts or roasted cashew nuts and $\frac{1}{4}$ cup salad oil. Purée all together until the mixture forms a smooth paste. Pesto will keep for 10-12 days in the fridge with a layer of oil on the top. Makes 1 cup.

Sun-dried Tomato Pesto

If you like sun-dried tomatoes, you'll find this a useful pesto. Into a food processor place $\frac{1}{2}$ cup sun-dried tomatoes in oil, 2 cloves garlic, $\frac{1}{4}$ cup olive oil, handful of fresh parsley sprigs (optional) and a pinch each of salt and pepper. Purée until smooth. Nuts such as toasted almonds or walnuts may be added as desired, thinning with more oil as needed. Makes $\frac{3}{4}$ cup. Store in the fridge. Without parsley, mix will keep indefinitely; with parsley it will last about 2 weeks.

Roasted Peppers

This is an excellent way to preserve peppers when they are in peak supply. Wash red, yellow or green peppers and place in a 250°C oven for 15-20 minutes until they start to blister and brown. Remove and place in a covered container or plastic bag until cool enough to handle. Remove skin, seeds and pith from peppers under cold running water. Slice peppers into strips and mix with a little olive oil. Refrigerate for up to 1 week or freeze.

Salsa Verde

This useful green sauce is a summer fridge staple. Purée together 1 packed cup parsley leaves, ½ packed cup mint leaves, 1 bunch chopped chives, ¾ cup olive oil, ¼ cup capers, 3 cloves garlic, 2 tsp Dijon mustard, 2-3 tbsp lemon juice, ¼ medium onion, chopped and a small can of anchovies. Store in the fridge. Keeps for several weeks. Makes about 1½ cups.

Caramelized Onions

This wonderful condiment is likely to become a kitchen staple. It goes well with bread, pastry, cheese and meats. It can be used as the basis of a great onion soup, as a sauce for grills and steaks and as a yummy pie filling. To make, use the recipe on page 108. Adding a tablespoon of mustard seed to the onions when they cook is also delicious. Cover and chill. They will keep for about 2 weeks.

Hot and Spicy Red Salsa

A useful summer salsa to make when peppers are cheap and plentiful. Purée flesh of 3 roasted peppers (see above for method), pith and seeds removed, with 2 cloves garlic, 1-2 tbsp hot pepper or hot chilli sauce to taste, salt to taste, 1 tsp fine black pepper, ¼ cup olive oil and 1 large bunch of coriander leaves and soft stems. Blend until smooth. It will keep for 2 weeks in the fridge. Makes about 1½ cups.

Harissa

From the heart of North African cooking comes this spicy red-hot paste. Its fiery lift adds wonderful richness. In a dry fry-pan heat 2 tsp each of cumin and coriander seeds, 1 tsp garlic flakes and 1 tsp cayenne pepper. Stir over medium heat for about 1 minute until the smell of the spices starts to flow – don't let them burn. Grind finely in a mortar and pestle then place in blender with the flesh of 2 roasted red peppers or 1 cup tomato purée. Purée until smooth, season to taste. Spoon into a jar, cover with a layer of oil and refrigerate. Makes about 1¼ cups. Harissa will keep for several weeks in the fridge.

Home-made Mayonnaise

Place 2 tsp dry mustard, 1 tsp salt, ½ tsp white pepper, 1 tsp sugar, ¼ cup lemon juice, ½ finely grated lemon rind and 3 egg yolks in a blender and blend to mix. With the motor running, add about 2 cups of canola or soy oil slowly in a thin stream until it is fully incorporated and the mayonnaise is very thick. Makes 3 cups. Mayonnaise can be thinned with hot water. Kept refrigerated, it lasts about 4 weeks.

Aïoli

Prepare home-made mayonnaise using olive oil instead of canola oil, add 1 extra egg yolk and blend in 3 cloves of crushed garlic.

Variations:
● *Saffron Aïoli – Add 10-12 threads of finely crumbed saffron to aïoli.*
● *Roasted Garlic Aïoli – In place of fresh garlic, blend in the flesh of 1 head of roasted garlic.*
● *Chilli Lime Aïoli – Use 3 tbsp lime juice in place of lemon juice, the finely grated rind of ½ lime and ½-1 small red chilli, finely chopped.*

Basic Vinaigrette Dressing

Combine in a jar 3 tbsp spiced vinegar or lemon juice, ½ cup extra virgin olive oil, ½ tsp each mustard and sugar, and salt and pepper to taste. Store in the fridge. It will keep for weeks.

Favourite Vinaigrette Dressing

Shake together 1 broken fresh free-range egg yolk, ⅓ cup soy or salad oil, 2 tbsp red or white wine vinegar, 1 tsp Dijon mustard, 1 tsp brown sugar, juice of ½ lemon, and salt and ground black pepper to taste. Keep chilled and use within 24 hours of making. Makes about ½ cup.

Useful Preserves

RETURN TO THE OLD FASHIONED RITUALS OF GOOD HOUSEKEEPING WITH A RANGE OF SCRUMPTIOUS HOME-MADE PRESERVES. A STORE OF YOUR OWN CONDIMENTS ALLOWS YOU TO GIVE FOOD A VERY PERSONAL TOUCH AND PROVIDES A SUPPLY OF GREAT GIFTS.

Pickled Lemons

This is great to make when lemons are plentiful. Pickled lemons are useful to add to casseroles, salads, fish or vegetable dishes, and make a great condiment for summer barbecues.

To Prepare: 10 minutes
Time Until Ready: at least a week

> *6 lemons*
> *6 tbsp coarse salt*
> *a little paprika*
> *a couple of bay leaves*
> *soy or corn oil to cover*

Cut lemons in wedges and freeze until firm. Take out of freezer, put on a shallow tray, sprinkle with salt and leave for about an hour. Layer the wedges into sterilised jars, sprinkling a little paprika between each and pour on any brine that has collected on the plate. Tuck in a bay leaf or two, cover with soy or corn oil and leave for about a week. They will keep 3-4 months in the fridge. The liquid is a good alternative to vinegar in dressings. To use, discard the pulp and slice rinds finely. Makes 1 big jar.

Red Pepper Sauce

This brilliant red sauce is so useful. Its sweet spicy flavour makes a terrific partner for cooked chicken or lamb as well as pasta. Thinned with vinaigrette it makes a sparky dressing.

To Prepare: 15 minutes
To Cook: about 1¼ hours

> *16-20 red or yellow peppers*
> *2 cups cider or rice vinegar*
> *2 cups white wine vinegar*
> *6 cups sugar*
> *1 tsp salt*

Above: Red Pepper Sauce, Preserved Figs and Tomato Kasundi

Remove seeds and roughly chop peppers. Put in a large heavy saucepan with cider or rice vinegar and white wine vinegar. Bring to the boil. Reduce heat and simmer for 15 minutes. Transfer to food processor and process until smooth. Return juice to washed saucepan, add sugar and salt and stir over low heat until sugar dissolves. Gradually bring to the boil and simmer very gently for a further 15-20 minutes until lightly thickened. Ladle into warm, sterilised glass containers or jars and seal while hot. Makes 6 medium jars.

Right: Chilli Jam with Grilled Crayfish

Tomato Kasundi

Adapted from Attai Hosian and Sita Pasricha's *Indian Cooking*, this wonderful aromatic sauce offers a stunning blend of flavours. You won't make another tomato sauce once you have discovered this one, and you can use it in so many ways, as a flavour booster and a sauce. Traditionally Indian pickles and chutneys use an enormous amount of oil. I have reduced the oil by over half with no loss of flavour.

To Prepare: 20 minutes
To Cook: 40-45 minutes
Time Until Ready: 2 weeks

> 225g green ginger, peeled
> 100g garlic cloves, peeled
> 50g green chillies, sliced in half
>   lengthwise, seeds removed
> 2½ cups malt vinegar
> 1 cup canola or safflower oil
> 2 tbsp turmeric
> 5 tbsp ground cumin
> 3 tbsp chilli powder
> 5 tbsp mustard seeds, ground to a
>   powder
> 2kg tomatoes, washed and chopped
> 2¼ cups sugar
> about 3 tbsp salt

Purée the ginger, garlic and chillies with a little of the vinegar to make a paste. Heat the oil in a very big pot or preserving pan. Add all the ground spices and fry until they exude a fragrant aroma. Add the puréed paste, tomatoes, the rest of the vinegar, sugar and half of the salt (check near the end of cooking to see if more is required). Cook over a low heat, stirring occasionally, until the oil floats on the top (about half an hour). Bottle in sterilised jars while hot with a thin film of hot oil on the top of each jar (to prevent top from drying out) and cover with screw-top seal lids. Leave for a couple of weeks for flavours to develop before using. Stored in a cool place, it will keep indefinitely. Makes about 2 litres.

Chilli Jam

With a jar of this on hand, great tasting meals just don't get any simpler. Slather over fish before roasting or grilling, or serve on the side. It keeps in the fridge for months.

To Prepare: 15 minutes
To Cook: 1½ hours

> 4 onions, peeled and chopped
> 8 cloves garlic, crushed
> 8 small red chillies, stems removed
> 2 red peppers, cut in strips
> 1 cup vegetable oil
> 2 tbsp tamarind concentrate
> ¼ cup packed brown sugar
> 2 tbsp fish sauce

Place onions, garlic, chillies, peppers and oil in a large heavy pot. Cook slowly for 30-40 minutes until onion is very soft. Purée. Return to the pot with tamarind, sugar and fish sauce and cook a further 45-50 minutes until very thick, stirring occasionally, taking care the mixture does not catch. Store in the fridge. Spoon a little oil over the top to form a film. Chilli Jam will keep for over a month.

Preserved Figs

Preserved in a heavy sugar syrup with ginger, lemon and a little dash of vinegar, these figs are unbelievably good. It is worth going out of your way to get fresh mascarpone to serve with them. Greek yoghurt is good but mascarpone is better.

To Prepare: 10 minutes
To Cook: 3½ hours

> 3 lemons, halved and thinly sliced
> 50g preserved ginger
> 300mls malt vinegar
> 1.2 litres water
> 3¼kg sugar
> 6kg figs

Place the sliced lemons, ginger, vinegar, water and sugar in a large preserving pan or pot. Bring to a boil, stirring until sugar has dissolved. Add figs and simmer gently for 3 hours until figs are soft. Bottle in about eight sterilised preserving jars, filled to overflowing with a little syrup or boiling water and sealed. Wipe jars clean and store in a cool dark place.

Pickled Watermelon Rind

Try and find organically grown melons for this delicious and pretty pickle. It is wonderful with cold meats, terrines and pâtés, and also makes a great gift. Best of all, you get to eat the watermelon first.

To Prepare: ½ hour, plus overnight soaking
To Cook: 30 minutes
Time Until Ready: 1 week

> rind of 1 large watermelon
> ¼ cup salt
> 1 litre water

Pickling Syrup
> 5 cups sugar
> 3 cups white wine vinegar
> 4 cups water
> 1 lemon thinly sliced
> 2-3 whole cinnamon quills
> 1 tsp whole cloves

> 1 tbsp whole allspice

Cut the flesh from the rind of the melon leaving just a hint of pink. Cut rind into strips about 1cm wide and 4-5cm long and place in a non-corrosive container. Mix through the salt and water and soak overnight. Next day, drain the rind, put into a pot, cover with cold water and simmer for 30 minutes, or until the skin is easily pierced with a pin. Combine all the pickling syrup ingredients in a large pot or preserving pan. Add the drained rind and simmer until it is translucent. Pour into hot sterilised jars and cover with syrup. Cover with screw-top seal lids and leave at least a week before eating. Pickle will keep for months in a cool place. Once opened, store in the fridge.

Pete's Lemon Pickle

This wonderful yellow lemon pickle from talented cook Peter Johnstone goes well with cold meats, chicken and fish.

To Prepare: 5 minutes
To Cook: about 1 hour

> 2 whole lemons, chopped and pips
>   removed
> 5 large onions, roughly chopped
> 4 cups white vinegar
> 1 cup lemon juice
> 3 tsp salt
> 5 cups sugar
> 1 tsp turmeric
> 4 tsp horseradish
> finely grated rind of 2 lemons
> 5-6 cloves garlic, crushed
> 2 tsp ground ginger

Purée lemons and onions with some of the vinegar until very smooth. Place in a large non-corrosive pot with all other ingredients and bring to a boil. Reduce heat to a simmer and cook for about 45 minutes until reduced to a spoonable consistency. Bottle while hot in sterilised jars.

APPETISERS AND SNACKS

Goat's Cheese
Pesto Tartlets

Pita Pizzas

Anne's Croûtons

Cheese and Almond Dreams

Cheese Straws

Crostini

Boursin Cheese

Blue Cheese Dip

Canapés

Cream Cheese Schmear

Cashew and Cream Cheese Pesto

Feta and Fennel Spread

Hummus

Smoked Mussel and Chilli Pâté

Smoked Mackerel Pâté

White Bean Spread

Dukkah

Hot Cheese Dip

Classic Country Terrine

Greek Pumpkin Spread

Vegetable Crudités

BBQ Pita Bread

Garlic Pita Crisps

Poppadom Bites

Cheat's Lavosh

Greek Roasted Minted Carrots

Roasted Eggplant

Roasted Asparagus or Green Beans

Fritters

Herb Pikelets

Pan Bagna

Platters

Thai Prawn Fritters

Chilled Oysters with Asian Dressing

Oysters on the Half Shell with Sour
Cream and Smoked Salmon

Rock Oysters with
Spinach and Bacon

Sushi Rice

Sesame Sushi Rice Balls

Salmon and Avocado Sushi Rolls

Sushi Dipping Sauce

Whitebait Fritters

Mussels on the Half Shell with
Pesto Vinaigrette

Vodka Cured Salmon
or Trout

Horseradish Cream

Vietnamese Glass
Noodle Rolls

Sludgy Margaritas

DIY Dirty Martini

Champagne Cocktails

Champagne Bellinis

Cuban Mojito

60s Fruit Punch

Summer Passion

Seabreeze Cocktail

Summer Sangria

Hot Baked

Hot crispy bites of flavour are a great way to whet the appetite before a meal.
These quick, easy recipes are ideal fare for parties and can be prepared ahead for last
minute re-heating. Most of these items also freeze well.

Goat's Cheese Pesto Tartlets

The mini tart pans or muffin trays can be lined with pastry and chilled or frozen, so all you need to do is pull them out, pop in the filling and bake them.

To Prepare: 5 minutes
To Cook: 12-15 minutes

> 250g savoury shortcrust pastry
> 120-150g soft goat's cheese or feta
> 4 tbsp pesto

Roll out pastry thinly and cut into small rounds to line base and sides of 24 mini muffin cups. Chill. Fill each with small pieces of goat's cheese and top with about $1/2$ tsp pesto. Bake at 220°C for 12-15 minutes. Serve hot or warm. Makes 24.

Pita Pizzas

Pita breads make quick easy pizza bases. Spread mixture over individual pitas. Bake at 220°C for 10-15 minutes or until topping is cooked through and lightly golden brown. Each of the following toppings will make enough for about 12 mini pizzas. Serve whole or in wedges.

Variations:
- *Spinach and Blue Cheese:* Blend $1/2$ cup cooked chopped spinach, squeezed dry, 100g blue cheese, crumbled, and 3 tbsp sour cream.
- *Mediterranean Topping:* Prepare Tapenade.❂ Spread over pita breads and top with goat's cheese.

- *Shrimp and Mozzarella:* Mix $2/3$ cup prepared tomato pasta sauce, 100g chopped shrimps, $3/4$ cup grated mozzarella cheese, 1 tsp oregano.
- *Smoked Salmon and Sour Cream:* Spread toasted pita breads with sour cream, then top with sliced smoked salmon and garnish with fresh dill.

Anne's Croûtons

My mother makes incredibly moreish croûtons using very thinly sliced French bread. Stored in an airtight container they will keep for weeks – if they last that long. Great for pre-dinner drinks and to serve with soup.

To Prepare: 15 minutes
To Cook: about 1 hour

> 1 small loaf of soft crusted French bread, very thinly sliced
> 400g grated tasty cheese
> 75g cold grated butter
> *Optional:* 2 tsp Vegemite, miso or pesto, or other flavour paste

Grate the cheese and butter in layers into a microwave bowl and microwave for 30 seconds to soften slightly. Don't overdo it. Mix the cheese, butter and optional spread with a heavy spoon to evenly combine. Spread a little onto each piece of bread. Place on a baking tray spread side up and bake at 130°C for about 1 hour until crisp, dry and crunchy. Makes about 50. Store in an airtight container.

An Easy Shortcrust Pastry

For an easy shortcrust pastry blend 2 cups high grade flour with a pinch of salt and 125g cold diced butter in the food processor and then mix in $1/2$ cup cold water to make a softish dough. Makes about 500 grams.

Chill Out

Pastry needs to be chilled before it is cooked to prevent shrinking and toughness. Press into tins and refrigerate for half an hour or freeze for 15 minutes.

Opposite: Goat's Cheese Pesto Tartlets

Previous page: Herb Pancakes topped with Smoked Salmon and Artichokes.

Right: Cheese and Almond Dreams

Cheese and Almond Dreams

Here's a scrummy filling from friend and one time caterer, Allison Budd in Toronto. Have it made up ready for crisp bread cases or pile on toasts then quickly bake. It keeps for about a week in the fridge.

To Prepare: 5 minutes

To Cook: 8-10 minutes

> *3 dozen bread cases (see side panel)*
> *300g grated tasty cheese*
> *½ cup toasted slivered almonds, chopped*
> *3 rashers bacon, cooked and crumbled*
> *2 egg yolks*
> *2 tsp mustard*
> *½ cup mayonnaise*

Mix all the filling ingredients together. Put walnut-sized nuggets into pre-cooked bread cases and bake at 180°C for 8-10 minutes. Makes 3 dozen.

Cheese Straws

An all-time favourite, cheese straws take just a few minutes to prepare in a blender. The mixture of equal parts flour, butter and grated cheese can be used to make straws or flat biscuits or rolled around pitted olives.

To Prepare: 5 minutes

To Cook: 12-15 minutes

> *250g each plain flour, grated tasty cheese and frozen butter*
> *1 tsp salt and a pinch cayenne*

Place flour and cheese in a blender. Grate over frozen butter. Add salt and cayenne. Blend until mixture forms a ball. Turn mixture onto a lightly floured board or chill if not using at once. Roll out to 1cm thickness. Cut into finger-sized strips or other shapes. Chill for 10 minutes before cooking. Bake at 200°C for 15-20 minutes until golden. Stored in an airtight container, biscuits will keep for 2 weeks. Refresh in a hot oven for a few minutes if needed. Makes about 40.

Crisp Bread Cases

Butter thin slices of white bread or spray with olive oil spray. Press into small muffin tins, butter side down, to fit base and sides. Bake at 160°C for 20-30 minutes until crisp. Store in an airtight container. Refresh in a hot oven for 5 minutes if stale. They will keep in a cool place for several weeks. Can also be frozen.

Re-heating Pastry

Re-heat pastry based appetisers and fritters in a 200°C oven for about 5-8 minutes.

Opposite: Crostini with assorted toppings

CROSTINI

Crostini, Italian for little snacks, originated as a clever way to use up stale bread. Simply brushing slices of French bread with a little olive oil and toasting, grilling or baking for 5-10 minutes produces a crisp base that won't fall apart when people eat them. Alternatively, you can fry sliced French bread with a touch of olive oil until golden on each side. Store in an airtight tin and refresh in a warm oven if they become a little stale. Add a selection of tempting toppings and serve.

- Cream cheese, roasted peppers and anchovies
- Sun-dried tomato pesto, marinated mozzarella and watercress
- Smoked salmon, mashed egg flavoured with horseradish and radish, spring onion garnish
- Tapenade, roasted peppers or roasted eggplant and anchovy
- Prosciutto with mozzarella and watercress
- Goat's cheese, pesto and watercress
- Smoked salmon, Tapenade, red onion and capers
- Hummus, sundried tomatoes and pesto

- Rocket, mozzarella and spicy sausage
- Pesto, tomato and Brie
- Roasted pepper, cream cheese and anchovy
- Roasted eggplant and pesto
- Cream Cheese Schmear and smoked salmon
- Walnut Paste, matchstick-cut cheese and rocket
- Olive paste, goat's cheese and roasted peppers
- Pesto and semi-dried or slow-roasted tomatoes
- Roasted courgettes, pesto, salami and marinated mushrooms
- Feta and Fennel Spread, salami and roasted peppers

Spread It Around

KEEP A SUPPLY OF USEFUL CANS IN THE PANTRY TO MAKE SPREADABLE,
DUNKABLE INSTANT SNACKS AND FINGER FOOD. MAKE TWO OR THREE DIPS OR SPREADS FOR AN
ANTIPASTO PLATTER AND SERVE WITH BREADS AND CRISP VEGETABLES.

Boursin Cheese

Freezing Cheese

Grated cheddar freezes well, so does parmesan. Spread on a tray to freeze, then free flow into bags and seal. Use straight from the freezer.

This versatile spread is great on bread or crackers. Use it also as a tangy filling for chicken breasts, melted over steaks for a quick sauce, or piled onto a mixed platter with roasted and fresh vegetables, breads and olives.

To Prepare: 5 minutes

> *250g cream cheese*
> *2 cloves chopped garlic*
> *4 fillets of anchovies*
> *1 tbsp capers*
> *1/4 - 1/2 cup cream*
> *2 tsp chopped fresh tarragon or
>   parsley*

Anchovy Storage

Store canned or bottled anchovies in the fridge once opened. Kept covered with oil, they will last for months.

Purée together all ingredients. Thin to taste with extra cream for a dipping sauce. Mixture will keep for a week in the fridge. Makes 1¼ cups.

Below: Canapé with roasted red peppers, cream cheese and anchovies

Blue Cheese Dip

Any kind of blue cheese can be used – some are stronger than others.

To Prepare: 5 minutes

> *150g blue cheese*
> *100g cream cheese*
> *1 tsp dijon mustard*
> *dash Tabasco or hot sauce*

Blend the cheeses and mustard until smooth, season with Tabasco to taste. Serve with crackers and crisp vegetables. Makes about 2 cups. Store in the fridge.

Canapés

If you have some cream cheese in the fridge, or one of the flavoured cream cheeses included in this section, you can whip up tasty canapés at the drop of a hat. The combinations are as endless as your imagination – you might like to try some of the crostini topping ideas mentioned on the previous page. One of my favourite combinations is cream cheese with strips of roasted red peppers and anchovies. Use a variety of bases – bread, toast, crostini, or small crackers.

Cream Cheese Schmear

One great schmear. Don't just think bagels. Spread it on anything.

To Prepare: 5 minutes

> 150g smoked salmon pieces
> 250g cream cheese
> dash of lemon juice
> ground black pepper
> Optional: 2 tbsp capers

Purée all ingredients. It will keep for 4-5 days in the fridge.

Cashew and Cream Cheese Pesto

Here's an elegant spread with a subtle creamy texture.

To Prepare: 5 minutes

> 100g roasted, salted cashew nuts
> 500g cream cheese
> 1 tbsp basil or other herb pesto
> few grinds of black pepper
> a little cream to thin

Blend together all ingredients. Thin to taste with cream. Makes about 2½ cups. Store in the fridge for up to a week.

Feta and Fennel Spread

Another scrumptious spread that exploits the versatility of feta cheese.

To Prepare: 5 minutes

> 1 tbsp fennel seeds
> 250g feta cheese
> a little water

Toast fennel seeds in a dry fry-pan over medium heat until they start to pop. Place on a chopping board and crush with a rolling pin. Combine in the bowl of a food processor with feta cheese, adding a little cold water until you have a smooth creamy texture. Store in refrigerator until ready to use. Makes about 1½ cups. It will keep for several weeks in the fridge in a covered container.

Variation: Use 1 tbsp chopped fresh rosemary in place of fennel seeds.

Above: Cream Cheese Schmear, Cashew and Cream Cheese Pesto and Feta and Fennel Dip

Marinating Feta Cheese

This is so easy to do and so tasty. Cut up cubes of feta and layer into a jar with flavours such as rosemary, chilli, garlic and peppercorns. Cover with oil and keep in a cool cupboard.

Marinating Olives

Cover olives with oil and add flavours of your choice. Try green olives with strips of orange rind and a few crushed cardamoms. Black olives are delicious with a couple of dried chillies, rosemary and 3-4 peeled garlic cloves. Leave at least 1 week before using. They will keep for months in oil mix.

Right: Hummus and Cheese Straws

Freezing Dips

Dips like Hummus, Smoked Mackerel Pâté, White Bean Spread, Chicken Liver Pâté and Greek Pumpkin Spread all freeze well. For convenience, freeze in small serving containers, tightly covered with plastic wrap.

Hummus

Make this easy purée with canned or home cooked chick peas.

To Prepare: 5 minutes

> *2 cups cooked chickpeas (2 x 310g cans rinsed and drained)*
> *3 cloves garlic, chopped*
> *2 tsp ground cumin*
> *pinch cayenne pepper*
> *¼ cup extra virgin olive oil*
> *1 tsp sesame oil*
> *2 tbsp lemon juice*
> *salt and ground black pepper*
> *Optional: 1-2 tbsp tahini*

Blend together all ingredients until smooth. Hummus will keep 4-5 days in fridge and freezes well. Makes 2 big cups.

Smoked Mussel and Chilli Pâté

Made using the same method as in the following recipe for Smoked Mackerel Pâté, but substitute 125g smoked mussels for smoked fish and add 1 tsp each of crushed garlic and chilli paste.

Smoked Mackerel Pâté

This lemony smoked fish pâté makes great use of any hot-smoked fish. Serve it with crackers or as part of a platter.

To Prepare: 5 minutes

> *200g smoked mackerel or other hot-smoked fish, flaked, no bones or skin*
> *250g light cream cheese*
> *¼ cup lemon juice*
> *ground black pepper*
> *a good pinch cayenne pepper*

Place half the smoked fish in a blender with cream cheese, lemon juice, freshly ground black pepper and cayenne pepper to taste. Purée until smooth. Mix in remaining flaked fish. Pâté will keep 5-7 days in the fridge. Makes 2 cups. Freezes well.

White Bean Spread

Delicious and nutritious, a spread that can also be served hot with meat.

To Prepare: 15 minutes

> 2 x 310g cans white beans, rinsed
> and drained
> 1/4 cup extra virgin olive oil
> 2 cloves garlic, crushed
> 1 bay leaf
> 1 tsp fresh rosemary or thyme
> leaves
> juice and finely grated rind of
> 1/2 lemon
> salt and ground black pepper

Place beans in a microwave bowl or saucepan with olive oil, garlic, bay leaf and rosemary or thyme. Microwave covered on full power for 4-5 minutes, or cook in a saucepan over low heat for 5 minutes. Lift out and discard bay leaf. Purée mixture in a blender with lemon juice and rind, salt and pepper, adding a little olive oil or water as desired to get a smooth creamy texture. Allow to cool, then refrigerate. Spread will keep in the fridge for 4-5 days and freezes well. Makes 3 cups.

Dukkah

This wonderful dry Egyptian spiced nut mix is served with bread and a bowl of good olive oil. Dip bread into oil then dukkah. It will keep in a jar for weeks. Useful also as a topping to coat fish or chicken.

To Prepare: 5 minutes
To Cook: 15 minutes

> 1 cup hazelnuts
> 1/4 cup sesame seeds
> 1 cup almonds
> 1 tbsp coriander seeds
> 1 tbsp cumin powder
> 1 tsp sea salt
> 1 tbsp sweet paprika
> 1 tsp turmeric

Pre-heat oven to 160°C. Put the nuts and seeds on an oven tray, bake for 15 minutes, and do the same with the spices. Remove from oven and cool. When cold, put all ingredients into the food processor and pulse until the mixture is crumbly. Pause between pulses to prevent overheating and therefore oiling up the mixture. Makes 2 1/2 cups.

Hot Cheese Dip

A deliciously different hot dip to serve with corn chips or breads.

To Prepare: 5 minutes
To Cook: 10 minutes

> 1 onion, finely diced
> 1 red pepper, finely diced
> 1 tbsp tomato paste
> 1 tsp crushed garlic
> 1 tsp chilli paste
> 2 tbsp olive oil
> 1 cup tasty cheese, grated
> 1 cup cream

Gently cook onion, red pepper, tomato paste, garlic and chilli paste in olive oil for about 10 minutes until onions are softened. Mix in cheese and cream and cook over a low heat until the cheese has melted and the sauce is thick. Serve hot with corn chips or vegetable crudités.

MENU IDEAS

After Work Drinks

platter of 3 spreads with breads
and crispbreads

goat's cheese pesto tartlets

oysters on the half shell with
balsamic vinegar

A Quick Chicken Liver Pâté

Heat 3 tbsp butter in a large fry-pan. Cook 500g cleaned and halved chicken livers, 2 rashers diced bacon, 1 clove crushed garlic for 3-4 minutes until livers are just pink in the centre. Add 2 tbsp brandy. Purée mixture with 1 tbsp fresh thyme, finely grated rind of 1/2 lemon and salt and pepper. Chill till ready to use. Freezes.

Classic Country Terrine

Terrines have the virtue of improving with age – at their best after 3-4 days.

To Prepare: 20 minutes

To Cook: about 1 hour

50g butter
250g chicken livers, cleaned
2 cloves garlic, crushed
1 onion, finely diced
2 tsp thyme leaves
1 cup fresh breadcrumbs
700g minced pork
1 tsp nutmeg, preferably fresh,
    finely grated
1/2 tsp allspice
1 tsp fine black pepper
2 tsp salt
2 eggs
1/4 cup port or brandy or sherry
2-3 bay leaves to garnish the top

Pre-heat oven to 180°C. Heat half the butter and cook livers over high heat for a minute until just browned each side. Remove from pan and chop up roughly. Add rest of butter, garlic and onion to pan and cook gently until soft. Mix onion and livers with all other ingredients except bay leaves using a heavy spoon. Press mixture into a greased 1.5 litre bak-ing dish or cast iron pan. Press bay leaves into the top. Cover with tinfoil or a lid. Place dish in a roasting pan and pour hot water around until it reaches half-way up the sides of the terrine dish. Bake for 1 hour or until a skewer inserted into the middle comes out clean and hot. Take ter-rine out of the oven and weight with cans or a filled bottle. Allow to cool overnight. It will keep in the fridge for about 7 days. Freezes well.

Greek Pumpkin Spread

This is good as a spread, or heated and served as a vege purée.

To Prepare: 10 minutes

To Cook: 8 minutes microwave, about 30 minutes oven

2 cups pumpkin (500g), diced,
    olive oil to drizzle over
1 tsp each of fennel and cumin
    seeds
1/2 cup feta cheese
salt and ground black pepper

Cook pumpkin on high in microwave in a covered dish for 8 minutes or roast at 200°C until tender. Heat fry-pan and toast fennel and cumin seeds over a medi-um heat until they start to pop. Do not burn. Put feta cheese and all other ingre-dients into blender. Purée until smooth. Add salt and black pepper to taste. Makes 3 1/2 cups. Freezes well.

Healthy Snacks for Kids

You don't have to rely on processed convenience foods to whet children's appetites, or when you need kids' snacks fast. Children always like foods that have been cut up or made into special shapes – sticks of carrot, celery and red pepper, cubes of cheese and crostini topped with things they like such as peanut butter. Popcorn is an excellent low fat snack that's quick and fun to make. Toss it with cinnamon sugar or finely chopped fried bacon. My children love Anne's Croûtons, Cheese Straws made without the cayenne pepper and fritters.

Below: Classic Country Terrine with Pickled Watermelon Rind

Dippers

WHETHER IT'S A PARTY, OR SIMPLY DINNER WITH FRIENDS, PARTNERING FLAVOURSOME DIPS AND SPREADS WITH A RANGE OF FRESH VEGETABLES, POPPADOMS, AND BAKED AND GRILLED BREADS IS A FUN, EASY WAY TO START A MEAL.

Vegetable Crudités

A platter laden with assorted fresh vegetables and a couple of delicious dips makes a great first course.

- *Baby potatoes, yams: scrub and simmer until just cooked then cool.*
- *Snow peas, courgettes and asparagus: drop in boiling water for 30 seconds, then refresh in iced water.*
- *Broccoli florets, cauliflower florets, green beans, broad beans: drop in boiling water for 1-2 minutes, then refresh in iced water.*
- *Carrots, celery, peppers, green onions: place in iced water to crisp.*
- *Mushrooms: marinate or serve raw.*
- *Cherry tomatoes and cucumbers: serve raw.*
- *Red peppers: serve raw or roasted in slices.*

Cheat's Lavosh

An easy shortcut to making crisp, thin lavosh-like flatbreads. Once made, they will keep for several weeks in an airtight container in a cool place and can be refreshed in a hot oven in 3-4 minutes.

Cut fresh tortillas into long thin wedges. Brush one side of each wedge with beaten egg. Sprinkle egg side generously with poppy seeds or sesame seeds. Place on a baking tray and bake at 200°C for 10-12 minutes until crisp.

BBQ Pita Bread

Great to serve with any kind of dip or spread.

To Prepare: 5 minutes
To Cook: 4 minutes

> *4 pieces pita bread*
> *50g butter, softened*
> *2 tsp crushed garlic*
> *2 tbsp chopped fresh herbs, eg parsley, basil, thyme, oreganum*

Combine the butter, garlic and herbs and spread over both sides of the pita bread. Place on the barbecue and grill for 1-2 minutes each side. Cut in wedges to serve.

Garlic Pita Crisps

Split large pita breads, cut into triangles and brush both sides of each piece liberally with garlic-flavoured oil (mix 2 tsp crushed garlic with ³⁄₄ cup olive oil). Place in a single layer on a baking tray and bake at 150°C for about 20-30 minutes until crisp. Store in an airtight container.

Poppadom Bites

Cut each poppadom into 4-6 wedges. Place on a paper towel in microwave. Microwave for about 1 minute until bubbled and crisp. Repeat for the remaining poppadoms until all are cooked. Cooked poppadoms will keep crisp in a tightly sealed container for about 1 week. Re-crisp in the microwave for a few seconds or in a 200°C oven for 5 minutes.

Melba Toast

Toast white sandwich bread in a toaster. Split in half through the width of the bread, remove crusts, cut into triangles and bake at 150°C for about 30 minutes until dry and crisp. Store in an airtight container.

Roasting Vegetables for flavour

Roasted vegetables have a wonderfully dense flavour and texture. Asparagus, mushrooms, green beans, peppers, carrots and eggplant are some of the vegetables that roast well. Use them in salads, on platters and as snack food in the fridge.

Great Grazing

A BIG PLATTER PILED HIGH WITH TASTY MORSELS MAKES GREAT FINGER FOOD OR

CASUAL BUFFET FARE. FOR A CROWD, SERVE A COUPLE OF MIXED PLATTERS WITH A BAKED GLAZED

HAM, A ROUND OF BRIE AND CRUSTY BREADS.

Greek Roasted Minted Carrots

Serve as part of any platter or toss through a salad.

To Prepare: 10 minutes
To Cook: 35-45 minutes

> 6 large juicy carrots, peeled and cut
> into thin slices (about 1cm)
> water to boil
> 2 tsp brown sugar
> 2 tbsp olive oil
> 2 cloves crushed garlic
> 1/2 cup white wine or water
> 1 tbsp balsamic vinegar
> 1/2 cup chopped mint
> Optional: 1/2 cup black olives

Pre-heat oven to 200°C. Boil carrots for 5 minutes and drain. Place carrots in a large roasting dish. Mix in all other ingredients and spread out evenly in dish. Cook for 35-45 minutes stirring occasionally until carrots are tender. Serves 6. Keeps in the fridge for 3-4 days.

Roasted Eggplant

Purée this yummy eggplant brew for a great tasting dip, serve chunky in sandwiches, or use as a salad accompaniment or as part of a platter.

To Prepare: 5 minutes
To Cook: 10-12 minutes

> 1 large eggplant, cut 1.5cm slices
> 3 tbsp olive oil puréed with
> 3 cloves of garlic
> salt and ground black pepper

Pre-heat oven to 220°C. Place eggplant in a roasting dish and mix through olive oil puréed with garlic. Season with salt and pepper and spread out to a single layer. Place under pre-heated grill and grill for 5-6 minutes each side or until browned and softened. Makes about 4-5 cups. Keeps in the fridge for 4-5 days.

Roasted Asparagus or Green Beans

This is a wonderful way to cook asparagus or fresh green beans, intensifying their delicate flavours and giving a dense satisfying texture. Serve as part of a platter or toss through a salad.

To Prepare: 5 minutes
To Cook: 12-15 minutes

> 2 big handfuls fresh asparagus,
> tough ends snapped off or an
> equal amount of green beans,
> topped and tailed
> 2 tbsp olive oil
> a few shavings of lemon peel cut
> with a vegetable peeler
> splash of water or white wine
> salt and freshly ground pepper

Pre-heat oven to 220°C. Place asparagus or beans in a large shallow roasting dish, mix through all other ingredients, seasoning with salt and pepper. Spread out into a single layer. Bake for about 12-15 minutes until they are just starting to shrivel. Cool and serve at room temperature. They will keep in the fridge for 4-5 days.

Glazing a Ham

Most hams you buy are already cooked and simply require glazing. First you need to take off the skin without removing the layer of fat underneath. This is most easily done by pushing carefully between the skin and the fat with your thumb. Leave a ring of skin around the shank bone. Lightly score the fat in a diamond pattern and stud with whole cloves. Glaze with either melted golden syrup, or apricot jam mixed with a little brandy, or marmalade mixed with a little coarse grained mustard. Bake at 200°C for 30-45 minutes until golden, brushing with more glaze every 15 minutes.

Fritters

Tender little fritters are great finger food while larger versions make a light lunch served with salad greens and salsa.

To Prepare: 5 minutes, plus standing
To Cook: 10-15 minutes

Base Batter

> 1 cup self-raising flour
> 2 eggs
> 1 tsp salt
> $^1/_2$ cup soda water
> freshly ground pepper

Mix all ingredients until smooth. Stir in chosen flavours and ingredients. Stand for 10 minutes. Cook spoonfuls in $^1/_2$cm hot oil in a pan over medium heat until golden on each side.

Fritter flavours:

Corn and Feta Fritters: *To base batter add 2 cups corn kernels, 2 tbsp chopped mint, $^1/_2$ cup crumbled feta cheese.*

Chilli Mussel Fritters: *To base batter add 2 cups chopped cooked mussels, $^1/_4$ cup chopped coriander and 2-3 tbsp sweet Thai chilli sauce.*

Smoked Fish Fritters: *To base batter add 1$^1/_2$ cups flaked smoked fish, $^1/_4$ cup chopped fresh parsley or coriander and $^1/_2$ tsp finely grated lemon rind.*

Courgette Pesto Fritters: *To base batter add 4 grated courgettes, $^1/_4$ cup parmesan cheese, 2 tbsp pesto.*

Coconut Fish Fritters: *To base batter add $^1/_2$ cup fine coconut, grated rind and juice of $^1/_2$ lemon, 2 tbsp chopped parsley and 200g fresh, raw diced fish or seafood.*

Above: Corn and Feta Fritters served with sliced avocado and Hot and Spicy Red Salsa

Right: Pan Bagna

Tender Batters

Batters such as the one used here for herb pikelets produce much more tender pikelets if allowed to rest for 10-15 minutes before cooking.

Savoury Pikelet Topping Ideas

- smoked salmon, artichokes and caper berries
- goat's cheese and Salsa Verde
- smoked chicken and tarragon mayonnaise
- roasted peppers and cream cheese

Opposite: Platter of roasted asparagus, roasted eggplant, peppers, Greek minted carrots and toasted flour tortillas

Herb Pikelets

This easy tender textured batter can be cooked a few hours before serving time. Cooked pikelets can be frozen.

To Prepare: 5 minutes, plus resting

To Cook: 10-15 minutes

>   1 cup plain flour
>   1 tsp baking powder
>   1/4 tsp salt
>   1/4 cup finely chopped soft herbs,
>   eg parsley, chervil, basil
>   3/4 cup milk
>   1 egg
>   2 tbsp melted butter

In a mixing bowl combine the flour, baking powder, salt and herbs. In another bowl, lightly beat together the milk and egg. Mix into the flour, beating until smooth. Mix in the melted butter. Rest for 10-15 minutes. Heat and lightly grease a heavy-based fry-pan. Drop small spoonfuls of batter into the fry-pan. Cook over medium heat until bubbles appear on the surface. Turn and cook for a further minute or until golden and cooked through. Place on a wire rack to cool. Makes about 18 mini pikelets.

Pan Bagna

This traditional French pressed sandwich is made ahead of time and weighted. Good sliced small for finger food or cut in thicker chunks for portable picnics.

To Prepare: 10 minutes, plus chilling

>   1 loaf French bread
>   about 1/2 cup Salsa Verde ○
> Filling
>   4-5 hard-boiled eggs, sliced
>   1 tbsp capers, chopped
>   flesh of 1-2 roasted red peppers,
>   cut in thick strips
>   salt and ground black pepper

Slice the loaf lengthwise. Spread both cut sides with Salsa Verde. Slice the eggs over one half, top with capers and red peppers and season with salt and pepper. Cover with the other half of the bread, wrap up tightly and then weight the loaf down with something heavy and chill for several hours. To serve, slice with a sharp knife. Serves 2 for lunch or makes about 20 thin slices for finger food.

PLATTERS

The platter approach is a simple and stylish way to feed a large number of people at parties or big events. Serve 5-7 different items on a large platter to provide a variation of flavours, colours and textures. Accompany with breads for a casual lunch or supper. For a party, add a baked ham.

- Wedges of frittata, marinated olives mixed with slices of roasted red peppers and feta cheese, roasted asparagus or beans, hummus and wedges of bread.
- Cashew and Cream Cheese Pesto, dried figs and apricots, sliced smoked ham, roasted green beans, wedges of fresh melon and Garlic Pita Crisps.

- Roasted asparagus, roasted eggplant, roasted peppers, toasted flour tortillas, Greek Pumpkin Spread.
- Corn and Feta Fritters, roasted asparagus, sliced spicy salami, roasted peppers, marinated olives, Feta and Fennel Dip and baby boiled potatoes.

Seafood Pleasures

The temptingly tangy flavours of fresh seafood evoke the ocean and all its pleasures.

With divine natural flavours, many fresh seafoods need little embellishment.

Frying Hint

When frying batters, don't have the heat too high – the mixture needs to cook through to the centre before the outside gets too brown. For larger pieces of food, finish for a few minutes in a hot oven.

Rice Flour

Rice flour makes fritters and batters crisp. Buy it at any Asian food shop and store like regular flour.

Coconut Cream

If coconut cream is very thick, which can make it hard to mix into dry ingredients, simply warm and it will thin. Any left-over coconut cream can be transferred to a jar and kept in the fridge for a few days or frozen.

Opposite: Thai Prawn Fritters

Thai Prawn Fritters

These fritters are sensational. The Thai flavoured batter can be mixed with other seafoods or used to make vegetarian fritters by omitting seafood altogether. Make the fritters ahead of time if desired and re-heat in a hot oven for a few minutes.

To Prepare: 10 minutes

To Cook: 15 minutes

> *300g raw de-shelled prawn tails, cut in half or quarters (drain well, if frozen)*
> *1 generous tbsp minced fresh ginger*
> *2 tbsp Thai sweet chilli sauce*
> *greens of 1 spring onion, finely chopped*
> *small handful coriander, finely chopped*
> *1/3 cup each self-raising flour and rice flour*
> *1 cup coconut cream*
> *1 tsp salt and plenty of freshly ground black pepper*
> *big pinch turmeric*
> *1 medium large kumara, about 180g, peeled and grated*
> *vegetable oil to fry*

Place chopped prawns in a bowl with ginger, chilli sauce, spring onion and coriander. Mix well so that prawns can absorb flavours of the aromatics before they are mixed into the batter. In a large bowl combine the flours with coconut cream, salt, pepper and turmeric, mixing to a smooth batter. Add grated kumara and chopped prawns in their marinade and mix evenly. Rest for 5 minutes before cooking, or chill for up to 1 hour. Heat about 1cm of oil in a heavy pan and cook small spoonfuls of the batter over medium heat for a couple of minutes on each side, turning as they brown and bubbles start to form on the top. Drain well on paper towels or brown paper. Serve hot or warm with a dipping sauce of Thai sweet chilli sauce. Makes about 24.

Variation: For vegetarian fritters omit prawns and add all flavourings straight into batter.

Note: Fritters can be cooked ahead of time and re-heated in a hot oven for 5 minutes.

Chilled Oysters with Asian Dressing

This light Asian style dressing tastes beautiful with chilled raw oysters and raw fish. It will keep in the fridge for weeks without vegetables.

To Prepare: 5 minutes

> *2 dozen oysters on the half shell*

Dressing

> *1/4 cup rice wine vinegar*
> *2 tbsp dry sherry*
> *1/2-2 tsp sugar*
> *1/2 tsp fresh grated ginger or wasabi powder*
> *1/2 tsp sesame oil*
> *finely shredded carrot and spring onion*

Combine the sauce ingredients with carrot and spring onion and chill. Just before serving the oysters, spoon a teaspoon of sauce over each and garnish with a little of the shredded vegetables. Makes 24.

Oysters on the Half Shell with Sour Cream and Smoked Salmon

A truly luxurious combination which can be prepared in a few minutes.

To Prepare: 5 minutes

> 3 dozen oysters on the half shell
> 150g sour cream
> 100g smoked salmon cut in fine
>   strips
> finely chopped chives for garnish

Spoon a little sour cream onto each oyster, top with salmon julienne and garnish with chives. Makes 3 dozen.

Rock Oysters with Spinach and Bacon

Oysters freeze very well, so buy extra for the freezer when you happen on a really fresh supply.

To Prepare: 10 minutes
To Cook: 4-5 minutes

> 12 fresh or frozen oysters on the
>   half shell
> 1 tbsp olive oil
> 2 rashers bacon, finely chopped
> 2-3 heads fresh spinach, washed
>   and dried
> 2 tbsp cream or sour cream
> salt and freshly ground pepper to
>   taste

Heat oil in a pan. Fry bacon until it starts to brown. Slice spinach, add to pan and cook until wilted. Mix in cream or sour cream and stir until evenly incorporated. Season to taste. Spoon mixture onto oysters. Place under pre-heated grill for 4-5 minutes until oyster flesh firms. Serves 2. *Note: Topping can be prepared and chilled, ready to place onto the oysters just before grilling.*

Sushi Rice

Sushi is such an easy thing to make, provided you have the right ingredients. Sushi rice can be prepared well ahead of time, as can the rolls themselves.

To Prepare: 2 minutes and 30 minutes standing
To Cook: 30 minutes

> 1 cup short grain rice,
>   eg Japanese sushi rice
> 3 tbsp rice wine vinegar
> 1½ tbsp sugar
> 2 tsp salt

Wash rice then stand in cold water for 30 minutes. Drain thoroughly. Heat together the vinegar, sugar and salt in a small pot, stirring until dissolved. Put to one side. Place rice in a medium size pot with a tight fitting lid, cover with 1 cup water and place on a high heat. As soon as rice comes to the boil, reduce the heat to lowest setting, cover pot and cook for 12 minutes. Remove from heat and stand 15 minutes without uncovering. Mix through vinegar seasoning with a fork. Turn out onto a large, flat, clean tray to cool. Use a fan to quicken the cooling. The rice is now ready to use. It can be refrigerated for up to 48 hours, covered in plastic wrap to prevent drying. To stop it sticking to your hands when you are assembling sushi, wet your hands with cold water, then clap to remove any excess water before picking up rice. Makes 2 cups cooked rice, enough for 6 filled sushi rolls or about 36 small sushi rice balls.

Sesame Sushi Rice Balls

Mix cooked, seasoned sushi rice with ½ cup finely diced cucumber, 3 tbsp finely chopped pickled ginger, and 2 tbsp toasted sesame seeds. Use wet hands to roll into balls. Makes about 36.

Freezing Oysters

Oysters freeze well for up to 3 months. For best results, thaw in the fridge. Only freeze the freshest of oysters and never freeze twice.

Oysters on the Half Shell with...

- sake and thin sliced pickled ginger
- lime or lemon juice and ground black pepper
- equal parts fish sauce, Thai chilli sauce and lime juice
- balsamic vinegar
- a splash of sherry or vodka

Rice Wine Vinegar

Made from sake, it has a mild sweet taste and is good in Asian dishes or as a replacement for lemon juice in dressings.

Salmon and Avocado Sushi Rolls

These are a favourite amongst sushi fans. You can also make them with smoked salmon, if preferred.

To Prepare: 10 minutes

6 sheets nori seaweed, sushi grade
1 quantity cooked sushi rice
a little wasabi paste, thinned with a
*   little water so it spreads*
150-200g freshest raw salmon, skin
*   and bones removed, cut in finger*
*   strips*
1 avocado, mashed

Toast the shiny side of the nori by passing over an open flame – the nori will become crisp and develop flavour. Lay one sheet of nori on a bamboo mat or clean tea towel, shiny side down. Place a handful of rice on sheet and pat out until rice covers all but a 5cm wide strip at the top edge of each nori sheet. Dip your finger into thinned wasabi paste, and about 4cm from the bottom and nearest edge of the rice, rub a line of wasabi from left to right in a thin strip of flavour. Lay salmon strips, 2-3 thick, along the wasabi line. Spread a little mashed avocado on top of the salmon. Starting with the edge nearest you, roll up as tightly as possible using the sushi mat or tea towel to help roll tightly. When you get to the border at the top edge, wet the nori and then roll up. Chill, joined side down, for at least 30 minutes, or up to 24 hours. Serve each roll sliced crosswise into 6 pieces and accompany with a dipping sauce. Makes 36 pieces.

Sushi Dipping Sauce

Mix ¼ cup good quality soy sauce, preferably Japanese, with 2 tsp wasabi paste.

Whitebait Fritters

Chinese whitebait is very bland. Add a squeeze of lemon juice as well as rind.

To Prepare: 5 minutes
To Cook: 4-5 minutes

400g whitebait
1 egg
½ tsp finely grated lemon rind
1 tbsp flour
salt and ground black pepper
butter for cooking

Combine the whitebait, egg, lemon rind and flour and season with salt and pepper. Melt a knob of butter evenly over the base of the pan. When the butter is sizzling, drop small spoonfuls of the mixture into the pan. Cook for 1-2 minutes on each side, or until golden brown. Serve warm or at room temperature. Makes 24 small fritters.

Above: Salmon and Avocado Sushi Rolls

Wasabi

Forget chillies. This is the stuff that sends your tastebuds into outer space. Its wonderful bite is an asset to any raw seafood or sushi. Fresh wasabi can be hard to find. Use paste or mix powder to a paste with a little cold water. Go easy, it's sinus-searingly hot.

Nori

Seaweed wrapper made of laver seaweed, used to wrap sushi. Look for sushi grade. Also sold shredded for garnish in Asian food stores. Keeps for years unopened. Once opened it absorbs moisture and may soften.

Mussels on the Half Shell with Pesto Vinaigrette

Cooked mussels on the half shell offer a superb base for a variety of toppings.

To Prepare: 5 minutes
To Cook: 10 minutes

> 3 dozen fresh or cooked mussels on the half shell
> 2-3 tbsp pesto of your choice, eg basil or sun-dried tomato pesto
> 1/2 cup vinaigrette dressing
> Optional: 1/4 cup finely diced roasted red peppers

On a high heat, steam open the fresh mussels in 1/4 cup water in a pot with a tight-fitting lid. Remove as they open. Take off the top shell. Mix together the pesto with the dressing and season with freshly ground black pepper. Arrange the mussel shells on a plate and spoon over the pesto dressing. Garnish with peppers. Chill until ready to serve. Makes 36.

Vodka-cured Salmon or Trout

This is really easy to make and fabulously impressive. Once cured, the side of fish will keep for about a week in the fridge. Ideal at Christmas or when there are likely to be streams of impromptu guests. Other herbs such as parsley or chives can be used instead of dill.

To Prepare: 10 minutes, 36-48 hours curing

> 2 sides salmon or trout, skin on, pin bones removed
> 2-3 tbsp vodka or brandy
> 2 tbsp sea salt
> 1 tbsp brown sugar
> 2 tbsp fresh dill, chopped
> 1 tsp coarse black pepper
> grated rind of 1 lemon, no pith

Use clean tweezers or bull nose pliers to pull out the line of pin bones that run about two-thirds the length of the salmon, just off centre. Rub vodka into the flesh of each side (not skin side). Mix salt, sugar, pepper, dill and lemon rind and sprinkle evenly over both cut surfaces. Sandwich together, skin sides out. Wrap fish tightly in tinfoil and put into a shallow dish. Weight the top with something heavy. Leave in the fridge for 36-48 hours before using. To serve, drain off liquid and carve very thin slices on an angle using a very sharp, thin-bladed knife. Serve with olive oil focaccia flavoured with capers and Horseradish Cream, or rye bread, or toasted bagels with a garnish of horseradish cream and sliced red onion. Serves 15-20.

Horseradish Cream

Mix 250g sour cream with 2 tbsp horseradish sauce, juice of 1/2 lemon, salt and pepper to season. Store in the fridge until ready to use – it will keep for about a week. A teaspoon of wasabi paste gives an extra kick.

MENU 🍴 IDEAS

Christmas Drinks

vodka-cured salmon,
horseradish cream and flatbread

marinated olives

goat's cheese pesto tarts

iced vodka

champagne cocktails

Advance preparations

- *marinate olives*
- *cure salmon in vodka (2-3 days before)*
- *make tarts*
- *make horseradish cream and bread*

Eating for Two

Pregnant women should avoid raw and marinated fish, rare cooked meats, raw eggs, commercial pâtés and unpasteurised cheeses.

Fish Sauce

The soy sauce of South East Asia, fish sauce is not unlike the garam used so widely by the ancient Romans. Smells dreadful, keeps for ever and is fabulous – use 1-2 tbsp in a curry, salad, sauce or dressing for an amazing lift. It is very salty so taste food before adding extra salt – the Thai Squid brand is good and not too salty.

Left: Vietnamese Glass Noodle Rolls

Vietnamese Dipping Sauce

Mix 3 tbsp fish sauce, 1 tbsp sugar, 2 tbsp rice wine vinegar and 2 tbsp Thai sweet chilli sauce. Keeps in the fridge for weeks.

Handling Rice Paper

Brittle and crisp when dry, rice paper softens to a pliable texture when dipped quickly into hot water. Shake off excess water and lay on a clean towel to soften. Don't soak in water; they will fall apart.

Vietnamese Glass Noodle Rolls

These pretty little rolls taste wonderfully fresh and light. The shrimps can be replaced with cooked chicken, or left out entirely and other salad ingredients such as cucumber or sprouts added instead.

To Prepare: 15 minutes plus soaking

1 large handful clear glass noodles
2 spring onions, finely sliced
1 cup lettuce leaves, freshly sliced
1/4 cup coriander or mint, finely chopped
1 large carrot, shredded
1/2 cucumber, cut in matchstick strips
1 1/2 cups cooked shrimps, chopped
1 tsp sugar
1 tbsp fish sauce
1 tsp sweet Thai chilli sauce
juice of 1 lime or lemon
8 sheets of rice paper

Soak noodles in warm water for 15 minutes to soften. Drain thoroughly. Place in a bowl with vegetables, herbs and shrimps. Mix in sugar, fish sauce, sweet Thai chilli sauce and lime juice until everything is evenly combined. Dip each rice paper sheet one at a time into hot water, just to wet. Lay on a damp clean tea towel. Leave for about 1 minute until they soften to a rollable texture. Take a small handful of filling and form a 3cm band across one edge of each softened sheet of rice paper, leaving about 2cm clear at either side. Roll up tightly to enclose the filling, folding in the ends on either side as you go. Chill until ready to serve. Slice each roll into 3. Arrange on a serving platter and accompany with dipping sauce. Can be made up to 6 hours ahead and kept in the fridge covered with a damp tea towel. Makes 35-40 pieces.

The Bar

IF YOU'RE IN A PARTY MOOD, A COUPLE OF FUN COCKTAILS WILL ALWAYS BREAK THE ICE. SOME PEOPLE PREFER NOT TO DRINK ALCOHOL, SO ALWAYS OFFER NON-ALCOHOLIC CHOICES TOO.

Sludgy Margaritas
(by the blender full)

Traditionally a sugar syrup is used to blend cocktails. Icing sugar streamlines the process.

> *3/4 cup fresh lime or lemon juice*
> *1/4 cup icing sugar*
> *1 cup tequila*
> *3 tbsp triple sec*
> *3 trays ice cubes*

Blend all ingredients together until they form a smooth purée. Serve immediately in a jug or pour into wide rimmed cocktail glasses that have had the rims dipped in lemon juice and then salt (optional). Makes 1 litre (enough for 4-5 cocktails).

DIY Dirty Martini

Fill a big glass with ice, cover with chilled vodka, strain into a martini glass, stir in about 1 tbsp green olive brine, top with 3 fat green olives and add a twist of lemon.

Champagne Cocktails

Some of the less expensive methode champenoise wines are perfect for cocktails. Here are some yummy suggestions:

- *Dash of bitters, sugar lump and a strip of orange or lemon peel*
- *Sugar lump, 2 dashes bitters, 1 tbsp Dubbonet, strip of lemon peel*
- *A little syrup from sliced tamarillos macerated in sugar*
- *1 tsp of cassis*
- *A little syrup from sweetened stewed rhubarb*

Cocktail Parties: How much drink?

Cocktail parties start and end at specific times and usually run for 2-3 hours. Over that period allow an average of 4-6 drinks per person. A 750ml bottle of wine contains 5 glasses and a 750ml bottle of spirits enough for about 25 drinks if you use double nip servings. A single nip at a bar is only 15mls. Always offer plenty of non-alcoholic choices – chilled club soda, ginger beer and fruit juices.

Champagne Bellinis

Here's another divine way to enjoy a less expensive champagne.

> *2 fresh peaches, stoned*
> *1/2 cup peach schnapps or kirsch*
> *2 cups ice*
> *1 bottle sparkling wine, chilled*

Blend peaches, schnapps and ice until smooth, then slowly add sparkling wine.

Cuban Mojito

The Cubans are famous for their cocktails, notably the daiquiri which they invented. This refreshing rum, mint and lime cooler is another favourite.

> *3 tbsp very finely chopped fresh mint leaves*
> *2 tsp sugar*
> *2 tbsp fresh lime juice*
> *crushed ice*
> *1/4 cup white rum*
> *chilled club soda*
> *2 fresh mint sprigs to garnish*

Mix the chopped mint leaves, sugar and lime juice in a small jug. Fill 2 tall glasses with crushed ice. Pour the mint mixture over the ice, add rum to each glass and top up with club soda. Garnish each glass with a mint sprig. Makes 2 drinks.

60s Fruit Punch

Cold tea is a traditional base for punches, both fruit and alcoholic.

> 1 litre cold tea, strained
> 2 litres orange and apple juice
> 1 litre grapefruit juice
> 1 litre ginger ale
> 1 litre lemonade
> $^1/_2$ cup lime cordial
> $^1/_4$ cup chopped fresh mint
> 1 each orange, lemon and
>   grapefruit, sliced
> ice, about 1 tray full
> Optional: 3 passionfruit (or 3 tbsp pulp)

Mix all together in a large bowl. Serves about 30. Serve straight or with lots of alcohol.

Above: Dirty Martini

Summer Passion

Canned coconut milk adds a silky, smooth flavour to any cocktail or fruit drink. This delicious brew is great on its own, but it is especially delicious as a base for a rum cocktail.

> 1 tin coconut milk, chilled
> 500ml chilled orange juice
> 227g can unsweetened crushed
>   pineapple
> 2 cups white rum (optional)

Purée all ingredients together until smooth. Makes about 1.3 litres. Serve immediately.

Seabreeze Cocktail

Mix chilled vodka with equal parts chilled cranberry juice and grapefruit juice.

Summer Sangria

This is great for a summer BBQ. You can make it with white wine instead of red.

> 1 litre red or white wine
> $^1/_2$ litre soda water
> $^1/_2$ litre orange juice (or orange and
>   mango)
> 1-2 fresh oranges quartered and
>   sliced thinly
> 1 tsp sugar
> Optional: 1 cinnamon quill

Mix all the ingredients together, stirring to dissolve the sugar. Serve in a large jug with some ice cubes. Makes 2 litres.

Cocktail Parties: How much food needed?

Plan to serve 4-5 different food items and allow 2-3 servings of each. Choose a variety of different food styles – some hot, some cold. Provide 'blotting paper' in the form of little pies and savouries and other filling foods.

SOUPS AND BREADS

Chinese Roast Duck
Noodle Soup

Chicken Laksa

Miso Soup

Vietnamese Pho Bo

Winter Lentil Soup

El Paso Chicken and
Vegetable Soup

White Bean and
Smoked Ham Soup with
Winter Pesto

Spicy Sausage and
Chickpea Minestrone

Black Bean Soup

Country Lamb,
Barley and Vegetable
Soup

Traditional Pea and
Ham Soup

Fast Track Lentil Soup

Smoked Fish and Potato
Chowder

Tomato and Orange Soup

Tom Yum Soup

French Onion Soup

Fred's Tomato Soup

Gazpacho Soup

Jilly's Roasted Pepper Soup

Pistou of Spring Vegetables
with Diablotins

Thai Pumpkin Soup

Classic Pumpkin Soup

Two Mushroom Soup

Quick Fresh
Mushroom Soup

Blue Bayou Gumbo

Mussel and Corn
Chowder

Bouillabaisse

West Coast Mussel Soup

Naan Bread

Olive Oil Focaccia

Chilli Cheese Bread

Grilled Chinese Pancakes

Coconut Onion Roti

Pizza

Pizza Toppings

Asian Soups

THE INTENSE FLAVOURS OF ASIA – GINGER, CHILLIES, CITRUS RINDS AND FISH SAUCE LEND

THEMSELVES TO THE QUICK CREATION OF WONDERFUL ASIAN-STYLE SOUPS.

Vermicelli Noodles

The clear brittle strands of bean thread noodles, known commonly as vermicelli, soften quickly to a palatable texture after a few minutes in hot water. Often found in the produce department at the supermarket, these noodles are tied into a large hank which needs to be broken up before using. It's easiest to transfer them to a large bag and use sharp scissors to separate them as they can make a huge mess.

Marvellous Miso

The fermented bean pastes of Japan, known collectively as miso, are rich in protein, B vitamins and minerals. There are many different kinds of miso offering differing flavours and textures. White miso tends to be quite light and sweet in flavour and is good for dressings and soups, while darker misos such as Hatcho-miso are very rich and salty and best for soup. To maximise its nutrition benefits, miso should not be boiled. Use miso as a spread or as flavouring for soups and stews, adding at the end of cooking.

Previous page: White Bean and Smoked Ham Soup with Winter Pesto

Chinese Roast Duck Noodle Soup

Count yourself lucky if you have ready access to freshly roasted Chinese ducks. Serve the duck in chunks on the bone, or de-bone and de-skin for a more elegant and lower fat version.

To Prepare: 10 minutes

To Cook: 25 minutes

> 1/2 roasted Chinese duck or chicken (purchase chopped up)
> 3 cups chicken stock
> 3 cups water
> rind of 1/4 orange, cut in very thin strips, no pith
> 1 tbsp fresh ginger, minced
> 2 tbsp oyster sauce
> 4 'nests' dried Chinese egg noodles (250g)
> 2 heads baby bok choy, washed and sliced
> 1 spring onion, finely sliced
> handful fresh coriander leaves

Place duck in a pot, pour over stock and water, add orange rind, ginger and oyster sauce. Bring to a simmer, cover. Cook for 20 minutes. Skim off any fat. Lift out duck from broth, shred meat into bite sized pieces (or you can leave in pieces on the bone). Add noodles to broth and cook according to manufacturer's instructions. Two minutes before noodles are ready, return cooked duck meat to the pot along with bok choy, spring onions and coriander. Simmer 2 minutes and serve at once. Serves 4 as a meal.

Chicken Laksa

A delicate, creamy Malaysian noodle meal in a bowl. The beauty of this dish is its flexibility – change ingredients according to taste and availability. To the creamy, spicy sauce, add sliced raw chicken (or seafood) and then a choice of vegetables.

To Prepare: 10 minutes

To Cook: 12-15 minutes

> 300g rice or egg noodles, or fresh noodles
> 1 tbsp vegetable oil
> 1 tbsp Thai curry paste
> 1 tbsp each minced fresh ginger and garlic
> 400mls coconut cream
> 1 1/2 cups chicken stock, or water
> 2 tbsp fish sauce
> 2 tbsp peanut butter
> 500g boneless chicken, cut in very thin strips
> vegetables: eg snow peas, sliced peppers, mung bean sprouts, spring onions, coriander or mint,
> Optional: *chopped peanuts to garnish*

Cook the noodles according to manufacturer's instructions. While they cook, heat the oil in a large wok or fry-pan. Add the curry paste, ginger and garlic and cook for 30 seconds. Add the coconut cream, stock or water and peanut butter and bring to a simmer. Stir until smooth. Mix in the chicken and simmer for a further 2 minutes. Add the vegetables and bring back to a simmer before serving, or serve the vegetables and chopped peanuts on a separate plate so each diner can garnish their own. Serves 4 as a one dish meal.

Above: Chicken Laksa

Miso Soup

Miso is to the Japanese cook what butter is to the French kitchen or olive oil to the Italians. Miso's omnipresence in the Japanese kitchen is justified by its incredible nutritional value (a bowl of miso soup provides about $\frac{1}{6}$ of an adult's daily protein requirement) as well as its ability to instantly add delicious flavour.

To Prepare: 5 minutes
To Cook: 5 minutes

> *3 cups chicken or fish stock*
> *small handful of dried seaweed*
> *3-4 sliced mushrooms*
> *2 tbsp miso paste*
> *2 spring onions, sliced*

Heat chicken or fish stock, or make up dashi. Add dried seaweed and sliced mushrooms. Simmer for 5 minutes. Soften miso paste in a little of the hot broth and add to soup with spring onions. Serve at once without re-boiling. Makes 2 servings. Recipe doubles easily.

Vietnamese Pho Bo

This substantial staple of the Vietnamese diet combines vegetables, clear noodles and slivers of chicken in a spicy clear broth, and takes just minutes to prepare and cook. Lean, good quality steak can be used in place of chicken, in which case use beef stock.

To Prepare: 10 minutes

To Cook: 10 minutes

3 cups chicken stock
2 tbsp fish sauce
1 chicken breast, skinned and sliced as thinly as possible
1-2 chillies, thinly sliced
2 handfuls clear vermicelli noodles
vegetables: 6 sliced mushrooms, 1 diced tomato, 1 packed cup thinly sliced spinach
salt and ground black pepper
1 tbsp minced lemon grass or finely grated rind of $1/2$ lemon
$1/4$ cup chopped fresh mint and/or coriander, beansprouts

Bring chicken stock to a simmer in a large pot. Add fish sauce and noodles and simmer for 5 minutes. Mix in vegetables and bring back to a boil. Add sliced chicken and simmer for 2 minutes. Mix through fresh herbs and beansprouts, season to taste and serve at once. Serves 2.

Right: Vietnamese Pho Bo

Rib Stickers for Cold Days

DENSE HEARTY SOUPS DELIVER THAT OLD FASHIONED COMFORT WE CRAVE YET SO SELDOM HAVE
TIME FOR. MAKE IN BULK AND KEEP IN A BIG JAR IN THE FRIDGE OR FREEZE FOR AN INSTANT FIX
WHEN YOU ARRIVE HOME EXHAUSTED, HUNGRY AND COLD.

Winter Lentil Soup

Lentils are wonderful comfort food –
they're nourishing, thoroughly satisfying
to eat and unlike many other pulses, they
don't require soaking or long cooking.

To Prepare: 10 minutes
To Cook: 1-1½ hours

> 2 tbsp olive oil
> 1 large onion, finely diced
> 1 carrot, peeled and finely chopped
> ¼ cup tomato paste
> 2 tsp smoked paprika
> 2 large cloves garlic, crushed
> 120g smoked Kransky or chorizo
>   sausages, diced; or spicy
>   salami, diced
> 2½ litres good chicken stock
> 2 x 400g cans crushed tomatoes

> 2 cups brown lentils, washed
> 2 bay leaves
> salt and pepper
> 1 tbsp lemon juice
> chopped fresh coriander

In a large pot heat oil and gently fry
onion and carrot until soft. Add tomato
paste, garlic, paprika and diced sausage
and stir over heat for another minute.
Add chicken stock, tomatoes, bay leaves
and lentils. Simmer gently until the lentils
are very soft; this will take 1-1½ hours
depending on their age and dryness.
Season to taste and mix in lemon juice
and coriander. Serves 6. Can be made in
bulk and freezes well. Accompany if you
like with creme fraîche or sour cream.

Above: Winter Lentil Soup

Nutrition –
Lentil Power

*You don't need to be
vegetarian to enjoy lentils.
Unlike many pulses, they
require no pre-soaking which
makes them ideal for busy
cooks. Recent research has
shown the riboflavins in
lentils offer protective
benefits against prostate
cancer. Ditto for chickpeas.*

El Paso Chicken and Vegetable Soup

Combine a piece of tender chicken on the bone with root vegetables in a spicy chicken broth and you have a satisfying soup dinner, ideal cold weather fare.

To Prepare: 15 minutes

To Cook: 20 minutes

> 8 cups well-flavoured chicken stock
> 6 chicken quarters or chicken supremes
> 1/2 buttercup pumpkin (600-800g), peeled and cut in 4cm chunks
> 3 medium potatoes, peeled and cut in 4cm chunks
> small bunch baby carrots, trimmed, or 2 carrots cut in thin strips
> 3 corn cobs, cut into 2cm rounds
> salt and ground black pepper
> 2-3 tomatoes, peeled, cores removed, flesh cut in eighths
> 1-2 fresh chillies, very finely chopped
> 2 spring onions, very finely chopped
> 2-3 tbsp Asian Pesto ✿ or Winter Pesto ✿

Bring chicken stock to a simmer in a large pot, seasoning to taste with salt and pepper. Add chicken, pumpkin, potatoes, carrots and corn, season with salt and pepper, cover and simmer for 12-15 minutes until chicken and vegetables are cooked. Season to taste and mix in tomatoes, chillies, spring onions and pesto just prior to serving. Bring back to a simmer. To serve, place a portion of chicken in six deep bowls. Spoon over vegetables and ladle over broth. Serves 6.

White Bean and Smoked Ham Soup with Winter Pesto

You may think this type of soup takes hours to prepare but canned beans streamline the process without compromising the results. Follow it with a salad for a simple elegant meal or special lunch.

To Prepare: 20 minutes

To Cook: 20 minutes

> 1 tbsp olive oil
> 300g smoked ham, diced
> 1 medium onion, chopped
> 1 tbsp minced garlic
> 6 tomatoes, peeled, seeded and chopped (or 1 x 400g can Italian plum tomatoes, chopped)
> 6 cups chicken stock
> 3 cups cooked white beans, drained and rinsed, eg lima beans, haricot or soy beans
> 6 stems of both parsley and mint
> pinch dry thyme
> 2 bay leaves
> salt and freshly ground pepper
> 1/2 cup Winter Pesto ✿ to serve

Heat the oil in a soup pot and add the ham and onion. Cook about 8-10 minutes, until onion is soft. Add the garlic and continue to cook for 3 minutes until ham begins to turn golden. Add the tomatoes, chicken stock, beans and herbs. Simmer for 20 minutes. Lift out the parsley stems, mint stems and bay leaves. Season to taste and mix in the pesto. Serves 6. Freezes well.

Washing Pulses

Pulses such as lentils, dried peas and beans should be sorted and washed before using to remove dirt and small stones.

Smoked Paprika

Smoked paprika has a far richer, more intense flavour than regular paprika. It is sold in cans and comes in a range of styles – from dulce, which is sweet and smoky through to picante – which is spicy. Gives a wonderful flavour lift to rice dishes and hearty sauces.

Opposite: El Paso Chicken and Vegetable Soup

Spicy Sausage and Chickpea Minestrone

This richly flavoured, chunky soup is great to have on hand in the fridge for a quick warming fix. It freezes well.

To Prepare: 10 minutes
To Cook: 12-15 minutes

> 2 tbsp oil
> about 150g spicy sausages, diced,
>   eg Julia Colbasse
> 1 tsp crushed garlic
> ½ tsp chilli powder
> 500g jar tomato pasta sauce
> 3 cups chicken stock
> 2 cups water
> 2 cups chopped vegetables,
>   eg pumpkin, leeks, carrots, etc
> 1 can chickpeas, drained and rinsed
>   (or 1 ½ cups cooked chickpeas)
> ¼ cup herb pesto
> 2-3 tbsp grated parmesan cheese

In a soup pot, heat the oil and cook the sausage, garlic and chilli for a few seconds. Add the tomato pasta sauce, chicken stock, water, vegetables and chickpeas. Bring to a simmer, and cook for 12-15 minutes until the vegetables are tender. Just before serving, mix in the pesto and parmesan and season to taste with salt and pepper. Serves 6. If freezing, omit pesto and parmesan and add before serving.

Black Bean Soup

Like lentils, black beans don't require pre-soaking before cooking. Another good brew for the freezer.

To Prepare: 5 minutes
To Cook: 2 hours 15 minutes

> 4 cups dried black beans
> 16 cups water, or more as needed
> 500g piece boiling bacon or
>   2 bacon hocks
> 6 cloves garlic, peeled and crushed
> 2 tsp ground cumin
> 2 cups tomato pasta sauce
> 2 tbsp hot chilli sauce, to taste
> salt and ground black pepper
> ½ cup fresh coriander or parsley,
>   chopped
> Optional: mild red chillies, thinly sliced
>   and lightly fried in a little oil

Wash, rinse and drain beans. Place beans in a pot with water, bacon or hocks, garlic, cumin, tomato pasta sauce and chilli sauce. Bring to the boil, removing any scum that rises. Simmer on lowest heat uncovered for 2 hours – once fully cooked, soup should have thickened slightly. Take care during last half hour of cooking that soup does not catch. Remove bacon and cut into small chunks, discarding skin and fat. Return pieces to soup pot. Season to taste with 1-2 tsp salt and plenty of freshly ground black pepper. Mix in coriander. If desired, garnish with red chillies which have been lightly fried. Serves 8-10. Allow to cool fully before refrigerating or freezing.

Freezable Beans

Cooked beans, lentils, chickpeas and other pulses can be frozen for easy use anytime. Cook up a big brew, then drain thoroughly, cool and freeze onto trays before transferring free flow into plastic bags.

Soaking and Cooking Beans

For information on soaking and cooking beans see the side panel on page 122.

Classic Country Lamb, Barley and Vegetable Soup

This postwar classic is unlikely to date – generations have been nurtured on its soothing flavours. When we were children, it was the mainstay of our after school winter sustenance. For an adult kick, stir in a good dollop of Harissa or some Winter Pesto.

To Prepare: 15 minutes

To Cook: 2 hours

> 4 lamb shanks, trimmed of any fat
> 2 cups pearl barley or dried
>   soup mix
> 3 bay leaves
> 16 cups water
> salt and freshly ground black
>   pepper to taste
> 3 cups each of grated carrots and
>   kumara or pumpkin
> 2 onions, finely diced
> 4 stalks celery, finely chopped
> 1/4 cup tomato paste
> 1 x 400g can tomatoes in juice,
>   roughly chopped
> Optional 2-3 tbsp Harissa ✪ or Winter
>   Pesto ✪ to serve

Place all ingredients in large pot, except for the optional garnish. Bring to a boil, removing any scum as it rises. Reduce heat to a simmer. Cook gently for 2 hours. Lift shanks from soup. When cool enough to handle, strip off meat and shred. Remove any fat from top of soup. Return shredded meat back to the soup. Season to taste and bring back to a simmer. Serve hot, topping each portion with a small dollop of harissa or pesto if desired. Makes 18 cups. Soup will keep in the fridge for 4-5 days and freezes well. Serves 12.

MENU IDEAS

Winter's Lunch

winter lentil soup

bruschetta with goat's cheese, rocket and roasted tomatoes

kisses and fresh persimmons

Advance preparations

- *make soup*
- *make kisses*
- *roast tomatoes*
- *toast bruschetta bases*

Traditional Pea and Ham Soup

Make up a big batch of this great and hearty soup and throw into the freezer for those cold winter nights.

To Prepare: 10 minutes

To Cook: 1¼ hours

> 1 tbsp oil
> 1 large onion, finely diced
> 1 bacon or ham hock
> 2 tsp curry powder
> 2 litres water
> 2 pkts dry pea and ham soup
>   powder
> Optional: 1 x 500g pkt frozen peas

Heat the oil in a large pot. Add the onion and cook gently until soft. Mix in the curry powder and cook a further minute, then add the water, bacon bone and soup powder. Bring to the boil and simmer for 1 hour or until meat is tender. Strip meat from bacon bone and return it to the soup. If using peas, cook in the microwave or in a pot, and purée. Add to the soup just before serving. Serves 6-8. Freezes well.

Keeping it Cool – Storage Tips

- *Cool hot soups or stews first before chilling in the fridge*
- *Once cool, don't leave food sitting around at room temperature, chill at once*
- *Always re-heat soup to a boil after chilling*

Streamlined Soups

HEARTY RICH FLAVOURS DON'T ALWAYS REQUIRE A LOT OF TIME IN PREPARATION.
THESE SOUPS DELIVER THE FLAVOUR WITH LITTLE EFFORT ON YOUR PART.

Left-overs for Soup

Left-over cooked vegetables make a good base for a tasty soup – like adding mashed potato and cooked leeks to a made-up packet leek and potato soup; or puréeing roasted pumpkin with stock and finishing with a spoon of pesto.

Fast-track Lentil Soup

If you have a pressure cooker cook everything together for 15 minutes.

To Prepare: 5 minutes

To Cook: 1½ hours

Place 3 cups lentils in a big pot with a bacon hock and 10 cups water. Bring to a boil then reduce heat to low and cook for an hour. Add a jar of prepared tomato pasta sauce and simmer another ½ hour, stirring occasionally. Lift hock out, strip off meat and dice finely. Return to the pot, add a spoonful of fruit chutney and another of hot chilli sauce.

Smoked Fish and Potato Chowder

Use any smoked seafoods for this easy chowder.

To Prepare: 10 minutes

To Cook: 30 minutes

In a big pot, heat a knob of butter and gently cook 1 large, finely diced onion until soft with ½ tsp curry powder. Add 1 tsp dried thyme, 2 bay leaves, 400g flaked smoked fish, 1½ litres water and 1 large, finely diced potato. Bring to a simmer and cook for 15 minutes. Mix in 1 pkt leek and potato soup powder mixed with 2 tbsp sherry or white wine. Stir until mixture has lightly thickened. Let cook a further 15 minutes. Add ¼ cup finely chopped parsley and season to taste with salt and pepper. Serves 6.

Tomato and Orange Soup

Here's one from the store cupboard.

To Prepare: 5 minutes

To Cook: 5 minutes

Purée an 800g tin of tomatoes in juice with 1½-2 cups orange juice and 1 tsp sugar. Heat 1 tbsp oil in a saucepan over gentle heat, cook 1 small, finely chopped onion until soft but not coloured. Add tomato mixture and bring to a simmer. Add a pinch of ground mace, coriander and the finely grated rind of ½ orange (no pith). Season with salt and pepper to taste. Just before serving, mix in ¼ cup chopped parsley. Serves 4.

Tom Yum Soup

The fresh clean flavours of Thai food come to the fore in this quick delicious soup.

To Prepare: 5 minutes

To Cook: 8 minutes

Heat 3 cups chicken stock, add 2 tbsp lemon juice, ½-1 tsp dried chilli flakes (or finely chopped dried chilli to taste), 1 tbsp minced lemon grass (or 1 tsp finely grated lemon rind) and 2 tbsp fish sauce. Simmer for 5 minutes. Add 150g of either raw shrimps, very thinly sliced raw chicken or thinly sliced beef and simmer 1 minute more. Mix in 2 tbsp chopped fresh coriander. Stand for a minute before serving. Makes 2 servings. Recipe doubles easily.

Vegetable Soups

CHOOSE FRESH SEASONAL VEGETABLES TO MAKE A RANGE OF CLEAN TASTING AND NUTRITIOUS SOUPS. PREPARING AHEAD ALLOWS FLAVOURS TO DEVELOP.

French Onion Soup

This timeless soup is best made a day or two ahead of serving to allow the flavours to fully develop. Caramelizing the onions first really brings out their sweet flavour. It freezes well.

To Prepare: 10 minutes

To Cook: 40 minutes-1 hour

4 large onions, preferably red
2 tbsp brown sugar
2 tbsp red wine vinegar
2 tbsp butter
1½ litres beef stock
2 cups water
¼ cup port or red wine
salt and ground black pepper
2 tbsp cornflour
a little water to mix

Place onions cut in half lengthwise and then in wedges, brown sugar, vinegar and butter in a covered microwave dish and cook on full power for 8 minutes. Transfer to a large pot and cook gently for 10 more minutes, stirring occasionally until it caramelizes. If not using microwave, cook slowly in the pot for about 40 minutes, stirring occasionally. Add stock, water and port or wine and simmer for 15 minutes. Season with pepper and salt if needed. Mix cornflour with a little water and stir into soup, simmer for 2-3 minutes to lightly thicken. Accompany with Anne's Croûtons.✿ Serves 6.

Above: French Onion Soup with Anne's Croûtons

Fred's Tomato Soup

Great hot or cold, this speedy soup full of summer flavours freezes well. Make it when tomatoes are in peak supply.

To Prepare: 5 minutes

To Cook: 5 minutes

> 1 kg really ripe tomatoes, preferably Italian
> 1 large clove garlic, peeled and lightly chopped
> 1 tbsp sugar
> 2 large handfuls fresh basil leaves, (or 3 tbsp basil pesto)
> 1 tsp each salt and black pepper
> 1 tbsp balsamic vinegar (or tarragon or spiced vinegar)
> 100ml fruity olive oil (to taste)
> about 250ml tomato juice to thin

Pierce the tomato skins in several places, place in a bowl and cover with boiling water. Leave for about 3 minutes, turning once or twice, then drain and peel. Place in a blender or food processor with all the other ingredients, except the tomato juice. Blend until smooth. Mix in the tomato juice, thinning to the consistency you prefer. Chill for at least 1 hour before serving. Alternatively heat to a boil. Serve with a spoon of pesto. Serves 6.

Gazpacho Soup

This wonderful chilled vegetable soup makes a refreshing summer meal. Partner with grilled pita bread and a wedge of washed rind cheese.

To Prepare: 10 minutes

> 500g ripe tomatoes, peeled and roughly chopped
> 1 tsp crushed garlic
> 1 tsp sugar
> salt and ground black pepper
> 1 tbsp chopped fresh mint
> 4-5 drops hot pepper sauce
> 1/4 cucumber, roughly chopped

> 1/4 small red onion, roughly chopped
> 1/4 red or green pepper, roughly chopped
> 2 tbsp balsamic, herb or spiced vinegar
> 1 litre chilled tomato juice

Place all the ingredients except juice in a blender bowl and pulse to blend until chunky. Mix in chilled juice and serve. Serves 4.

Jilly's Roasted Pepper Soup

My friend Jilly Jardine is famous for her picnics, her soups and her good company. This is one of her splendid soups.

To Prepare: 5 minutes

To Cook: 45 minutes

> 3 tbsp olive oil
> 3 large raw red peppers, diced
> 2 medium onions, halved and thinly sliced
> flesh of 3 large roasted red peppers
> 1 tsp chilli paste or minced chillies
> good pinch of cayenne
> 6 cups chicken or vegetable stock
> 1 cup fresh orange juice
> finely grated rind of 1 orange
> salt and ground black pepper
> Optional: handful of basil leaves, torn
> 1/2 cup cream

Heat oil in a large heavy soup pot over low heat. Add raw peppers and onions and cook gently for 15 minutes, stirring occasionally. Add diced roast peppers, chillies, cayenne and stock and simmer for about 25 minutes, stirring occasionally. Stir in orange juice and rind, season to taste and simmer another 5 minutes. Purée in batches. Mix through torn basil leaves and optional cream. Serves 4-6. Freezes well.

Preserving Tomatoes

There's no doubt tomatoes taste best grown outdoors and harvested after a summer of sun. Freeze peak season tomatoes on trays then free flow in plastic bags for winter use or make a big brew of Country Tomato Sauce ✿ to bottle or freeze.

Vegetable Thickenings

Potato, kumara and pumpkin provide good thickeners for soups and stews. Add at the start of cooking so they break down fully.

A Quick Soup Base

The carcass of a roasted chicken or turkey makes a good soup base. Place in a pot, cover with water, add a couple of carrots, an onion and a bay leaf and simmer for one hour. Strain and use as stock.

Pistou of Spring Vegetables with Diablotins

Here's a substantial soup, ideal for lunch or supper, that I've adapted from a recipe of Adelaide cook Sandra Crawley. The Diablotins are a fun idea but not essential.

To Prepare: 20 minutes

To Cook: 20 minutes plus overnight standing

150g carrots, finely chopped
500g onions, finely chopped
1/3 cup extra virgin olive oil
250g courgettes, chopped into
*   1cm rounds*
500g skinned and chopped
*   tomatoes*
500g mixed fresh green beans,
*   runner or French, stringed and*
*   chopped in 4cm lengths*
250g freshly shelled broad beans
*   (or shelled frozen broad beans)*
500mls tomato juice
1 litre good chicken stock
salt and ground black pepper
1/2 tsp chopped fresh thyme
125g short tube macaroni or other
*   dried pasta*
pesto and shaved parmesan to serve
Optional: *Diablotins*

In a large heavy pot, cook onions and carrots in olive oil until onions begin to soften. Add remaining ingredients except macaroni. Bring to a boil then add macaroni. Simmer gently for 5 minutes then remove from heat and leave covered to stand overnight (in the fridge once cooled). The flavours of soup when made this way are much better. Simply re-heat to serve. If you are in a rush, continue to simmer soup another 10 minutes until vegetables and pasta are cooked and serve at once. Accompany with Diablotins, pesto and shaved parmesan on the side. Serves 6.

Diablotins

Mix 1 cup thick White Sauce❂ with pinch cayenne, 1 cup grated cheddar cheese, 1/2 cup grated parmesan or any other good tasty dry cheese. Beat in well until cheese has fully melted and sauce is smooth. (Sauce can be made ahead of time and chilled.) Pre-heat grill. Lay 12 thin slices French bread on a lightly greased tray. Butter top sides and grill until lightly browned. Remove from oven and turn over. Spread with cheese sauce, sprinkle with either parmesan and paprika or a little more cayenne. Place under the grill and cook until brown and bubbling. Allow to cool slightly before serving on a platter.

Below: Pistou of Spring Vegetables with Diablotins

Thai Pumpkin Soup

The most time consuming part of this recipe is cutting up the pumpkin. You can short circuit this by buying chopped pumpkin pieces. Microwaving a whole pumpkin for 10 minutes makes cutting easier.

To Prepare: 10 minutes
To Cook: 30 minutes

> 2 tbsp olive oil
> 1 onion, finely chopped
> 1 tbsp brown sugar
> 2 cloves garlic, crushed
> 1 medium pumpkin (about 1.2kg), eg buttercup, peeled and diced
> 2 cups water
> 1 x 400ml can coconut milk
> 1-2 fresh or dried chillies, finely chopped
> 1 tbsp lemongrass, minced, or 1/2 tsp finely grated lemon rind
> 1 tbsp fish sauce
> salt and ground black pepper
> 1/4 cup fresh coriander or parsley, chopped

Heat oil in a big pot and gently cook onion, sugar and garlic until softened (8-10 minutes). Add all other ingredients except fresh coriander and simmer until tender, about 20 minutes. Mash roughly, adjust seasonings to taste and mix through coriander. Serves 4. Freezes.

Classic Pumpkin Soup

The essence of a good pumpkin soup lies in the pumpkin – you need a dry texture and good nutty flavour.

To Prepare: 15 minutes
To Cook: 25 minutes

Base Soup

> 1 tbsp butter
> 1 large onion, finely diced
> 3 cloves garlic, crushed
> 1kg buttercup pumpkin, peeled and diced into 2cm cubes
> 5 cups chicken stock (or make up with water 1 pkt soup mix and 2 tsp stock powder)
> 1 tsp finely chopped fresh thyme
> 1/2 tsp nutmeg
> 1/2 tsp finely grated orange rind
> salt and pepper
> chopped parsley or chives to garnish

Heat the butter in a large pot and cook the diced onion and garlic over low heat until softened. Add the diced pumpkin with the chicken stock, nutmeg, rind and thyme. Simmer for about 15 minutes until tender. Just before serving stir in 1/2 cup of chopped parsley or some chopped chives. If preferred, blend the soup until smooth before serving. Serves 6.

Variations:

- **Bacon and Gruyère Pumpkin Soup:** Cook 3 rashers diced bacon with the onion and add 1/2 cup grated gruyère to cooked soup.
- **Moroccan Pumpkin Soup:** Omit thyme and add 2 tbsp Moroccan Spice Rub.☺
- **Orange and Walnut Soup:** Add 1 cup fresh orange juice and 1/2 cup ground toasted walnuts.

Opposite: Thai Pumpkin Soup with Coconut Sambal

Two Mushroom Soup

This elegant soup gets a real boost of flavour from the addition of a handful of dried Chinese mushrooms.

To Prepare: 40 minutes (includes 30 minutes soaking time)

To Cook: 20 minutes

> 8 dried Chinese mushrooms
> ½ cup port
> 2 tbsp butter
> 1 tsp crushed garlic
> 500g field mushrooms, finely sliced
> 6 cups chicken stock
> black pepper and a pinch of nutmeg
> ¼ cup finely chopped parsley
> 2 tsp cornflour mixed with water

Optional: 1 cup cream

Soak the Chinese mushrooms in port for at least 30 minutes, or until soft enough to slice finely. Lift out of the liquid and slice, discarding stalks. Return to the liquid and reserve. Heat the butter and cook the garlic for a few seconds. Add the field mushrooms and cook until dry and just starting to brown. Add the soaked mushrooms and their liquid and cook until dry. Add the chicken stock and simmer for 15 minutes over a low heat. Thicken with cornflour paste. Season well with black pepper and nutmeg and mix in the chopped parsley. If using cream, add and allow to heat through. Serves 4. Freezes.

Variation: For a special occasion use an equal quantity of dried ceps or 2-3 dried morels in place of dried Chinese mushrooms.

Quick Fresh Mushroom Soup

When fresh field mushrooms are plentiful and darkly flavoursome, make this delicious quick soup. Heat 2 tbsp butter, add 1kg chopped dark mushrooms and 2 cloves crushed garlic and a spoon of chopped fresh herbs, eg tarragon, parsley, basil. Cook until mushrooms have exuded all their liquid and are starting to brown. Add 4 cups chicken stock and simmer for 10 minutes. Mix 2 tbsp cornflour with ½ cup milk and stir into soup until it is lightly thickened. Simmer for 5 minutes. Season well with salt and ground black pepper and add the juice of ½ lemon. Serves 4. Freezes.

Using Dried Mushrooms

Dried mushrooms have an intense flavour unmatched by fresh. Chinese dried mushrooms are much cheaper than European mushrooms such as ceps or morels, and although their flavour differs, can be substituted wherever dried mushrooms are called for to give a more intense mushroom flavour. Store dried mushrooms in a sealed container. To use, soak mushrooms in water, wine or port until pliable. With Chinese shiitakes, remove and discard the stems. Add the soaking liquid with the mushrooms for extra flavour.

Right: Two Mushroom Soup with Naan Bread

Seafood Soups

ADDING SEAFOOD TO A SOUP TURNS IT INTO A SUSTAINING MEAL. TAKE CARE NOT TO OVER COOK AND SERVE FRESH RATHER THAN MAKING AHEAD AND THEN RE-HEATING.

Blue Bayou Gumbo

Depending on the type of sausage you use, this dish varies from hot to fiery!

To Prepare: 20 minutes
To Cook: about 1 hour

> 50g butter
> 3 tbsp flour
> 2 large onions, diced finely
> 1 green pepper, cut into 2cm dice
> 1 tbsp crushed garlic
> 2 stalks celery, diced finely
> 1/2 cup tomato paste
> 8 cups chicken stock
> 2 chicken pieces
> 300g pepperoni or chilli sausage (hottest), diced in 1/2cm cubes
> 2 tsp each thyme, basil and smoked paprika
> 1/2 tsp each allspice, cloves, cayenne, salt
> 2 bay leaves
> 2 tbsp finely chopped parsley
> 1kg mixed diced seafood eg prawns, diced fish and squid
> 6 spring onions, thinly sliced
> Optional: 4-6 okra, thinly sliced

Heat the butter in a large heavy pot until smoking hot. Mix in the flour, stirring constantly over heat until the roux turns a darkish red-brown colour, which will take about 3 minutes. When the roux reaches the desired colour add the onions, pepper, garlic, celery and tomato paste. Cook over medium heat 2 to 3 minutes, stirring constantly. Add the chicken stock and stir over heat until it is fully absorbed. Add the chicken, diced sausage and all the remaining seasonings. Bring the mixture to a low simmer. Cook ingredients for about 1 hour, skimming frequently. The sauce should be reduced until it is semi-thick. If using okra, reduce cooking time slightly and add in the last half-hour of cooking. Lift out chicken pieces, shred flesh and add to soup. Add seafood to soup in last 5 minutes of cooking. Garnish with spring onions and parsley. Serves 6 as a meal.

West Coast Mussel Soup

If collecting wild mussels be sure they are from a safe, unpolluted source.

To Prepare: 5 minutes
To Cook: 10 minutes

> 2kg mussels in shell
> 2 cups water
> 2 tsp crushed garlic
> 1 cup white wine
> 1 cup cream
> ground black pepper
> 1/4 cup finely chopped parsley

Scrub the mussels and place in a large, lidded pot with the water. Cover and cook over high heat, removing as they open. Remove mussels from shells, saving all the cooking juice. Purée the mussels and garlic in batches. Place the purée in a pot with reserved cooking juices, wine and cream and bring to a simmer. Season to taste with lots of pepper. Stir through the parsley. Serves 6.

Dashi for Fish Stock

Dashi is Japan's all purpose soup stock and flavouring, which is made from dried bonito fillet. These days Japanese food stores sell packets of instant dashi – granules which dissolve in hot water. They make a great instant fish stock.

Okra

Okra is an interesting vegetable with an extraordinary gummy texture when sliced. This is used to thicken soups and stews. The word gumbo comes from the Bantu word for okra – 'gombo'.

Bouillabaisse

This is a special soup, great for a week-end dinner or when you have been lucky with your fishing line. Bouillabaisse tastes better if you can use 2-3 different kinds of fish. In France, the fish is usually served first on a plate, with the broth to follow, topped with garlicky, hot rouille croûtons.

To Prepare: 20 minutes
To Cook: 45 minutes

> ½ cup olive oil
> 2 medium onions, finely chopped
> 1 leek, finely chopped
> 1 stalk celery, chopped
> 2-3 bay leaves
> 4 large garlic cloves, minced
> 2 tbsp tomato paste
> 1-2 tsp chilli paste, to taste
> 2 cups dry white wine
> big pinch saffron threads
> 1 tsp honey
> 2 x 400g cans tomatoes in juice,
>   chopped or 1kg fresh tomatoes,
>   peeled and chopped
> 12 cups fish stock ✿
> salt and ground black pepper
> 1kg various firm fish, boneless
>   fillets, cut in 4cm pieces
> 500-700g fresh mussels, scrubbed
> Rouille and croûtons to serve
> *Optional: 8-16 large raw prawns*

Heat oil in a large pot and gently cook onions for 10-15 minutes until clear. Add leek and celery and cook a further 10 minutes. Add bay leaves, garlic, tomato paste and chilli paste. Sizzle a few seconds. Mix in wine, saffron, honey and tomatoes. Cook for 20 minutes over low heat. Add fish stock and season to taste. Bring back to a simmer and add mussels (or steam separately then add them to the soup with their juices). Discard any mussels that don't open. Add fish fillets and simmer gently for 2-3 minutes until just cooked. Divide between hot soup bowls and top with a croûton spread with Rouille. Pass around extra Rouille and croûtons separately. Makes 8 large servings.

Mussel and Corn Chowder

This chunky, substantial chowder makes a great winter meal. Use chilli or garlic flavoured mussels as a variation.

To Prepare: 10 minutes
To Cook: 20 minutes

> 1 tbsp butter
> 1 large onion, diced
> 2 stalks celery, finely diced
> 2 potatoes, diced in 1cm cubes
> 3 cups chicken stock
> 1 tsp dried thyme
> 2 bay leaves
> 1 cup whole kernel corn, drained
> 200g smoked mussels, chopped
> 1 tbsp cornflour mixed with 2 tbsp
>   sherry or water
> 2 cups milk
> ¼ cup chopped parsley
> salt and black pepper to taste

In a large saucepan heat the butter and cook the onion and celery over a low heat until the onion is soft. Add the potato, stock, thyme, bay leaves, corn and smoked mussels and simmer over low heat until the potato is cooked (about 10 minutes). Mix in the cornflour paste until it thickens, then add the milk and parsley. Allow to simmer for 3-4 minutes. Season to taste with salt and pepper. Serve with hot, crisp bread. Serves 6.

Rouille

The classic accompaniment to Bouillabaisse, this spicy, creamy purée makes delicious dunking for bread as well as a topping for croûtons. Purée 1 large boiled potato, 6 cloves garlic, peeled and minced, 1-2 tsp minced chillies, 1 egg yolk, ¼ tsp paprika and ½ cup extra virgin olive oil, adding salt to taste. Stored in the fridge, rouille will keep for 2-3 days.

Handling Saffron

Toasting the dried saffron pistils and then grinding them makes the saffron release its colour much more quickly. Use a dry pan, microwave or hot oven and toast until crumbly. Take care not to burn. Pulverize threads in the palm of your hand and add to the cooking pot or sauce as required. Store fresh saffron in an airtight container out of the light.

Opposite: Bouillabaisse

Bread

FEW SMELLS EVOKE THE SENSE OF HOME AND HEARTH LIKE THOSE OF BAKING BREAD. YEAST-RISEN DOUGHS ARE WONDERFUL, BUT IF YOU DON'T HAVE TIME TO RISE DOUGHS MAKE YEAST-FREE RECIPES LIKE ROTI AND CHILLI CHEESE BREAD.

Naan Bread

This soft puffy bread is terrific for mopping up winter soups and stews.

To Prepare: 15 minutes and 30-40 minutes rising

To Cook: 4-5 minutes

> 6 cups high grade flour, plus a little extra flour for kneading
> 2 tsp salt
> 1 cup hot water
> 1 tbsp sugar
> 1 cup unsweetened yoghurt
> 1 tbsp dried yeast
> 2 eggs
> 100g butter, melted

Combine flour and salt in a large mixing bowl. Mix hot water, sugar and yoghurt in another bowl – the mix should be lukewarm. Stir in yeast and leave for 5 minutes. Beat eggs and melted butter into yeast mixture. Combine with flour, stirring until mixture has combined. Turn out onto a lightly floured board and continue kneading until mix has come together into a smooth soft dough (10 minutes). Extra flour may be required for kneading. Place in an oiled bowl in a warm place, covered until doubled in bulk (30-40 minutes). Lightly flour a board and turn out the dough. Knead for 2-3 minutes until smooth, silky and elastic. Take golfball-sized pieces of dough and work into balls. Roll or press balls on a lightly floured surface, flattening to 1cm thickness. Give them a light pull to stretch dough a little. Place 3 or 4 breads (as will fit) on a lightly floured oven tray or baking stone and grill under high heat until golden brown and puffy on one side (1-2 minutes). Watch like a hawk. Turn over and cook other sides. Repeat until all breads are cooked. Re-heat in tinfoil if required. Serve plain or brush with butter or oil (plain or flavoured). Makes about 22-24 large naans. Dough freezes well – roll into balls, and free flow freeze.

Olive Oil Focaccia

This is a wonderfully gratifying bread to prepare. Both raw dough and cooked bread can be frozen.

To Prepare: 15 minutes plus 30 minutes rising

To Cook: 20 minutes

> 2 cups warm water
> 2 tsp dry yeast
> 1 tsp sugar
> $1/2$ cup olive oil
> $5^1/2$ cups high grade flour
> $1^1/2$ tsp salt
> Optional: $1/2$ cup chopped olives or capers

Mix yeast and sugar into warm water. Stand for 5 minutes to dissolve. Mix in oil and $3/4$ of flour, then add rest of flour and optional olives. Rub your hands with oil and work the dough, kneading until smooth – it will be quite sticky. Use a little olive oil if necessary to stop sticking. Divide dough into 2 and form each into a flat oblong. Leave in a warm place for 30 minutes, then brush top of loaf with water as it goes into the oven and bake at 220°C for about 20 minutes or until golden and loaf sounds hollow when tapped.

Which Flour?

The difference between high grade and plain flour is not in the quality but in the amount of protein the different flours contain. High grade flour has a higher level of protein than plain flour. This affects its take up of water. Mixing 1 cup water with 2 cups high grade flour gives the same texture as mixing 1 cup water with about $2^1/2$ cups plain flour. Use high grade flour for breads and heavy fruit cakes and plain flour for general baking and thickening.

Garlic Infused Oil

Gently heat $1/2$ cup extra virgin olive oil, 2 crushed cloves garlic and 1 fresh bay leaf, just allowing garlic to come to a gentle sizzle. Cool and store in a clean sealed bottle. It will keep for a couple of months.

Chilli Cheese Bread

Here's a moist quick loaf spiked with cheese and chillies. It's extra good when toasted and made into sandwiches with avocado, tomato, spinach and cheese. Makes an excellent partner with barbecues and roasts or served toasted, under Gumbo.

To Prepare: 10 minutes

To Cook: 30-35 minutes

> 1 tbsp sugar
> 1 egg
> 2 tsp salt
> 1 tsp black pepper
> 100g melted butter
> 2 cups milk
> 1/2 tsp baking soda, mixed with 2 tbsp hot milk
> 1 red pepper, finely diced

> 1 tbsp minced chillies
> 4 cups self-raising flour
> 1 cup coarse cornmeal
> 2 cups grated tasty cheese
> beaten egg

Pre-heat oven to 200°C. Beat together sugar, egg, salt and pepper. Mix in butter, milk and soda which has been mixed with hot milk. Add red peppers, chillies, flour, cornmeal and cheese and mix until just combined. Spoon into 2 greased loaf pans, brush with beaten egg and bake in pre-heated oven for 30-35 minutes, or until a skewer inserted into the middle comes out clean. Leave to cool in the tins before tipping out. Makes 2 loaves. Freezes well.

Above: Olive Oil Focaccia

Testing doneness of breads

One of the easiest ways to determine whether a loaf is cooked is to tap it on the top — if it sounds hollow then the dough is fully cooked through. If you want a crisp crust on a loaf, spray the dough finely with water as you put it into the oven and again about half-way through cooking.

Grilled Chinese Pancakes

Roll up these wonderful chewy little pancakes with a tasty filling for an easy lunch or supper.

To Prepare: 10 minutes
To Cook: about 15 minutes

> 2 cups high grade flour
> 1/2 tsp sugar
> 1 tsp salt
> 1/2 cup cold water
> 1 tsp sesame oil
> a little extra sesame oil to brush

Combine flour, sugar and salt in a bowl. Mix in water and oil, kneading to form a smooth firm dough. Divide dough in half and form each half into a sausage shape. Cut each sausage into 12 equal portions, then form each portion into a ball. Pat into flat circles. Brush top of one round with a little sesame oil, then top with another like a sandwich. Repeat with the other balls to make 12 'sandwiches'. Roll out each 'sandwich' as thinly as possible to form 10cm rounds. Cook on a preheated barbecue plate for 2-3 minutes each side. Split pancakes in half to serve and fill with toppings of your choice. Makes 12 pancakes.

Coconut Onion Roti

The coconut and onion in these roti make them delicious enough to serve on their own, or as a tasty accompaniment to soups.

To Prepare: 10 minutes
To Cook: 15 minutes

> 1 1/2 cups desiccated coconut
> 2 cups plain flour
> 3/4 tsp salt
> 2 eggs
> 1/2 cup finely chopped onion cooked in oil until soft
> about 3 tbsp water to make a stiff dough

Mix together the coconut, flour and salt in a large bowl. Make a well in the middle and mix in the eggs, cooked onion and enough water to make a firm dough. Mix well, then knead dough about 20 times. Divide dough in half, then roll each piece into a log and cut each log into 20 pieces. Roll out very thinly. (Alternatively, roll out dough and use a cutter to cut small rounds.) Heat a grill plate or heavy pan and cook roti on both sides until lightly golden. Makes about 20 roti.

Pizza

Good pizza has a crisp crust and not too much topping. The base dough can be made ahead of time. Raw dough freezes well. Thaw and press out into pizza shapes before topping.

To Prepare: 25 minutes plus
30 minutes rising
To Cook: 25 minutes

> 2 tsp sugar
> 1 1/3 cups warm water
> 2 tbsp dry yeast
> 4 cups high grade flour
> 2 tsp salt
> 2 tbsp olive oil

To prepare the base, dissolve the sugar in the warm water. Sprinkle the yeast over the water and stand in a warm place for 10 minutes. Combine the flour and salt in a mixing bowl. Stir in the yeast mixture and oil until well combined. Knead on a lightly floured surface for 10 minutes until smooth. Place the dough in a lightly oiled bowl. Cover and stand in a warm place for 30 minutes or until the dough has doubled in size. Push a clenched fist into the middle of the dough to deflate and turn onto a lightly floured surface. Roll out into 2 x 28cm rounds. Sprinkle with your chosen toppings. Bake at 220°C for 25-30 minutes until crisp and golden.

PIZZA TOPPINGS

- garlic, spinach, red peppers and parmesan
- crumbled spicy sausage, mozzarella and peppers
- sun-dried tomato pesto, peppers, cherry tomatoes, basil and garlic oil
- peppers, blue cheese, salami and cherry tomatoes
- peppers, capers, olives and mozzarella
- garlic oil, tomato sauce, roasted eggplant slices and mozzarella
- tapenade, wilted greens (spinach, watercress or rocket), red peppers, olives and mozzarella

- basil pesto, roasted eggplant, tomatoes and mozzarella
- fresh mozzarella, herbs and extra virgin olive oil
- crème fraîche, mozzarella, smoked salmon and watercress
- sun-dried tomato pesto, salami, olives and feta
- havarti cheese, stewed artichoke hearts, cooked garlic and ham
- roasted onions, feta cheese, herbs and mozzarella
- leeks, goat's cheese and toasted pinenuts

SEAFOOD

Flash-roasted Fish with Red Pepper
Sauce

Genoese Baked Fish with
Parmesan and Herbs

Veracruz Baked Fish

Soy and Ginger Glazed Salmon

Fish Fillets with Toasted Almonds
and Lime Juice

Roasted Crayfish with Herb Butter

Flash-roasted Salmon with
Chilli Lime Glaze

Sesame Ginger Butter

Pesto Butter

Chilli Ginger Whole Fish

Thai Fish Parcels

Creamy Pasta and Scallops

Chilli Mussel Fettuccine

Fresh Fish Pasta with
Ginger Nut Butter

Spicy Peanut Shrimp Noodles

Pasta with Smoked Salmon
and Peppercorns

Cockles or Mussels with Pesto
Cream Sauce

Provençal Fish

Crab Cakes with Aïoli

Mediterranean Stir-fried Squid

Battered Fish

Steamed Mussels with Aromatics

Cantonese Paua Stir-fry

Indian Spiced Fish

Mussels with Chilli, Coconut
and Coriander

Brazilian Fish with
Cashew Sauce

Hellish Mango Fish

Thai Fish Curry

Sichuan Stir-fried Crab

Smoked Fish and
Kumara Pie

Lemon Fish Pie

Kedgeree

Salmon and Lemon Risotto

Spicy Steamed Seafood

Whole Fish with
East Asian Marinade

BBQ Crayfish with Brazilian
Seasoning

Scallops Cooked in the
Half Shell with Cumin Chilli
Tomato Sauce

Skewered Mediterranean Fish and
Vegetables

Oriental Barbecue
Tuna Steaks

BBQ Pipi Fritters

Potato Rosti with Hot-smoked
Salmon and Salsa Verde

Pan-fried Paua with Roasted Corn
and Red Peppers

Hot-smoked Salmon with Asparagus
and Rocket

Smoked Fish Salad with Aïoli, Cucumber
and Spring Onions

Smoked Salmon, Avocado and
Grapefruit Salad

Thai Marinated Grilled Salmon
with a Crisp Noodle Salad

Marinated Fish Salad

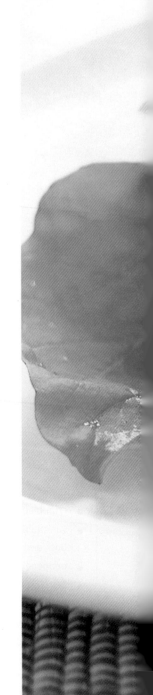

Quick Oven Treatments

BAKING FISH IN A REALLY HOT OVEN IS ONE OF THE QUICKEST WAYS TO COOK — A DELICIOUS DINNER ON THE TABLE IN UNDER 10 MINUTES. COVER BONELESS FILLETS WITH A TOPPING, COATING OR MARINADE BEFORE BAKING AND SERVE WITH RICE, MASH OR COUS COUS AND LIGHTLY COOKED GREENS.

Testing Fish for Doneness

Fish is so easily over cooked. The result is dry and mealy instead of being juicy and tender. Press a piece of raw fish before you start cooking to ascertain its texture. When fish is cooked, it should no longer have any 'bounce', but should give with pressure. Cooked fish will also show no resistance when skewered – choose the deepest part. Another way to tell whether fish is cooked is when small fine white beads of protein start to appear on the surface.

For whole fish, cook until the eye starts to whiten and test with a skewer up in the deepest part behind the gills.

Previous page: Rosti with Hot-smoked Salmon and Salsa Verde

Flash-roasted Fish with Red Pepper Sauce

This dish is ideal when you want a quick, elegant dinner. The sauce will keep for a few days in the fridge and is also excellent mixed through seafood and pasta, or served with grilled meats.

To Prepare: 10 minutes
To Cook: 5-8 minutes

Red Pepper Sauce

> flesh of 2 roasted red peppers
> 1/4 cup stock or orange juice
> salt and ground black pepper
> 4 x 180-200g boneless fish fillets
> 1/4 cup good olive paste, or herb pesto or other flavour paste
> 4-6 sliced courgettes or a large bunch green beans, ends trimmed off

Pre-heat oven to 250°C. To prepare sauce, purée red peppers with stock or juice until smooth. Season to taste with salt and pepper. Put to one side (it will keep for several days in the fridge and can also be frozen). To cook fish, place fillets in a lightly oiled baking dish and fold under any thin edges. Spread with olive paste or another paste or pesto. Bake fish for 5-8 minutes until flesh shows very little resistance when pressed. Check after 5 minutes. Do not over cook – the fish should still be slightly translucent in the centre and not flake too easily. While fish cooks, heat red pepper sauce and cook courgettes or beans.

To serve, spoon red pepper sauce into the centre of each plate. Top with a mound of beans and place fish on top. Serves 4.
Busy Day Dinner Idea: Accompany fish with mashed potato, rice or noodles.

Genoese Baked Fish with Parmesan and Herbs

Parmesan cheese makes a great coating for fish. If preferred, the fish can also be pan fried rather than baked.

To Prepare: 5 minutes
To Cook: 10-12 minutes

> 4 fresh boneless fish fillets
> 1 egg, lightly beaten
> 1/2 cup grated parmesan cheese
> 1/2 cup fresh breadcrumbs
> 1 tbsp olive oil
> 1 tsp dried oregano
> pinch each of salt and ground black pepper

Pre-heat oven to 220°C. Dip fish into egg. Combine other ingredients and coat fish pieces. Place on a baking tray and bake for 8-10 minutes, or until a skewer inserted into fish meets no resistance. Serves 4.
Busy Day Dinner Idea: Accompany with mashed potato and a fresh coleslaw.

Veracruz Baked Fish

Hot and Spicy Salsa from the fridge forms a piquant sauce base for this tasty fish bake. Use any form of white fish.

To Prepare: 5 minutes

To Cook: 15 minutes

> 6 thick firm white boneless fish
>   fillets
> 2 tomatoes, sliced thinly
> 2 red peppers, sliced thinly
> 1 cup Hot and Spicy Salsa ❂ or
>   1 cup taco sauce
> juice and finely grated rind of
> 1 orange
> 1 tsp minced chillies
> 2-3 tbsp chopped coriander

Pre-heat oven to 220°C. Arrange fish fillets in a single layer in a shallow baking dish. Season with salt and pepper. Spread over sliced tomatoes and peppers. Mix Hot and Spicy Salsa with orange juice, rind, coriander and chillies and pour over. Cover dish and bake for 15 minutes. Serves 6.

Busy Day Dinner Idea: *Accompany with rice and a green salad.*

Above: Flash-roasted Fish with Red Pepper Sauce

Right: Soy and Ginger Glazed Salmon

Removing Salmon Bones

A line of bones, known as pin bones, runs just off-centre of the spine of each salmon fillet for about two thirds of its length.
Use sterilised tweezers or pin-nosed pliers to remove, pulling them out at the same angle as they lie. Now you have a completely boneless fillet.

Soy and Ginger Glazed Salmon

Here's a really useful, great tasting glaze for fish or poultry. Use any firm fish.

To Prepare: 5 minutes
To Cook: 5-6 minutes

> ¼ *cup soy sauce*
> ¼ *cup rice wine or sake*
> 1 *tbsp minced fresh ginger*
> 2 *tbsp sugar*
> 1 *side salmon, cut in 6, pin bones removed, or 6 fillets of boneless salmon*

Place soy sauce, rice wine or sake, ginger and sugar in a pot and boil about 5 minutes until just lightly thickened. Cool. Pour over fish. Leave for 10 minutes or up to 2 hours in the fridge, turning once or twice. Pre-heat oven to 250°C. Place fish in a baking dish, spoon over marinade to coat. Bake 5-6 minutes until cooked. Serves 6.

Busy Day Dinner Idea: *Serve on a bed of rice with lightly cooked spinach.*

Fish Fillets with Toasted Almonds and Lime Juice

An update on an easy classic and great with delicate fish like orange roughy.

To Prepare: 3 minutes
To Cook: 6 minutes

> 2 *tbsp butter*
> ½ *cup flaked almonds*
> 2 *fresh firm fish fillets or steaks*
> *juice of 1 lime or lemon*
> *salt and ground black pepper*

Pre-heat oven to 220°C. Melt the butter in a pan or microwave and mix in the almonds. Cook for 2-3 minutes, stirring every 30-40 seconds until lightly toasted. Place fish fillets in a shallow baking dish, folding under any thin ends. Drain butter from almonds and brush over the fish. Squeeze over lemon or lime juice. Season with salt and pepper. Top with almonds, cover tightly and bake for 5-6 minutes until fish is cooked. Serves 2.

Roasted Crayfish with Herb Butter

Split a fresh crayfish in half, lengthwise, brush the cut flesh with flavoured oil or butter and throw into a super hot oven for about 10 minutes. It's divine with Sesame Ginger Butter or Pesto Butter.

To Prepare: 5 minutes
To Cook: 10 minutes

1-2 whole fresh crayfish, split in half lengthwise with a heavy knife or cleaver
2-4 tbsp flavoured butter, eg Sesame Ginger Butter ✿

Pre-heat oven to 250°C. Spread cut flesh of crayfish with flavoured butter. Place in a roasting dish cut side up and bake for 8-10 minutes until flesh is cooked through and no longer transparent at the thickest part. Stand for 3-4 minutes before serving. Serves 2-4.

Flash-roasted Salmon with Chilli Lime Glaze

So easy and so very good. Try the glaze with chicken too.

To Prepare: 5 minutes
To Cook: 5-6 minutes

1 side salmon, cut in 6 fillets, pin bones removed
salt and ground black pepper
1/2 cup Thai sweet chilli sauce
1/4 cup fresh lime juice
finely grated rind of 1 lime

Pre-heat oven to 250°C. Arrange fish in a baking dish, season with salt and pepper. Mix chilli sauce, lime juice and rind. Spread half over the fish. Bake for 5-6 minutes until cooked through. Heat rest of the sauce and spoon over. Serves 6.
Busy Day Dinner Idea: *Serve salmon fillets on rice with lightly cooked spinach.*

MENU IDEAS

Mid-week Guests
Dinner on the Run

pita breads with goat's cheese and salsa verde

flash-roasted salmon with chilli lime glaze

Thai rice

lightly cooked greens

fresh fruits with Greek yoghurt or cream

Advance preparations

- *make salsa verde and Greek yoghurt*
- *put rice on to cook*
- *spread fish with chilli lime glaze ready to bake*
- *wash greens and put wet in a fry-pan with a little grated ginger and a dash of oil*
- *make fruit salad while fish cooks*

Sesame Ginger Butter

Mix 50g soft butter, 2 tbsp minced ginger, 2 tsp sesame oil and 1 minced spring onion.

Pesto Butter

Mix 100g soft butter with 1 tbsp pesto, 1/2 tsp finely grated lemon rind and 1 tbsp lemon juice.

Dealing with a live crayfish

Crayfish can be killed by drowning in fresh cold water; by dropping into boiling water (they can tend to kick off their legs this way); by freezing for an hour or two; or by cutting through the head between the eyes with a sharp heavy knife.

Storing Flavoured Butters

Store flavoured butters covered in the fridge if not using at once. They will keep for about a week. They also freeze well.

Over: Flash-roasted Salmon with Chilli Lime Glaze

FAST FISH IN A FLASH

Spread fish with any one of these snappy seafood toppings and cook in a very hot oven – about 250°C. Fillets will cook in 4–6 minutes. For master recipe, see Flash-roasted Salmon with Chilli Lime Glaze on the previous page.

- Chilli Lime Glaze
- Winter Pesto
- Black Olive Tapenade
- Black Bean Sauce or Oyster Sauce
- Soy and Ginger Glaze
- Cajun Spice Mix

- East Asian Marinade
- Salsa Verde
- Thai Flavour Mix
- Hot and Spicy Salsa
- Sesame Ginger Butter
- Moroccan Sauce

Chilli Ginger Whole Fish

This classic Asian fish treatment is an easy and great way to cook whole fish. Don't be nervous about cooking a whole fish – its sweetness is unrivalled. To determine when the fish is cooked check the eye. As the eye starts to whiten the fish is generally cooked through – press the thickest part of the flesh up by the gills and if it no longer 'bounces' the fish is cooked. Stand for 5 minutes before serving.

To Prepare: 5 minutes

To Cook: 10 minutes

> 1 whole fish, scaled and cleaned, head and tail intact, eg red snapper approx 600-800g
> 1 tbsp Thai sweet chilli sauce
> 2 tbsp grated root ginger
> 2 tsp sesame oil
> 1 clove crushed garlic
> 1 tsp each salt and brown sugar

Pre-heat oven to 250°C. Wash and pat the fish dry. Make criss-cross slashes on each side of the body. Mix seasonings together and rub over skin, into slashes and inside cavity of fish. Place in an oiled baking dish. Bake for 8-10 minutes, or grill for about 4-5 minutes per side until the fish is cooked. Serves 1.

Variation: Mediterranean Grilled Whole Fish – Prepare and cook fish as above but with the following seasoning paste. Combine 2 chopped cloves of garlic, 1 tbsp chopped fresh rosemary, 1 tsp fennel seed, 1 tbsp chopped parsley and 3 tbsp olive oil.

Thai Fish Parcels

Fish parcels take all kinds of flavours and are so easy to make. Use tinfoil or baking paper as a wrap, or if you have access to them, banana leaves. If prepared in tinfoil, they can also be cooked on the barbecue – allow about 10 minutes, and shake occasionally to distribute heat.

To Prepare: 5 minutes

To Cook: 10 minutes

Thai Flavour Mix

> 1 tsp green curry paste
> 2 tbsp Thai sweet chilli sauce
> 2 tsp fish sauce
> juice and finely grated rind of $^1/_2$ lemon
> 1 diced spring onion
>
> 4 fresh, boneless fish fillets

Pre-heat oven to 250°C. Combine flavourings. Place each boneless fish fillet on a large circle of tinfoil or baking paper. Spread over 1 tbsp of flavour mix. Pull up sides of paper to make a pouch, tie tightly with string, or twist tinfoil at the top to seal. Bake for 10-12 minutes. Serves 4.

Other Fish Parcel Combinations

- tomatoes, peppers and pesto
- cooked leeks, garlic, tomatoes and fennel seeds
- shredded spinach, orange rind and tarragon
- banana, coconut, coriander and lemon juice
- coconut cream, spring onions, coriander, curry paste
- sweet chilli sauce and spring onions
- cream cheese and pesto
- olive paste and sliced tomatoes
- tomatoes, olives, red peppers, pesto and capers

Left: Chilli Ginger Whole Fish

Seafood Pasta & Noodles

AROMATICS SUCH AS LEMON OR LIME RIND, SAFFRON AND FRESH HERBS
ENHANCE SEAFOOD'S SUCCULENT FLAVOURS WITHOUT OVERPOWERING. ALWAYS COOK THE
SEAFOOD JUST BEFORE YOU PLAN TO EAT IT.

Re-heating Pasta

Purists will raise their
eyebrows, but cooked pasta
can be successfully re-heated.
Cover and microwave for 2-3
minutes or place in a bowl
and cover pasta with boiling
water for 1 minute.

Cream or Not

Cream adds richness and
texture to everything,
including pasta sauces. It also
adds fat and calories. Ditto
for coconut cream. If you
wish to live a creamless
existence, then go for a
tomato based sauce or serve
pasta drier, using lemon
juice, fresh herbs and a little
olive oil combined with fish,
chicken or vegetables.

Creamy Pasta and Scallops

Perfect for a dinner party or special occasion. The sauce and pasta can be prepared ahead of time and re-heated. Cook the scallops just before serving. Fresh cubes of fish can also be used.

To Prepare: 5 minutes
To Cook: 10-15 minutes

> 1/4 cup finely chopped shallots
> 2 tbsp butter
> 1 tsp tomato paste
> 1 cup dry white wine
> 1 cup cream
> 600-800g fettuccine
> 30-50 fresh scallops, cleaned, or
>   1kg cubed fish
> finely diced red pepper
> 1/4 cup chopped chervil or dill
> salt and ground black pepper

Optional: pinch saffron threads

In a large heavy pan cook the shallots in the butter until soft but not browned. Add the tomato paste and cook a few seconds. Add the wine and bring to a fast boil. Mix in the cream and saffron, if using. Boil until the sauce has a light coating consistency (prepare ahead to this point if desired). Cook the pasta according to manufacturer's instructions, warm the pasta bowls. When the pasta is nearly cooked, add the scallops or fish and peppers to the hot sauce, cover and cook on lowest possible heat for about 2 minutes, stirring at the start to ensure even cooking. Do not over cook. Mix in the herbs and season to taste. Toss sauce through cooked pasta and divide between heated pasta bowls. Serves 6-8.

Busy Day Dinner Idea: *Accompany pasta with a green salad.*

Chilli Mussel Fettuccine

Smoked mussels add an intense flavour and richness to this easy pasta dish. Smoked mussels can be stored in the freezer.

To Prepare: 5 minutes
To Cook: 10-15 minutes

> 400g fettuccine or spaghetti
> 1 tbsp vegetable oil
> 1 tsp crushed garlic
> 2 cups prepared tomato pasta
>   sauce
> 200g smoked or chilli mussels,
>   sliced thinly
> 1-2 tbsp sweet chilli sauce, to taste
> salt, pepper and a pinch of sugar
> diced pepper and finely sliced
>   spring onions to garnish

Optional: 2-3 tbsp pesto

Cook the pasta according to manufacturer's instructions. Heat the oil in a fry-pan and cook the garlic for 30 seconds. Add the pasta sauce, mussels, chilli sauce and seasonings. Simmer for 5 minutes. Toss the sauce through the cooked pasta, add the peppers, spring onions and optional pesto and serve immediately. Serves 4-5.

Fresh Fish Pasta with Ginger Nut Butter

Dinner in five. A quick tasty toss of fresh salmon, green beans and a delectable nut butter.

To Prepare: 10 minutes

To Cook: 10 minutes

    400g dried linguini or fettuccine
    250g green beans or snowpeas
    2 tbsp olive oil
    400g boneless skinned salmon, in
      2cm pieces (or other dense fish)
    salt and pepper
    1 portion Ginger Nut Butter (see
      side panel)

Cook the pasta according to manufacturer's instructions, adding beans or peas in the last few minutes of cooking (snowpeas only take 1 minute). While pasta cooks, heat the oil, season salmon and cook over high heat for about 30-40 seconds on each side, just until it starts to change colour. Do not over cook. Drain pasta and beans, toss through Ginger Nut Butter, then lightly toss in the fish to combine evenly, taking care not to break it up. Serve at once. Serves 4.

Busy Day Dinner Idea: *Accompany with flatbread and grilled tomatoes.*

Above: Fresh Fish Pasta with Ginger Nut Butter

Ginger Nut Butter

Spread over fish before flash roasting, thin with oil and use as a BBQ baste, toss through pasta with seafood, or for a vegetarian pasta combine with lightly cooked beans and goat's cheese. Purée together 1 cup roasted almonds or walnuts, 2 tsp minced fresh ginger, juice of $^1/_2$ lemon, $^1/_4$ cup olive oil, 1 tsp chopped fresh rosemary and salt and pepper to season. Keeps in the fridge for a couple of weeks.

Spicy Peanut Shrimp Noodles

An easy combination of hot Chinese noodles with a creamy peanut sauce and shrimps. This method also works well with chicken.

To Prepare: 3 minutes
To Cook: 8-10 minutes

> 200g egg noodles
> 2 tbsp peanut butter
> 1 large clove garlic, crushed
> 1 can coconut cream (400ml)
> 1-2 tsp hot pepper sauce, to taste
> 200g shrimps, prawns or diced chicken
> 2 spring onions, thinly sliced
> 1/2 cup chopped, roasted peanuts
> 1 pkt (2 cups) bean sprouts or snowpeas
> 1/4 cup chopped coriander or mint to garnish

Cook noodles in plenty of salted water until tender, according to manufacturer's instructions. While they cook, prepare the sauce. Place peanut butter, garlic, coconut cream and hot pepper sauce in a microwave jug, or pot. Cook for 2 minutes on high, then stir until smooth and thick. Add shrimps or chicken and cook on 80% power another 2-3 minutes until prawns or chicken are cooked. Drain noodles, toss through the sauce with spring onions, sprouts or snowpeas and nuts, reserving a little for garnish. Pile into a serving dish. Sprinkle over the coriander or mint. Serves 2.
Variation: Add diced fish or very thinly sliced chicken to sauce and simmer gently until opaque and just cooked through.

Pasta with Smoked Salmon and Peppercorns

Heat some cream, add smoked salmon and flavourings and toss through cooked pasta. Rich, simple and very delicious.

To Prepare: 10 minutes
To Cook: 5 minutes

> 400g pasta, eg fettuccine or linguini
> 1 cup cream
> 150-200g smoked salmon, sliced
> 2 tbsp lemon juice
> 2 tbsp green peppercorns
> salt and ground black pepper
> 2 tbsp finely chopped fresh dill or chives
> a few drops hot pepper sauce
> Optional: bunch asparagus, angle sliced in 3cm pieces

Cook the pasta according to manufacturer's instructions. If using asparagus, add in the last 2 minutes of cooking. While pasta cooks, heat the cream in a pot or pan. When it boils add salmon, lemon juice and green peppercorns. Season and add herbs and hot pepper sauce. Toss through the cooked pasta and serve immediately. Serves 4.
Variation: Use 2 tbsp pesto to flavour cream instead of fresh herbs.

Cockles or Mussels with Pesto Cream Sauce

In a tightly covered pot, steam 2- 3 dozen cockles (or cleaned mussels) in 1/2 cup wine with 1 tsp crushed garlic until they open. Remove cockles and keep warm. To the pan liquids add 1 cup cream, 2 tbsp basil pesto. Mix through 400g cooked fettuccine and pile cockles on top. Serves 4.

To Oven Toast or Roast Nuts

Spread out in a roasting pan and bake at 180°C for 15 minutes until pale gold in the centre.

Bitterness in Citrus

The white pith under the skin of citrus is bitter and should be removed before rinds are used. A zesting tool is ideal to remove rind without the pith.

Flash in the Pan

I CAN STILL SEE MY GRANDFATHER OUT AT SEA HAULING IN COD FROM HIS HANDLINE.
MINUTES LATER HE WOULD BE DOWN IN THE GALLEY AND BEFORE THE KETTLE
HAD THE CHANCE TO BOIL PLATEFULS OF HOT PAN-FRIED COD WOULD BE PASSED BACK UP TO
THE DECK. DELICIOUS, FRESH AND FAST.

Provençal Fish

This easy tomato-based sauce can be cooked ahead of time and fish added just before you plan to serve. The sauce is also great with chicken.

To Prepare: 5 minutes
To Cook: 20 minutes

> 2 tbsp olive oil
> 1 clove garlic, crushed
> 2 anchovies
> 1 x 400g can tomatoes in juice, chopped
> 1 tsp sugar
> 2 tbsp each capers and olives
> pinch cayenne
> salt and ground black pepper
> 200-300g fresh firm fish fillets, diced into 3-4 pieces

In a heavy pot, heat oil and gently fry garlic and anchovies. Add tomatoes and sugar and simmer for 10 minutes. Add olives, capers, cayenne and salt and pepper, to taste. Mix in fish. Cover and cook about 4-6 minutes until fish is just cooked through. Serves 2.

Above: Provençal Fish

Olive oil or butter to fry?

Butter burns more easily than oil but it does taste delicious! Use olive oil or a mix of 50-50 oil and butter for pan frying.

Crab Cakes with Aïoli

These tender tasty cakes can be cooked ahead and re-heated. Use fish or crabs.

To Prepare: 10 minutes
To Cook: 15 minutes

> 250g crabmeat, or flaked cooked fish
> 1 cup fresh white breadcrumbs
> 2 tbsp Aïoli ✿ or mayonnaise
> 1 egg
> pinch cayenne
> salt and freshly ground pepper
> 1-2 tbsp sesame seeds
> a little olive oil and butter to cook

Blend crab or fish with half the breadcrumbs, Aïoli or mayonnaise, egg, cayenne and salt and pepper to evenly combine. Stand for at least 10 minutes before cooking (up to 3-4 hours in the fridge). Shape into balls (almost golf ball-sized) and dip into other half of breadcrumbs mixed with sesame seeds. Lightly flatten. Chill until ready to cook. Heat 2 tbsp oil and a small knob of butter in a heavy pan and cook cakes for a couple of minutes on each side until lightly golden. Makes 10-12 small cakes.
Busy Day Dinner Idea: *Accompany with Chilli Lime Aïoli* ✿ *and salad greens.*

Mediterranean Stir-fried Squid

Lots of flavours work well with squid – try it also with Asian style sauces, like the one in the Cantonese Paua Stir-fry recipe.

To Prepare: 10 minutes, plus marinating
To Cook: 2-3 minutes

> 4 squid tubes (approx 400g)
> 1/4 cup olive oil
> 2 tbsp lemon juice
> 1 tsp crushed garlic
> 2 tbsp chopped fresh rosemary
> salt and ground black pepper
> 2 tbsp chopped basil leaves

Cut open squid tubes, remove any cartilage and rinse well. Use a sharp knife to lightly score squid on the outside in a diamond pattern. Cut into strips about 2cm wide. Combine with all other ingredients, except basil, and marinate for at least 30 minutes, turning occasionally. Cook squid in an oiled pan or wok over high heat, tossing for about 2 minutes until flesh has whitened. Mix in the basil leaves. Serves 4.
Busy Day Dinner Idea: *Add cooked, sliced red peppers and green beans to stir-fry and serve with rice.*

Battered Fish

Chilled liquid and resting the mixture before cooking makes this a very light crisp batter. For hints on frying, see the end of this chapter.

To Prepare: 5 minutes and 15 minutes standing
To Cook: 10-15 minutes

> 1 cup self-raising flour
> 1 egg
> 1/2 cup chilled soda water, beer or water
> 1/2 tsp salt
> fine white pepper
> oil to fry
> 4 fresh boneless fish fillets or 2 dozen oysters

Beat flour, egg, the cold liquid and salt and pepper until smooth. The batter will be quite thick, but should drop from the spoon. If not, add another tablespoon or two of liquid. Heat about 3cm of oil in a large deep pot over medium high heat. Dip fish pieces (cut the size you prefer) into batter and drop straight into hot oil. Cook until crisp and browned on base, then turn to cook other side. Lift out of oil and drain on paper towels. Keep warm in a hot oven. Serves 4.

Fish Fillets – Crispy or Soft?

If you want pan-fried fish to be crispy on the outside, cook it uncovered over a high heat in a little butter or oil until lightly browned on each side and just cooked inside. If you want more of a steamed effect, put the fish into a hot lightly oiled pan, cover tightly, reduce the heat and cook just until white droplets start to form on the top surface of the fish and the flesh changes colour. There's no chance of it falling apart, because you don't have to turn it.

Cooking Squid

Squid is cooked when the flesh turns from opaque to white and becomes tender – in a couple of minutes. Over cooking will make it tough as old boots.

Opposite: Crab Cakes with Aïoli

*Right: Steamed Mussels
with Aromatics*

Handling
Paua / Abalone

To prepare fresh paua or abalone, use your thumb to prise live from the shell. Once you have loosened the fish from its shell remove the ring of gut that surrounds the foot. Don't forget to push out the two small red-cased teeth at the pointy end. Give 3-4 bashes with a clean heavy implement – you will feel the texture change from absolutely rigidly hard to limpish. Cook quickly over high heat for about 1 minute on each side.

Freshness in
Shellfish

Don't eat shellfish that have died before you cook them. Discard any that won't close when you tap them or those that won't open after cooking.

Steamed Mussels
with Aromatics

The classic way to cook mussels is with garlic and parsley in a little white wine. Here, Asian aromatics provide a fresh zingy flavour.

To Prepare: 5 minutes
To Cook: 5-6 minutes

> *3 dozen fresh live mussels*
> *1 tbsp olive oil*
> *2 cloves garlic, crushed*
> *finely grated rind 1 lemon, no pith*
> *1 tbsp minced fresh ginger*
> *2 tbsp Thai sweet chilli sauce*
> *2 spring onions, finely sliced*
> *Optional: ¼ cup fresh coriander, chopped*

Scrub mussels and remove beards. Heat oil in a large pot, add garlic, lemon rind and ginger and allow to sizzle for a few seconds. Add chilli sauce and mussels, cover tightly and cook 3-4 minutes until mussels start to open. Once mussels are open, mix in spring onions and optional coriander. Pile into deep serving bowls. Serves 4 with crusty bread.

Cantonese Paua
Stir-fry

This prized gastropod is known in many other countries as abalone. Use the same flavours for any kind of seafood stir-fry.

To Prepare: 5 minutes
To Cook: 5 minutes

> *2 tbsp oyster sauce*
> *1 tbsp minced fresh ginger*
> *1 tbsp sesame oil*
> *a little vegetable oil to cook*
> *2 spring onions, very thinly sliced*
> *3-4 paua, lightly pounded and cut in thin slices, or 3-4 fish fillets cut into bite-sized pieces, or 3-4 squid tubes, sliced*

Combine oyster sauce, ginger and sesame oil, mix through seafood and leave for 5-10 minutes. Add sliced spring onions when ready to cook. Heat a little oil on a barbecue plate or in a heavy pan and cook seafood over high heat, stir-frying until just cooked. Serve on a bed of rice or noodles. Serves 3-5.

Busy Day Dinner Idea: *Add sliced red peppers, courgettes and spring onions to stir-fry and serve on rice.*

Hot & Spicy Fish Flavours

SEAFOOD IS ALSO WELL SUITED TO SPICING UP; IT JUST LOVES CHILLIES, CURRIES, MUSTARD AND PEPPER. SAUCES CAN BE PREPARED WELL AHEAD OF TIME, READY TO BE ADDED TO SEAFOOD FOR QUICK LAST MINUTE COOKING.

Indian Spiced Fish

This traditional Indian method for preparing and cooking fish is incredibly useful. You can follow the same method using a Moroccan Spice Rub ♦ for a great variation.

To Prepare: 5 minutes plus marinating

To Cook: 6-8 minutes

> $1/4$ cup lemon juice
> 1 tsp each, salt and ground black pepper
> 1 tbsp garlic, crushed
> 4 boneless fish fillets (at least 1.5cm thick)
> $1/2$ cup cream
> 1 tsp prepared mustard
> 1 tsp garam masala
> chopped fresh coriander or fresh shreds of cucumber rind to garnish

Combine the lemon juice, salt, pepper and garlic and mix through the fish. Leave to marinate in the fridge for 30 minutes. Combine the cream, mustard and garam masala and add to the fish, mixing well. (At this stage the fish can be marinated in the fridge for longer if desired.) Pre-heat the oven to 250°C. Place the fish on a baking tray, spoon over marinade and bake for 6-8 minutes until fish shows no resistance when pressed. Garnish with sauce, coriander or fine shreds of cucumber rind. Serves 4.

Busy Day Dinner Idea: *Accompany with rice and poppadoms.*

Mussels with Chilli, Coconut and Coriander

This substantial, spicy brew falls into the category of a soup dinner that only requires some type of bread or rice accompaniment and, if desired, a salad or dessert to follow. Bulk it up for a crowd.

To Prepare: 10 minutes

To Cook: 15 minutes

> 16-20 fresh mussels
> 1 large onion, finely diced
> 1 tbsp vegetable oil
> 1 tsp crushed garlic
> 2 tbsp hot chilli sauce
> 400ml can coconut cream
> 2 cups water
> 2 tbsp chopped coriander
> extra fresh coriander to garnish

Scrub the mussels under running water and discard the beards. Cook the onion in oil in a big pot over low heat until soft. Add the garlic and chilli sauce and stir over heat for a minute. Add the coconut cream, water and cleaned mussels, cover tightly and boil until the mussels start to open, removing them as they do. Mix in the coriander just before serving. Put 4-5 mussels per person in deep bowls and spoon over the broth. Garnish with extra fresh coriander. Serves 4 as a soup and 2-3 as a main course.

Busy Day Dinner Idea: *Accompany with rice or hot naan bread and a cucumber and rocket salad.*

Garam Masala

At the heart of every Indian and Pakistani kitchen is this aromatic spice mixture. It combines cardamom, cloves, cinnamon, pepper and nutmeg, which are thought to 'heat' the body. Unlike other spices garam masala is generally added right at the end of cooking.

Opening Shellfish

If you want shellfish opened without cooking them or having to shuck them, simply freeze in a single layer for an hour. They will pop open, making it very easy to remove the top shell.

Cooking Fish in a Sauce

Avoid stirring fish which is cooked in a sauce towards the end of cooking, as it will break up.

Perfect Thai Rice

For every cup of unwashed long grain rice add 1½ cups water and a good pinch of salt. Bring to a boil, stir, cover and reduce heat to lowest setting. Cook for 12 minutes then remove from heat and leave without uncovering for another 10-15 minutes. It will stay hot for up to ½ hour. Fluff up with a fork before serving.

To Crush Cashews

Place roasted nuts in a bag and crush using a rolling pin or bottle.

Freezing Fish

Fish can be frozen for short periods – up to 1 month. Make sure it is tightly wrapped to prevent water loss or freezer burn. Thaw in the fridge to prevent water loss.

Brazilian Fish with Cashew Sauce

The wonderful cashew sauce in this recipe can be used as a base in which to simmer fish or served over pan-fried fish.

To Prepare: 5 minutes
To Cook: 8 minutes

> 1 tbsp oil
> 1 large clove garlic, crushed
> 2 tsp garam masala
> 2-3 tsp hot pepper sauce, to taste
> 400ml coconut cream
> 100g roasted, salted cashew nuts, crushed
> 600g firm fish, cut 4cm pieces
> salt and ground black pepper
> finely grated rind of ½ lemon or lime
> 2 tbsp chopped coriander

Place oil, garlic and spices and pepper sauce in a pan or microwave jug and cook for 1 minute to bring out flavours. Add coconut cream and cashew nuts and cook for 3 minutes. Mix in diced fish, cover and cook 3 minutes more, stirring gently after 2 minutes. Season with pepper and a little lemon or lime rind to taste and garnish with chopped coriander. Serves 4.

Busy Day Dinner Idea: *Serve on a bed of rice and accompany with a salad of rocket and cucumber batons.*

PREPARING FRESH CRAB

Crabs, like crayfish, should be alive when you purchase them. To kill, freeze for ½ an hour or drown in fresh water. The fish retailer will often prepare crabs for you, but if you need to do it yourself, remove and discard the top shell and gills. Cut small crabs in half and large ones in quarters.

Hellish Mango Fish

Looks like a big list of ingredients but easy to make and tastes wonderful. The sauce is fantastic with seafood and chicken.

To Prepare: 10 minutes
To Cook: 5 minutes

Sauce

> flesh of 2 ripe mangoes, chopped
> 1-2 chillies, minced
> 1-2 tsp hot pepper sauce
> 2 large cloves garlic, minced
> 1 tbsp ginger, finely minced
> ¼ cup desiccated coconut
> 1 tsp ground cumin
> 1 cup coconut cream
> ¼ cup lemon juice
> 3 tbsp chopped fresh coriander

To Cook

> 2 tbsp peanut oil
> 1 each red and yellow peppers, finely diced
> 500g boneless fish, cut in 4cm pieces, or 500g green prawns

Purée all the sauce ingredients. Transfer the mixture to a saucepan and simmer for 3 minutes. Heat the oil and cook the peppers for 2-3 minutes until their colour changes. Add the mango sauce and bring to a simmer. Mix in the seafood and cook for about 3-4 minutes covered, without stirring, until fish is cooked. Do not over cook. Serves 4-6.

Busy Day Dinner Idea: *Accompany with rice and poppadoms.*

Thai Fish Curry

With a can of coconut cream, fish curries become one of the simplest, great tasting one-pot dinners. If desired, add a few curry leaves, fresh lemon leaves or a tablespoon of minced lemongrass to the sauce.

To Prepare: 5 minutes

To Cook: 5 minutes

> *1 tbsp vegetable oil*
> *1-2 tbsp green curry paste, to taste*
> *2 tbsp fish sauce*
> *400ml can coconut cream*
> *500-600g boneless fresh fish, diced*
> *salt and ground black pepper*
> *2-3 tbsp chopped coriander*
> *Optional: 2-3 fresh lime leaves*

Heat the oil and cook the curry paste for a few seconds. Add the fish sauce, coconut cream and lime leaves and simmer for 5 minutes. Add fish, stirring well to combine. Cover and cook without stirring for 4-5 minutes until the fish is just cooked. Season, garnish with coriander and serve. Serves 4.

Sichuan Stir-fried Crab

Try this wonderful formula with a variety of seafoods. Regardless of what seafood you use, the method is the same – shake up the Sichuan flavours, fry the aromatics, then add seafood, spring onions and mixed flavour base.

To Prepare: 10 minutes

To Cook: 10 minutes

Sichuan Flavour Base

> *2 tbsp black bean sauce*
> *1 tbsp dry sherry*
> *1 tbsp soy sauce*
> *1 small red chilli, minced*
> *½ tsp sugar*
> *1 tsp sesame oil*

To Cook

> *2 tbsp soy or peanut oil*

> *2 tbsp minced ginger*
> *1 tbsp crushed garlic*
> *3 dried red chillies*
> *2 spring onions, finely chopped*
> *6-8 large paddle crabs or*
> *1 kg mussels or 1 kg diced fish*

Shake first 6 ingredients together in a jar. Heat oil in a very large pan or pot, add ginger, garlic and chillies and cook a few seconds, then add all the cut up crabs (or other seafood). Cover and cook about 5 minutes, stirring frequently. Remove lid and check if done – if shells have turned fully red, you can proceed. Add mixed Sichuan sauce ingredients and spring onions. Stir well to combine, cover and cook 2-3 minutes more. Serve in a deep bowl or straight from the pan and provide everyone with fingerbowls of hot water with sliced lemon. Serves 4.

Variation: Use crayfish, scallops, boneless gamefish or shellfish in place of crabs.

Busy Day Dinner Idea: *Accompany with rice and a fresh spinach salad with crunchy sprouts, red peppers, oranges and caramelized onions.*

Above: Sichuan Stir-fried Crab

Is It Cooked?

To check fish is cooked, press with your finger. Fish should 'give' and just start to break apart to the centre.

Oven-grilling Fish

Suitable for firm to medium textured fish steaks or fillets less than 2cm thick. The high heat of the grill can dry out the top surface of the fish, so you may wish to brush it with butter or oil before cooking. Cook the fish 6-10cm from the heat source without turning.

SEAFOOD SORCERY

Make your favourite sauce ahead of time. That way there's little last minute preparation. Bring sauce to a gentle simmer and add pieces of fish or other seafood. Mix into sauce well. Cover and simmer without stirring for no more than 4-6 minutes until seafood is just cooked. Apply the same method and flavours to chicken – slice it very thinly and cook until it turns opaque.

- Thai Fish Curry
- Red Pepper Sauce
- Sauce used for Creamy Pasta and Scallops
- Sauce used for Chilli Mussel Fettuccine
- Provençal Fish Sauce
- Sauce used for Spicy Peanut Shrimp Noodles

- Pesto Cream Sauce
- Mango Glaze
- Sauce used for Cantonese Paua Stir-fry
- Hellish Mango Fish
- Cumin Chilli Tomato Sauce
- Moroccan Sauce

One-dish Fish

BE IT A TASTY SEAFOOD RISOTTO OR A HEARTY FISH PIE, A MEAL IN A DISH MAKES A
REALLY EASY AND INFORMAL WAY TO DINE. ADD A GREEN SALAD AND FINISH WITH A LIGHT
DESSERT SUCH AS FRESH OR ROASTED FRUIT.

Smoked Fish and Kumara Pie

For a rainy Sunday lunch or dinner, a flavoursome golden-topped fish pie delivers the necessary level of comfort.

To Prepare: 20 minutes

To Cook: 15-20 minutes

White Sauce

> *5 tbsp butter*
> *1 large onion, finely sliced*
> *1/4 cup flour*
> *3 cups milk*
> *1/2 tsp nutmeg*
> *salt and ground black pepper*
> *450g smoked fish, flaked,*
> *or drained and flaked canned*
> *smoked fish*
> *1 1/2 cups grated, tasty cheese*
> *2 medium kumara and 2 potatoes*

Optional: 2 cups cooked rice, 1/4 cup capers

Cook the kumara and potato in boiling salted water for about 15 minutes until tender. To make white sauce, melt the butter in a heavy-based saucepan. Cook the onion for 5 minutes until soft. Stir in the flour and cook for 1 minute. Gradually add the milk, stirring continuously. Season with nutmeg and salt and pepper. Cook, stirring constantly until the sauce thickens and comes to the boil. Stir in the flaked smoked fish and rice and capers if wanted. Place the mixture in a greased, medium oven-proof dish. Drain kumara and potato and mash with a little milk, seasoning to taste with salt and pepper. Spread over the fish mixture. Sprinkle the cheese over the topping. (Dish can be prepared ahead to this point.) Bake at 220°C for 15-20 minutes until golden brown; or cover and microwave for 5 minutes, then place under a grill to brown. Serves 4-5.

Busy Day Dinner Idea: *Accompany with a spinach and orange salad.*

Lemon Fish Pie

Here's a taste of nostalgia. Fresh fish and hard-boiled eggs cooked in a lemony sauce topped with a crust of golden mashed potato.

To Prepare: 15 minutes

To Cook: 25-30 minutes

> *3 cups White Sauce (see side panel)*
> *3-4 tbsp fresh lemon juice*
> *about 500g boneless fish, cut in*
> *4cm chunks*
> *3 hard-boiled eggs, quartered*
> *4 cups of mashed potato, seasoned*

Make White Sauce recipe in side panel. Mix through lemon juice. It should taste quite lemony. Pour about half the sauce into a shallow baking dish. Cover with fish and hard-boiled eggs. Pour over rest of sauce. Cover with a layer of mashed potato. Bake at 220°C for 25-30 minutes, until sauce is bubbling and potato is golden on top. Serves 4.

Busy Day Dinner Idea: *Accompany with green peas or a salad.*

Freshness in Fish

- *When buying whole fish look for a clear eye and shiny scales. If the eye has sunken or is cloudy the fish isn't fresh. The gills should be red, if they are brown or pinkish the fish has started to deteriorate.*

- *When you press a whole fish it should feel springy and bouncy, otherwise it is not fresh. Fish fillets should feel springy and look translucent and shiny. Don't buy them if they look dull and limp.*

- *Fresh fish should smell of the sea, it should never have a fishy or strong smell.*

White Sauce

Heat 70g butter and 1/2 cup flour. Once melted, stir over heat for about a minute. Add 1/2 tsp mustard powder and a pinch nutmeg. Gradually whisk in 3 cups milk, stirring until a thick smooth sauce is produced. Season to taste. Sauce thickens as it cools. Makes 3 1/2 cups.

Opposite: Thai Fish Curry

Right: Kedgeree

Left-over Rice

Kedgeree is a great way to use left-over rice. Use it also for fried rice with egg, chicken and vegetables; or make a frittata with raw eggs, herbs or smoked fish, left-over rice and seasonings. Left-over rice re-heats well in the microwave. Sprinkle with a few drops of water, cover tightly and microwave on full power for a minute or two, until hot.

Kedgeree

A version of the Indian dish kicheri, kedgeree found its place as a classic in the breakfast kitchens of England and Scotland during the 18th and 19th centuries. This revamp is a great way to use smoked fish and cooked rice for a filling lunch or supper.

To Prepare 10 minutes
To Cook: 10 minutes

> *200g boneless smoked fish, flaked*
> *4 cups cooked long grain rice*
> *4 hard-boiled eggs, quartered*
> *50g butter*
> *2 onions, finely sliced*
> *1 tsp finely grated lemon rind*
> *2 tsp each curry powder, garam*
>   *masala, cumin, coriander*
> *2 spring onions, finely diced*
> *¼ cup finely chopped parsley*
> *salt and ground black pepper*
> *2 tbsp lemon juice*

Mix the fish, rice and eggs lightly together. Heat the butter in a large pot and cook onion until browned. Lift out half to use as garnish. Add the rind and spices and cook for a few more seconds, then mix in the fish, egg and rice and toss over medium heat until hot right through. Mix in spring onions and parsley, season with salt and black pepper to taste, squeeze over lemon juice and sprinkle with rest of onion. Serves 4.

Busy Day Dinner Idea: *Accompany with a salad of sliced cucumber, orange and bananas, tossed in lemon juice and sprinkled with toasted coconut.*

Salmon and Lemon Risotto

Mixing the salmon with lemon rind and pepper before cooking gives it a lot more flavour when it is cooked. Use any kind of fresh fish with leeks, asparagus or beans. For a plain lemon risotto to serve with grilled or roasted seafoods or meats, leave out the fish and vegetables.

To Prepare: 5 minutes
To Cook: 25 minutes

> finely grated rind of 1 lemon,
>   no pith
> salt and ground black pepper
> 300-400g boneless fresh salmon,
>   cut into 2cm cubes
> 2 tbsp olive oil
> 1 onion, finely diced
> 1 leek, halved, washed and sliced in
>   thin rounds, including green ends
> 2 cups Italian short grain rice, eg
>   Carnaroli or Arborio
> 1/2 cup white wine
> 4 cups fish or chicken stock, hot
> big pinch saffron threads
> 2 tbsp lemon juice
> lemon wedges to serve
> Optional: 2 cups sliced asparagus or
>   beans, boiled for 1 minute

Mix lemon rind and pepper through fish. Heat oil in a largish heavy pot and cook onion and leek gently until onion is clear. Add rice and stir over heat a minute. Add wine then mix in hot stock, saffron and salt to taste. Once it boils, reduce heat to low simmer. Simmer for exactly 18 minutes, stirring now and then. Rice should be sloppy. Add a dash more stock if it looks dry. Mix in fish, optional vegetables and lemon juice and adjust seasoning. Cover the fish with rice, cover pot and cook a further 2 minutes without stirring. Remove from heat and stand, without uncovering, for 1-2 minutes before serving. Serve with fresh lemon wedges. Serves 4.

Spicy Steamed Seafood

Light and fresh, this easy steam-pot takes its cue from the sand bakes of old.

To Prepare: 10 minutes
To Cook: about 20 minutes

> 3 potatoes, scrubbed and quartered
> 1 kumara, peeled, cut in 2cm slices
> 2 corn cobs, cut in 3cm slices
> 1-2 tsp Cajun spice mix, to taste
> 1 red pepper, sliced
> fresh seafood as available,
>   eg shellfish, halved crayfish and
>   fish fillets, enough for 2
> Green Goddess Dressing ° to
>   accompany

Put 1 cup water in the bottom of a big pot or steamer. Place potatoes, kumara and corn on top of a rack or steamer tray. Season with cajun spice and salt and pepper, cover tightly and cook over high heat for 10 minutes. Check water, adding more if needed. Add red pepper and seafoods. Season with a little more Cajun spice, salt and pepper. Cover and cook for another 10 minutes or until vegetables and seafoods are cooked through. Serve with Green Goddess Dressing. Serves 2.

MENU IDEAS

A Spring Dinner

salmon and lemon risotto with asparagus

rhubarb and raspberry pie

Advance preparation

- prepare dessert

Steaming

If you don't own a steamer, improvise. Place a cake rack in the bottom of a big pot and keep water level just below it. Or you can buy bamboo steamer trays in Asian stores very cheaply. They come in many sizes to fit most saucepans.

Which Rice for Risotto?

You need to use good quality Italian rice to make creamy risottos that won't turn to sludge. Arborio, Carnaroli or Vialone Nano are all good types of rice for risotto. Calasparra, the Spanish paella rice, also works but is less creamy.

Microwaving Fish

Due to its high water content, fish cooks really well in the microwave. Cover tightly and cook on full power. A single fillet will take about 1-1½ minutes. Check every minute. Fish should look slightly under cooked. Leave covered and wait 3-4 minutes. Over the standing time it will cook through.

BBQ & Grilled Seafood

To cook delicious, juicy fish successfully on the BBQ, have the grill plate lightly oiled and hot before you start so the fish forms a light crust and does not tear or stick. Take great care not to over cook.

Bamboo Skewers

Bamboo skewers require soaking for about 10 minutes in cold water before using or else they will char. Bamboo skewers are also useful for holding together chicken cavities and meat, chicken or seafood rolls.

Leaves as Wrappers

Banana leaves, lotus leaves, grape leaves and fresh herbs can all be used to wrap fish before grilling. In times gone by, whole fish such as trout and salmon were wrapped in 10-12 layers of brown paper. This was then dunked into water to wet and the whole fish package cooked in the embers for about 10 minutes each side. It's still a good trick for camping.

Opposite: BBQ Crayfish with Brazilian Seasoning

Whole Fish with East Asian Marinade

I particularly like this spicy paste with its clean fresh flavours. It is excellent with seafoods as well as pork or chicken.

To Prepare: 5 minutes

To Cook: 10-25 minutes

East Asian Marinade:

> *2 fingers fresh ginger, chopped*
> *4 large cloves garlic, peeled*
> *1 spring onion, chopped*
> *leaves of 1 coriander plant*
> *1-2 small red chillies*
> *1 tsp each salt, brown sugar and fine black pepper*
> *juice and finely grated rind of 1 lime (no pith)*
> *1/4 cup coconut cream or oil*
>
> *1 whole fish, scaled and cleaned, head and tail intact, 600g-700g*

Pound or purée all flavouring ingredients together to a fine paste. Slash a criss-cross pattern with a sharp knife on either side of fish. Rub marinade into skin and cavity of fish. Marinate in the fridge up to 6 hours. Grill for about 8-10 minutes each side, covered, or bake fish for 15-25 minutes in a 220°C oven until eye starts to whiten and fish is just cooked. Serves 1-2.

BBQ Crayfish with Brazilian Seasoning

From the beaches of Buzios, where I lived for a year, a wonderfully simple seasoning to flavour all kinds of seafood.

To Prepare: 5 minutes

To Cook: 5-8 minutes

> *3 small to medium live crayfish, cut in half lengthwise or 2 dozen green king prawns, tails shelled*
> *3 cloves garlic, crushed*
> *1 tbsp crushed black peppercorns*
> *finely grated rind of 1/2 a lime*
> *1 small hot red chilli, chopped*
> *1/4 cup extra virgin olive oil*
> *1 tsp sea salt*

In a non-corrosive bowl, pound or purée together all ingredients and spread over cut surface of crayfish, or mix through peeled prawn tails. Pre-heat a grill or barbecue and cook crays (cut side up) for 4-6 minutes until shells turn red, then brush cut surface with left-over marinade, turn and cook another 1-2 minutes. Green prawns need only 1-2 minutes to cook. Pair with a lime risotto. Serves 6.

To make Lime Risotto: *follow the recipe for Salmon and Lemon Risotto omitting salmon and leeks and adding finely grated rind of half a lime with the chicken stock. Stir in 2-3 tbsp fresh lime juice at the end with grated parmesan.*

Right: Scallops Cooked in the Half Shell with Cumin Chilli Tomato Sauce

Scallop Anatomy

There is a small knob on the side of each scallop which hinges the scallop to its shell. This should be removed before cooking as it is tough.

Freezing Scallops

Scallops freeze well. Like all seafood they should be thawed slowly – in the fridge is ideal.

Dishy Shells

Scallop shells make a great cooking and serving utensil. They wash and recycle well.

Chilli Chat

Chillies freeze well, but they mush when thawed. Keep a store in the freezer for anytime use.

Scallops Cooked in the Half Shell with Cumin Chilli Tomato Sauce

The single most important thing to remember about this dish is to take great care not to over cook the scallops. Cook just until they turn opaque. The sauce is great with all kinds of seafood and can be made well in advance.

To Prepare: 10 minutes

To Cook: sauce 7-8 minutes,
scallops 2 minutes

Sauce

> *1 tsp cumin seeds*
> *5 tomatoes, cores removed*
> *2 spring onions, roughly chopped*
> *1 large clove garlic, peeled*
> *½ minced chilli, or ½ tsp chilli paste*
> *2 tbsp extra virgin olive oil*
> *pinch sugar, salt and ground black pepper*
> *juice of 1 lime or lemon*

> *36-48 fresh scallops, remove small attached side muscle*
> To serve: *18-24 clean scallop shells*

To make the sauce, toast the cumin seeds in a dry pan over medium heat for 1-2 minutes until they start to pop, taking care not to burn. Grind finely. Purée all other ingredients until smooth and then place in a pot with ground cumin. Simmer gently for 5 minutes. Season to taste. Sauce can be prepared and refrigerated for up to 3 days before using. To cook scallops, place about 1 big teaspoon of sauce in the base of each cleaned scallop shell. Place 2 scallops in each shell, turn to coat lightly in the sauce and place onto pre-heated barbecue. Once the sauce starts to bubble turn scallops inside shells and cook another 30-60 seconds. Don't over cook. Squeeze over lime juice.

To cook scallops in a pan, lightly oil a hot pan and add scallops in batches without overcrowding. Cook for about 1½ minutes over high heat. Mix through hot sauces. Serve on rice or pasta. Serves 8.

Skewered Mediterranean Fish and Vegetables

Assemble these kebabs in the afternoon and chill, ready for dinner outdoors.

To Prepare: 10 minutes

To Cook: 4-5 minutes

> 500g medium or firm textured white fish fillets
> 1 small eggplant, diced into 8cm pieces
> 2-3 tbsp olive oil
> 2 red peppers, cut into 3cm dice
> 1 lemon, sliced thinly
> 2 tbsp Pesto,✿ mixed with 2 tbsp olive oil or ¼ cup Chilli Jam ✿
> ground black pepper
> bamboo skewers soaked in water for 10 minutes

Soak skewers while preparing fish. Cut the fish into 3cm cubes. Halve the eggplant slices and fry in the first measure of oil until softened. Thread all the ingredients onto skewers, alternating them. Chill until ready to cook. Combine Chilli Jam or Pesto and oil with black pepper. Brush over kebabs. Grill or barbecue for 4-5 minutes or until cooked through. Serves 4-5.
Busy Day Dinner Idea: *Serve kebabs with cous cous.*

Oriental Barbecue Tuna Steaks

The dense texture and flavour of all game fish make it ideal for marinating and quick cooking.

To Prepare: 5 minutes, plus marinating

To Cook: 2 minutes

> 6 fresh tuna steaks, or other gamefish, approx 1.5cm thick
> 2 tbsp soy sauce
> 2 tsp finely chopped fresh ginger
> 2 tbsp sesame oil (or plain oil)
> juice of 1 lemon

Combine the steaks with all other ingredients and leave to marinate in the fridge for at least 1 hour and up to 4 hours. Preheat a heavy pan or barbecue and oil lightly. Drain off the marinade and barbecue or pan fry steaks over a high heat for about 40 seconds per side, until just firm. Do not over cook – the flesh should be slightly translucent in the centre. Serves 6.
Busy Day Dinner Idea: *Serve steaks on rice with lightly cooked spinach.*
Variations: *Use other Asian sauces to marinate fish, eg Oyster Sauce or Black Bean Sauce.*

MENU 🍴 IDEAS

Summer BBQ at the beach

corn and feta fritters cooked on the hot plate

scallops or fish with cumin chilli tomato sauce

Mediterranean summer grill plate

French plum cake

Advance preparations

- make fritter batter
- make garlic, basil and anchovy dipping sauce
- make cumin chilli tomato sauce
- marinate meat and prepare vegetables for grill plate
- cook French plum cake

Game Fish

Tuna, kingfish and other 'game fish' require very light cooking as they easily become dry.

Keeping Seafood Cold

Don't ever underestimate the importance of keeping seafood chilled at all times. Fish which is caught, gutted and chilled immediately has a shelf life of around 12 days. Every hour at room temperature equates to a day's loss in shelf life.

BBQ Pipi Fritters

A commercial dry scone mix makes fast work of these light fluffy fritters.

To Prepare: 5 minutes
To Cook: 10 minutes

> *1 cup of packet scone mix*
> *¾ cup cold water*
> *½ tsp salt*
> *1 tsp pesto*
> *1 tsp hot chilli sauce*
> *1½ cups finely chopped cooked*
>   *mussels or pipis*
> *2 tbsp vegetable oil*

Mix packet scone mix with cold water, salt, pesto and hot chilli sauce. Add finely chopped, cooked mussels or pipis. Fry spoonfuls in an oiled pan over medium heat 2-3 minutes each side, until cooked through. Makes about 10.

Potato Rosti with Hot-smoked Salmon and Salsa Verde

These crisp potato cakes re-heat well in a hot oven. They can be served in a variety of ways. A splash of anchovy sauce gives them a slight richness but is not 'fishy'.

To Prepare: 10 minutes
To Cook: 10 minutes

Rosti

> *2 large potatoes, peeled and*
>   *grated, moisture squeezed out*
> *1 tsp salt*
> *olive oil to fry*

Optional: 2 tsp anchovy sauce

Topping

> *2 tsp of anchovy sauce*
> *1 bunch rocket or watercress*
> *200g hot-smoked salmon*
> *½ cup Salsa Verde ✿*

Heat 1cm oil in a large heavy pan. Season the potato with salt and anchovy sauce and drop handfuls into the oil. Spread out

rosti and cook over medium heat until golden and crispy. Flip to cook other side. Drain on paper towels. Serve 2-3 rosti in a stack, on a bed of rocket layered with smoked salmon. Accompany with Salsa Verde. Makes 8. Serve 2 per person.

Pan-fried Paua with Roasted Corn and Red Peppers

This has been a favourite recipe for paua for several years. It brings to the fore the flavours of summer when corn and onions are in abundant supply, and the first red peppers are appearing. Try it also with mussels.

To Prepare: 10 minutes
To Cook: 1½ minutes

> *2 cups corn kernels, preferably cut*
>   *fresh from the cob*
> *flesh of 2 red peppers, diced*
> *2 tbsp olive oil*
> *1 red onion, thinly sliced*
> *1 bunch coriander, chopped*
> *2 tbsp mayonnaise*
> *1-2 tbsp hot chilli sauce, to taste*
> *4 fresh paua, shucked and bashed*
>   *(see Handling Paua)*
> *2 tbsp butter*
> *salt and ground black pepper*
> *juice of 1 lemon*

Fry corn and peppers in oil until starting to brown. Combine with other salad ingredients in a large bowl. Heat a heavy pan with butter, season paua and cook for about 1-1½ minutes each side until they feel very tender. Do not over cook. Remove from pan, squeeze over lemon juice and rest for 1-2 minutes. Meanwhile, add salad to paua pan and toss over heat to just warm through. Spoon warm salad onto plates and top each with a cooked paua. Serves 4-6.

More Rosti Ideas

- Top potato rosti with poached eggs and roasted tomatoes
- Dip thick wedges of tomato into 1 tbsp brown sugar mixed with 1 tsp curry powder. Fry in butter. Serve on hot rosti with a little sour cream
- Make a smoked fish salad with aïoli cucumber and red onion and serve with rosti
- Serve hot rosti as finger food with a dipping sauce eg salsa or Cashew and Cream Cheese Pesto ✿

De-sanding Shellfish

To get pipis or other sand-dwelling shellfish to shed their sand, put them in a bucket of seawater with a handful of flour or oats and leave in a cool place overnight.

Hot-smoked Salmon with Asparagus and Rocket

This is so wonderfully easy. Buy the salmon hot-smoked or make your own, following the method given below.

To Prepare: 5 minutes

To Cook : 15 minutes

>   1 side hot-smoked salmon
>   2 big handfuls fresh asparagus, tough ends snapped off
>   2 tbsp olive oil
>   a few shavings of lemon peel cut with a vegetable peeler
>   splash of water or white wine
>   salt and freshly ground pepper
>   6 big handfuls rocket

Optional: Aïoli ✿ or Salsa Verde ✿ to serve

Pre-heat oven to 220°C. Place asparagus in a large shallow roasting dish, mix through oil, lemon rind, water or wine and season with salt and pepper. Cook for about 12-15 minutes until it just starts to brown. Remove any bones and skin from salmon and break into large flakes. Pile rocket onto plates, top with asparagus, salmon and, if desired, a spoonful of Aïoli or Salsa Verde. Serves 6.

Busy Day Dinner Idea: *Accompany with flatbread or Olive Oil Focaccia.*✿

Above: Hot-smoked Salmon with Asparagus and Rocket

SMOKING SEAFOOD

You don't need a commercial fish smoker to successfully hot-smoke seafood. Simply line a heavy roasting pan with tinfoil and sprinkle with a handful of untreated sawdust. Place fish or shellfish on a rack on top. Cover the pan tightly with tinfoil. Place dish over high heat on a barbecue hot plate or heated element for 5-6 minutes. Transfer to a hot oven for a few minutes. Allow to cool before removing lid.

Side of salmon: *5-6 minutes on hot plate, 6 minutes in 220°C oven, cool then remove lid.*

Fish fillets: *5 minutes on hot plate, cool then remove lid.*

Pipis and other shellfish: *5-6 minutes on hot plate, cool then remove lid.*

Seafood Salads

LAST MINUTE ASSEMBLY IS THE KEY TO ANY GOOD SALAD. THE TRICK IS TO PREPARE THE
COMPONENTS AHEAD OF TIME, THEN TOSS THEM TOGETHER JUST BEFORE SERVING.

Above: Smoked Fish Salad with Aïoli, Cucumber and Spring Onions

Avocado Ripeness

Avocados have a short period of optimum ripeness. Enjoy them as soon as they have reached a 'sliceable' texture. Overripe, they are mushy and acquire an unpleasant odour and 'off' flavour.

Smoked Fish Salad with Aïoli, Cucumber and Spring Onions

This quick, easy, mix and serve salad makes a great lunch with some home-made bread, or served with pre-dinner drinks.

To Prepare: 10 minutes

> 1 side hot-smoked fish, skin and bones removed, flesh flaked
> 1 telegraph cucumber, cut into small finger batons
> 1-2 spring onions, thinly sliced
> about ½ cup Aïoli,❂ just enough to bind
> salt and ground black pepper

Optional: 1 large cooked potato, diced

Combine all ingredients in a mixing bowl. Serve at once. Serves 4-6 as an appetiser or light lunch. Salad needs to be made and served at once; if prepared ahead, the cucumber will make the salad watery.

Smoked Salmon, Avocado and Grapefruit Salad

To Prepare: 5 minutes

> 3 large handfuls of watercress or rocket
> 1 medium head curly endive
> ¼ cup vinaigrette or Favourite Dressing ❂
> 1 side hot-smoked salmon, skin and bones removed, flesh broken in generous flakes
> 3 avocados, flesh sliced in wedges
> 2 grapefruit or oranges, peeled and sliced or segmented
> sea salt and ground black pepper
> ¼ cup caper berries or capers

Toss the salad greens with dressing. Strew the endive and cress over a flat dish. Scatter the avocados, grapefruit and salmon over the salad greens. Sprinkle with a little sea salt and ground black pepper. Garnish with caper berries or capers. Serves 6.

Busy Day Dinner Idea: *Toss through 400g cooked pasta shapes dressed with a little pesto.*

Left: Thai Marinated Grilled Salmon with a Crisp Noodle Salad

Thai Marinated Grilled Salmon with a Crisp Noodle Salad

Looks a million dollars, tastes like a dream, ideal for a special occasion. Everything can be prepared in advance. When ready to serve, cook the salmon and toss the salad.

To Prepare: 20 minutes

To Cook: noodles, 2 minutes, fish, 5-6 minutes

Marinade

> 1 batch Thai Shrimp Marinade ❂ or Thai curry paste
> 1 side of salmon, pin bones removed

Salad

> 3 carrots, peeled and grated
> 400-500g fresh mung bean sprouts
> 2 spring onions, finely sliced
> 1 red pepper, finely diced
> 1 large telegraph cucumber, cut in small batons
> 1/2 cup each finely chopped fresh coriander and mint

Optional: 100g bean thread vermicelli, deep fried (see side panel) or bought fried noodles

Dressing

> 2 tsp sugar
> 1-2 small red chillies, minced (or 1-2 tsp chilli paste)
> 2 tsp crushed garlic
> 1/4 cup fish sauce
> 1/4 cup fresh lime or lemon juice
> freshly ground pepper

Cut salmon on an angle into 12 pieces (allow 2 per person), leaving skin on. Mix through marinade. Cover with plastic wrap and chill for at least 6 hours. Prepare salad ingredients and refrigerate. Make dressing by combining all ingredients in a jar. Fifteen minutes before serving time pre-heat grill and drain salmon, place under a hot grill about 6cm from the heat source and cook without turning for 5-6 minutes, until just cooked through. Rest salmon for 3-5 minutes. While salmon rests, combine salad ingredients with dressing in a huge bowl. Mix through broken up noodles at the very last minute, tossing to combine. Pile salad into bowls and serve 1-2 pieces of salmon on top of each. Serves 6.

Deep-fried Noodles

To deep-fry vermicelli noodles, put whole shank of noodles into a big bag. Break noodles apart thoroughly. They are quite tough and will make a huge mess if you try and do this on the bench. Heat oil and fry noodles in handfuls. They will puff up into a 'nest' in under a minute. Remove with a slotted spoon and drain on paper towels. Cook in this way until all are done. Store in an airtight container and they will keep for weeks. If noodles soften, re-crisp in a 180°C oven for 5-6 minutes.

Above: Marinated Fish Salad

Marinated Fish Salad

This method of pickling cooked fish, known as 'escabese', was used in earlier times as a way of making fish last. It's a great recipe for fresh trout, salmon or any dense fish. It needs a day or two to marinate in the fridge, and then can quickly be assembled with fresh salad ingredients.

To Prepare: 15 minutes, and marinating
To Cook: 10 minutes

> *500-700g fresh, boneless fish, cut*
>   *in 4cm pieces*
> *salt and ground black pepper*
> *⅓ cup extra virgin olive oil*
> *½ cup each dry vermouth and*
>   *fresh orange juice*
> *¼ cup lime or lemon juice*
> *1 tbsp white wine vinegar*
> *finely grated rind of 1 lemon*
>   *and 1 orange, no pith*
> *To serve: several handfuls of watercress*
>   *or rocket*

> *3 oranges, peeled and segmented*
> *3-4 tbsp each of fresh coriander*
>   *and mint, chopped*
> *Optional: 2 bunches asparagus, with ends*
>   *snapped off, lightly cooked, sliced*
>   *flesh of 1 avocado*

Season fish with salt and ground black pepper. Heat oil in a fry-pan and once hot, quickly fry pieces for about 20-30 seconds on each side. Remove from pan at once to prevent further cooking – flesh should only be just cooked on the outside. Place in a shallow dish. Mix together vermouth, orange, lemon or lime juices, vinegar and rinds and pour over fish. Cover and refrigerate for 12-48 hours. Just before serving, check seasoning and adjust to taste. Mix through watercress, toss through oranges, herbs, asparagus and avocado. Serves 6 as a main course and 8-10 as a first course.

Segmenting Oranges

To segment oranges is somewhat boring, but for a special occasion, the effort is worth it. Remove all peel and pith. Using a sharp knife cut between the white lines to release small segments of pith free fruit.

MATCHING THE FISH
WITH THE METHOD

From species to species, fish vary tremendously in texture and flavour. When you purchase fish, be familiar with or enquire about its texture, as this will determine the best way to cook it. For example, delicate fish such as bottom-dwelling flounder and sole have a very fine white flake and fall apart easily, so should not be stir-fried.

Baking

Suitable for whole fish, fillets or steaks 2cm or more thick. A good method when cooking for a crowd. Suitable species – all types except gamefish, eg tuna and kingfish, which are best cooked quickly and served rare as they tend to dry out.

Flash-roasting

Ideal for whole fish and fish fillets or steaks. A very high temperature is required so the fish cooks quickly and does not dry out. Suitable species – all.

Pan-frying

Suitable for all species of boneless fillets and steaks, small whole fish and flat fish. For more delicate flaky species, cook in a covered pan without turning.

Deep-frying

Frying is one of the most difficult cooking methods to master. It's also dangerous because of the risk of fire. Use fresh pure olive oil or canola oil to prevent the oil deteriorating, which results in greasy, oily fish. Try to fry as quickly as possible to get the fish cooked through. Don't cook too much fish at once or heat is lost. Use high temperatures for small thin pieces of fish and reduce to medium high for larger pieces so they will cook through fully before over-browning on the outside. Don't over cook or fish will be greasy. If desired, transfer to a hot oven to finish cooking and keep hot.

Grilling *(in the oven)*

Suitable for firm to medium textured fish steaks or fillets less than 2cm thick. The high heat of the grill can dry out the top surface of the fish, so you may wish to brush it with butter or oil before cooking. Cook the fish 6-10cm from the heat source without turning.

Barbecuing

Excellent for fish steaks of dense or medium texture, game fish and other oily species, whole fish and shellfish. Oil grill well and have it hot before cooking to prevent seafood from sticking. Don't attempt to barbecue frozen fish as it tends to be dry and flaky. Shellfish can also be barbecued – use the hot plate and add a splash of water or wine.

Steaming & Microwaving

Ideal for species with a delicate flavour, plus all shellfish. The cooking vessel must be tightly covered.

Stir-frying

Suitable for species with a large flake and firm texture. The Chinese dust their fish in cornflour before cooking to provide a protective coating that prevents fillets and pieces from falling apart during the stir-frying process.

Poaching

Good for whole fish and fillets. Cover the fish by 2cm with cold liquid and bring just to a simmer. Once the liquid reaches a simmer, a whole fish will take 12 minutes to cook regardless of its size. The time remains the same because the water will only come to a simmer when the internal temperature of the fish has reached the right heat. To poach fish fillets, immerse in cold liquid, bring slowly to a simmer, simmer for 2 minutes then allow to cool in cooking liquid.

VEGETARIAN

Roasted Pepper and Asparagus
Frittata

Smoked Fish Frittata

Herb and Feta Frittata

Spinach Frittata

Felafels with Mint
Yoghurt Sauce

Mint Yoghurt Sauce

Tibetan Split Pea Cakes

Spiced Bean Quesadillas

Noodle Pancake with Spring
Onions and Herbs

Pan Fried Tofu

Roasted Vegetable Platter
with Aïoli

Greek Spinach Roll

Grilled Mushrooms with
Garlic Nut Topping

Anne's Spinach Tart

Roasted Tomato Tart

Pete's Potato Cake

Caramelized Onions

Roasted Onion and Goat's
Cheese Tart

Wild Mushroom Bruschetta

Double Baked Soufflés
with Blue Cheese
and Spinach

Vegetable Samosas

Pumpkin, Spinach and Goat's
Cheese Lasagne

Pasta with Spinach and Feta

Pasta with Asian Pesto and
Roasted Pumpkin

Roasted Walnut Blue
Cheese Polenta

Corn and Spinach
Polenta Slice

Péla

Mushroom Risotto

Pumpkin and Roast
Garlic Risotto

Asparagus and Fresh Rocket
Risotto

Provençal Ratatouille

Indonesian Peanut
Sauce

Country-style
Tomato Sauce

Moroccan Sauce

Double Mushroom Sauce

Avial
(Mixed Vegetable Curry)

Potato and Pea Curry

Indian Spicy Dhal

Sri Lankan Egg Curry
(Bitter Hoddie)

Mexican-style Chickpeas

Vegetable Platter with
Green Goddess Dressing

Harvest Salad of Roasted
Beets, Walnuts and Onions
with Goat's Cheese Croûtons

Salad of Roasted Carrots and
Beets with Rocket and
Pinenuts

Asian Deli Noodles

Greens, Pears, Spicy Pecans
and Blue Cheese

Raw Energy Salad

Light Meals

ERASE FOREVER THE PERCEPTION THAT VEGETARIAN FOOD IS A DULL LEGACY OF THE 70s

BEANSPROUT BRIGADE WITH THESE QUICK FLAVOURFUL PAN COOKED DISHES.

Quick Fix Omelettes

Watch the Mexicans behind the counter at any Mexican airport food bar for a lesson in delicious ultra-quick omelettes. Put 2 eggs in a bowl and season with salt and pepper. Pour this into a hot well buttered pan on medium heat and spread out so it forms a thin layer. Scatter over chopped herbs, sliced smoked salmon, some cooked chopped spinach or whatever flavours take your fancy. Once the egg sets on the bottom but is still liquid on top, fold in the sides like a parcel, then turn the whole thing over and cook for a couple of minutes until egg is almost firm. Serve with salsa or fresh tomatoes and toast.

Handling Asparagus

Even when it is really fresh asparagus has tough ends. To remove the tough bits bend the stalks at the base — the tough portion will snap off. If you ever find white asparagus, trim the ends and peel the stalks with a potato peeler.

Previous page: Roasted Tomato Tart

Roasted Pepper and Asparagus Frittata

The Italians call it Frittata, the Spanish, Tortilla. Whatever you choose to call this versatile filled omelette, it makes great portable food, can be prepared ahead of time and slices into portions easily. Using cooked potatoes makes it very quick.

To Prepare: 10 minutes
To Cook: 15 minutes

> *6-8 eggs, preferably free range,*
> *   lightly beaten*
> *3 tbsp chopped fresh herbs,*
> *   eg thyme, oregano, parsley*
> *2 cooked potatoes, diced 2cm*
> *sliced flesh of 1-2 roasted peppers*
> *2 handfuls lightly cooked asparagus*
> *2 tbsp parmesan*
> *salt and freshly ground black*
> *   pepper*
> *2 tbsp olive or cooking oil*
> *1 tsp crushed garlic*

Beat the eggs in a large bowl. Add the herbs, potatoes, peppers, parmesan and asparagus. Mix in parmesan and salt and pepper to taste. Heat the oil in a fry-pan with a heat-proof handle. Add the garlic and sizzle a few seconds. Pour the potato mixture into the bowl, season and mix well to combine. Re-heat the fry-pan. Pour in the mixture and cook over low heat for 6-8 minutes. Place under a pre-heated grill and cook for 5 minutes or until golden brown and set. Leave in the pan for a few minutes to cool before turning out. Cut into wedges and serve warm. Serves 4.

Smoked Fish Frittata

Use 200g boneless flaked smoked fish, in place of garlic, peppers, asparagus and parmesan.

Herb and Feta Frittata

Use 100g crumbled feta in place of peppers, asparagus and parmesan.

Spinach Frittata

Use 1 cup cooked spinach in place of peppers and asparagus.

MENU IDEAS

Sunday Night Supper

steamed mussels with aromatics

roasted pepper and artichoke frittata

salad of mixed greens with favourite vinaigrette

crusty bread

preserved figs with mascarpone

Advance preparations

- *prepare aromatics for mussels*

- *wash and dry salad greens and make dressing*

- *cook potatoes and peppers for frittata*

Felafels with Mint Yoghurt Sauce

Chickpeas, split peas or even lentils can be used to make tasty felafels.

To Prepare: 20 minutes, plus soaking
To Cook: 30 minutes

> *300g dried, split green peas*
> *1 small onion, finely diced*
> *1 tsp crushed garlic*
> *1/2-1 tsp chilli powder, to taste*
> *2 tsp cumin*
> *1 tsp lemon juice*
> *1 tsp salt and lots of freshly ground*
> *   black pepper*
> *1/4 cup sesame seeds*
> *oil for shallow frying*

Cover the green peas with water and leave to soak for a minimum of 1 hour. Chickpeas need longer – soak overnight or for 8 hours. Drain, place in a saucepan and cover with fresh water, bring to the boil and simmer for 15 minutes. Drain and place in a food processor with the onion, garlic, chilli powder, cumin and lemon juice. Process until smooth. Season well and roll into balls. Flatten a little then dip in sesame seeds. Fry on a well-greased barbecue plate or shallow fry in 1cm of hot oil for 1-2 minutes on either side, or until golden brown. Drain on paper towels. Makes 24. Felafels can be prepared in advance and re-heated in the oven at 180°C for 5-8 minutes.

Busy Day Dinner Idea: *Serve the felafels in lightly toasted pita pockets with bean sprouts, diced tomatoes, diced cucumber, yoghurt and chilli sauces.*

Mint Yoghurt Sauce

Combine in a bowl 1 cup unsweetened natural yoghurt, a pinch of chilli powder, 2 tbsp chopped mint, a little salt and plenty of freshly ground black pepper. Spoon over the felafel pockets.

Above: Roasted Pepper and Asparagus Frittata

Catch Some Culture

Nutritionally, low-fat yoghurt is a winner. High in protein, low in fat, with calcium, zinc and riboflavin and all those helpful bugs. Yoghurt is a great stomach settler — those bugs keep your insides very happy. Yoghurt makes a good marinade base and can be flavoured with all manner of herbs or spices. When you are cooking with yoghurt, remember it will curdle if boiled. A little cornflour mixed through prevents curdling; or add right at the end and don't allow to boil.

Tibetan Split Pea Cakes

These spicy little cakes can also be made with lentils or dried beans. They can be made ahead of time and re-heated.

Tibetan Yoghurt Sauce

1 tomato, peeled

1/2-1 tsp chilli powder

1 cup unsweetened yoghurt

2 cloves garlic, finely chopped

1 tsp fresh ginger, finely chopped

1/2-1 tsp salt (to taste)

1/4 cup chopped coriander or mint

Purée all ingredients together until smooth. Keep chilled until ready to serve. Makes approx 1 1/4 cups.

To Prepare: 10 minutes

To Cook: 10-15 minutes

1 cup split peas

2 cloves garlic, crushed

1 tsp root ginger, finely chopped

1 tsp grated lemon rind

1 tsp turmeric

2 tsp cumin

1/2 tsp chilli powder

1 tsp salt

1/4 cup onion, finely chopped

1 cup milk

1/2 tsp baking soda

2/3 cup self-raising flour

oil for deep frying

Soak the peas overnight in cold water. Rinse several times then drain thoroughly. Place in a blender and blend with all the other ingredients to a semi-smooth mixture. Heat a heavy-bottomed fry-pan over medium heat and oil it lightly. Drop spoonfuls of the mixture in the pan, flatten slightly into small pancakes and cook for about 2 minutes on each side until golden. Makes about 3 dozen. They will keep, covered for about 2 days in the fridge or they can be frozen. Re-heat for 5-8 minutes in oven at 220°C.

Busy Day Dinner Idea: *Serve with a salad of cherry tomatoes, roasted red pepper, cucumber and mint, with Tibetan Yoghurt Sauce drizzled over.*

Spiced Bean Quesadillas

Quesadillas are the Mexican equivalent of pizza, and as such provide the opportunity for all manner of tasty toppings. In their most basic traditional form, quesadillas are made by sprinkling some chillies and cheese onto half a tortilla, which is then folded over and fried on both sides.

To Prepare: 10 minutes
To Cook: 15 minutes

> splash of olive oil
> 2 cloves garlic, crushed
> 2 tsp cumin
> 1 tsp chilli powder
> 1 x 310g can kidney beans, rinsed
>   and drained
> 1/4 cup sweet chilli sauce
> salt and ground black pepper
> 1 cup grated tasty cheese
> 2 tbsp chopped fresh coriander or
>   spring onions
> 4 fresh flour tortillas

Heat oil and gently cook garlic, cumin and chilli powder for about a minute. Roughly mash drained beans and mix in garlic, spices and chilli sauce. Season to taste. Spread about 1/4 of the mixture onto a tortilla, sprinkle with cheese and coriander, and place in a heated fry-pan. Top with another tortilla and cook until golden then turn to brown other side. Makes 2 'sandwich' quesadillas.

Variations:

- *Olive Pepper and Cheese Quesadillas:* Sandwich tortillas with grated cheese, scattered with olives and peppers.
- *Pesto Pumpkin and Gruyère Quesadillas:* Sandwich tortillas with a spread of pesto, slices of roasted pumpkin and grated gruyère cheese.
- *Quesadillas with Feta and Roasted Vegetables:* Sandwich tortillas with Feta and Fennel Spread ✪ and roasted vegetables, eg peppers, kumara and beans.

Noodle Pancake with Spring Onions and Herbs

Left-over noodles take on fresh appeal with this easy pancake. Very good topped with sliced tomatoes and pan-fried tofu.

To Prepare: 5 minutes
To Cook: 10 minutes

> 1 tbsp sesame oil
> 2 cloves crushed garlic
> 3 spring onions, finely diced
> rind of 1/2 lemon, finely grated
> 3 tbsp fresh coriander, chopped
> 2 tbsp Asian Pesto ✪
> 2 eggs
> 250g cooked noodles, eg udon
> salt and ground black pepper

Heat sesame oil and gently fry garlic for a few seconds. Remove from heat and place in a bowl with other flavourings and eggs. Combine with a fork to combine. Stir in noodles. Heat a little vegetable oil in a large pan, pour in noodle mixture and spread out evenly. Cook over gentle heat for about 5 minutes, then flip to cook the other side. Serve in wedges. Serves 4.

Pan-fried Tofu

Forget bland. When you marinate tofu in aromatic Asian flavours it's wonderful. Great for burgers, salads and stir-fries.

To Prepare: 5 minutes
To Cook: 5 minutes

> 1 tbsp butter or oil
> 2 tbsp soy sauce
> 1 tbsp minced fresh ginger
> 2 cloves crushed garlic
> 150-200g firm tofu, thinly sliced
> 2 tbsp toasted sesame seeds

Heat all ingredients except tofu and sesame seeds in a pan. Add tofu and stir-fry for a couple of minutes until evenly coated with flavours. Add sesame seeds and serve. Serves 4.

Noodle Natter

These days even the supermarket sells bean thread noodles, rice sticks and Chinese egg noodles. The pasta of Asia offers tremendous scope to the cook at home – in stir-fries, soups and salads.

Glass Noodles

Known also as bean thread noodles, cellophane noodles or vermicelli. Require soaking in hot water for about 15 minutes to soften.

Chinese Egg Noodles

Sold fresh and dried, often in portion 'nests'. Cook like pasta in plenty of salted boiling water. They will take 2-4 minutes depending on thickness.

Soba

Made from buckwheat and traditionally used in soups and salads. Cook like pasta; they take about 7 minutes.

Udon

These very thick hearty wheat noodles are often sold fresh from the chiller in Asian food markets. They are already cooked and simply need re-heating in a bowl of hot water before using.

Rice Sticks

Soften in warm water. When ready to use boil in lightly salted water for 2-3 minutes until tender.

Vegetable Power

WE ALL KNOW WE SHOULD EAT MORE VEGETABLES, BUT SOMETIMES IT'S HARD TO THINK OF NEW WAYS TO TREAT THEM. HERE VEGES TAKE CENTRE STAGE IN A RANGE OF WONDERFUL DISHES TO TEMPT EVEN THE STAUNCH MEAT EATERS.

Nutrition – Vitamin C

Vitamin C aids in the absorption of iron and assists in healing. It also helps in the formation of collagen and the brain chemical serotonin. Best sources of Vitamin C include kiwifruit, citrus fruit, mangoes, rock melons, strawberries, pineapple, spinach and all members of the cabbage family – ie broccoli, brussel sprouts, Chinese greens, etc. When cooking vegetables or fruits cut just before cooking and use as little water as possible to retain vitamins.

Egg wash

A little beaten egg brushed over pastry before it cooks creates a shiny glaze. Brushing egg over the base of a pre-cooked pastry shell before it is cooked also helps to seal it and prevents the filling from sogging.

Roasted Vegetable Platter with Aïoli

Roasted vegetables are very appealing – their flavours are so dense and rich. Vary your selection according to preference and the season.

To Prepare: 10 minutes
To Cook: 35-40 minutes

> *2 medium kumara, peeled*
> *1/2 medium pumpkin, peeled*
> *2 carrots, peeled*
> *2 red peppers*
> *big handful of green beans*
> *2 tbsp olive oil*
> *2 cloves garlic, crushed*
> *2 tsp fresh rosemary leaves, chopped*
> *salt and ground black pepper*
> *2 tbsp balsamic vinegar, to toss*
> *Aïoli* ✿

Pre-heat oven to 220°C. Cut kumara and pumpkin into wedges about 2cm thick. Cut carrots and peppers in chunks. Remove stems from beans. Place vegetables in a large roasting dish and mix through oil, garlic, rosemary, salt and pepper. Spread out to a single layer and roast at 220°C for 35-40 minutes until tender and starting to brown. Remove and drizzle over balsamic vinegar. Leave until warm or at room temperature. Serves 4.

Busy Day Dinner Idea: *Pile roast vegetables onto serving plates. Top each with a dollop of Aïoli,✿ Salsa Verde,✿ or Asian Pesto ✿ mixed with a little mayonnaise.*

Greek Spinach Roll

A herby brew of spinach and feta cheese encased in a crisp pastry crust.

To Prepare: 15 minutes
To Cook: 35 minutes

> *2 tbsp olive oil*
> *1 small onion, finely chopped*
> *400g spinach washed and de-stemmed, or 1 x 480g pkt frozen, thawed and drained*
> *1 egg, lightly beaten*
> *200g cottage cheese*
> *100g feta cheese, crumbled*
> *1/4 cup grated parmesan cheese*
> *2 tbsp chopped parsley*
> *1/2 tsp nutmeg*
> *salt and freshly ground pepper, to taste*
> *3 sheets or 400g flaky pastry, thinly rolled*

Heat oil and cook onion over low heat until soft. Add spinach and cook until pan is dry. Take off heat and mix in all other ingredients except pastry. Roll out pastry to a 35cm x 25cm rectangle. (If using pre-rolled pastry, overlap it, brushing with a little egg wash to join.) Lay spinach mixture in a mound along nearest edge leaving a border at sides to turn in. Roll up to fully enclose filling, leaving about 3cm pastry clear to overlap. Seal this edge with egg wash and place roll, joined edge down, on baking sheet. Use any remaining pastry to garnish. Brush with a little milk or beaten egg. Bake at 200°C for approximately 35 minutes, or until pastry is golden brown. Serves 4-6.

Grilled Mushrooms with Garlic Nut Topping

Use this versatile topping for mushrooms, sprinkled over casseroles and oven bakes or in salads.

To Prepare: 5 minutes

To Cook: 20 minutes

> *1/4 cup olive oil*
>
> *2 cloves crushed garlic*
>
> *1/2 cup chopped parsley*
>
> *1/2 cup pinenuts*
>
> *2 cups fresh white breadcrumbs*
>
> *1/2 cup grated parmesan or tasty cheese*
>
> *8-10 large flat mushrooms, stalks trimmed off*

Blend olive oil, parsley and pinenuts until fine. Add breadcrumbs and cheese and pulse to mix. Pile onto mushrooms and bake at 200°C for about 20 minutes until crisp and golden. Makes 8-10.

Variations:

- *Sprinkle over a smoked fish pie made with Lemon White Sauce,✪ hard-boiled eggs and pasta.*
- *Roll up Garlic Nut Topping in slices of roasted eggplant, bake and serve with Country-style Tomato Sauce.✪*
- *Flash-roast fish topped with pesto and sprinkled with Garlic Nut Topping.*
- *Sprinkle over soup.*

Above: Grilled Mushrooms with Garlic Nut Topping

This fiery root is a member of the mustard family. It has a clear, almost sweet bite and is the traditional partner to roast beef. Sold as a bottled sauce, it makes a useful flavouring for sauces and fillings. Grows easily but be warned, it is extremely invasive.

Easy Cheese Pastry

In a food processor place 1 cup high grade flour, 1 tsp salt, pinch cayenne pepper, 130g cold butter cut in small pieces and 100g grated tasty cheese. Blend until the mixture comes together in a ball. Roll out and chill. Pastry freezes.

Quick Pesto Fixes

- *White Bean Soup with Winter Pesto* ✿
- *pasta tossed with Winter Pesto and roasted pumpkin wedges*
- *prepared tomato pasta sauce, marinara mix or other seafood, and Winter Pesto simmered and tossed through cooked pasta*
- *flash-roasted fish topped with Winter Pesto*
- *polenta bake made with roasted peppers and courgettes, and Winter Pesto*

Anne's Spinach Tart

My mother makes the best savoury tart I have ever tasted. It's quite quiche-like but has a denser texture and wonderful green colour. Double the recipe and freeze one – they freeze beautifully.

To Prepare: 20 minutes

To Cook: 30 minutes

Pastry

> *1 cup plain flour*
> *¼ tsp salt*
> *75g butter (or ½ butter, ½ lard)*
> *about 2 tbsp cold water*

Filling

> *⅓ cup cream cheese*
> *3 eggs*
> *½ cup cream or milk*
> *1 tbsp pesto*
> *1 spring onion, chopped*
> *1 tsp horseradish sauce*
> *½ tsp prepared mustard*
> *½ cup grated cheese*
> *leaves from 2-3 heads fresh spinach (use as much or as little as you like)*
> *salt, pepper and a pinch nutmeg*

Place the flour, salt and butter in the bowl of a blender and blend to fine crumbs. With the motor running, add the water until the mixture comes together in a ball. Press into a loose-bottomed quiche dish (about 20cm), cover with baking paper, weight with baking beans or rice and bake for about 12-15 minutes at 200°C. While pastry cooks, prepare the filling. Blend together the cream cheese, eggs and cream. Add all other ingredients, blending until the mixture forms a smooth, green purée. Pour into semi-cooked pastry shell and bake at 180°C for about 30 minutes until golden. Serves 4.

Variation: Alsace Onion Tart *– Fill the tart shell with a mixture made with ⅓ cup of cream cheese, blended with 3 eggs and ½ cup of cream or milk. Add 4 large sliced cooked onions, 1 tbsp finely chopped fresh thyme, 2 tsp crushed garlic and 100g grated tasty cheese. Season to taste and bake as above.*

Roasted Tomato Tart

Here's a wonderful combination – a crisp cheese crust with a filling of sweet, slow-roasted tomatoes. Both can be prepared and cooked ahead of time ready to assemble at the last minute.

To Prepare: 20 minutes

To Cook: 1 ½ hours (includes tomatoes)

> *1 quantity of cheese pastry (see side panel or you can use regular savoury shortcrust)*
> *8-10 medium tomatoes, cores removed, cut in 8-10 wedges*
> *2 tbsp olive oil*
> *2 tsp balsamic vinegar*
> *2 tsp sugar*
> *salt and ground black pepper*
> *about 50g crumbled blue cheese*
> *finely shredded sorrel, rocket or spinach to garnish*

Roll out pastry to fit a 28cm flan tin or cut 6 x 10cm discs and put on a baking tray. Chill in the fridge for 20 minutes or freeze for 10 minutes. Mix sliced tomatoes with oil, vinegar and sugar, and season with salt and pepper. Spread into a large shallow roasting dish and roast at 170°C for about 1 ½ hours or until tomatoes are shrivelled. Bake pastry at 200°C for 10 minutes, reduce heat to 180°C and bake a further 15-20 minutes until crisp and golden. Allow to cool and slip out of tin. Arrange roasted tomatoes on top of cooked pastry and scatter over crumbled cheese. Pile a small handful of thinly sliced greens on top. Serves 6.

Pete's Potato Cake

This easy mixture is terrific lunch fare; it slices well and goes a long way. The cooking time will vary depending on the type of potatoes – wetter potatoes take longer.

To Prepare: 15 minutes

To Cook: up to 1½ hours

> 2 eggs
> 250g cream cheese
> 2 tbsp cornflour
> 3 cups roughly mashed potato
> ½ cup chopped fresh dill
>   and chives
> 1 tbsp horseradish sauce
> salt and ground pepper

Beat together eggs and cream cheese. Fold in cornflour, mashed potato, dill, chives and horseradish. Season with salt and pepper. Spread into a well-greased 20cm loose-bottomed cake tin, sprinkle with sea salt. Bake at 150°C for 1¼-1½ hours depending on the wetness of the potatoes. Remove from baking tin and allow to cool. If desired, spread the top with sour cream and top with lightly boiled asparagus. Serve in wedges, warm or cold. Serves 6-8.

Busy Day Dinner Idea: *Accompany with salad greens, Pete's Lemon Pickle*⊙ *and fresh bread.*

Above: Pete's Potato Cake topped with baby spinach leaves and Lemon Pickle

*Above: Roasted Onion and
Goat's Cheese Tart*

Caramelized Onions

The cooked onion mix used in the filling
can be made ahead of time, and will hap-
pily keep in the fridge for up to a week.
It's useful for all manner of things – from
quick soups to steak sauces.

To Prepare: 5 minutes

To Cook: 45 minutes

> *3 large red onions, peeled, cut in*
> *thin wedges*
> *2 tbsp oil*
> *1 tbsp brown sugar*
> *2 tbsp balsamic vinegar*
> *salt and ground black pepper*

Mix sliced onion wedges with oil, sugar
and vinegar. Season with salt and pepper.
Spread out into a roasting dish. Bake at
170°C for 45 minutes until tender and
lightly golden. Remove and allow to cool.

Serving Ideas:

- *Add 1¹/₂ cups beef stock and a splash
  of port or brandy for a steak sauce.*
- *Toss through salad greens with
  roasted pears, beets or walnuts.*
- *Simmer with 4 cups beef stock and
  ¹/₄ cup port for a delicious soup.*
- *To make a delicious casserole: Add
  1 cup red wine, 1 cup beef stock and
  2 tbsp tomato paste. Spoon over
  browned diced meat and bake at
  170°C for 1- 1¹/₂ hours.*

Roasted Onion and Goat's Cheese Tart

You could use store bought pastry for this wonderful savoury tart, but the home-made version here is super easy and delivers a fabulously crisp, flaky result. Take care not to overwork the dough, or it will be tough. Pastry can be frozen.

To Prepare: 30 minutes

To Cook: 40-45 minutes

Flaky Pastry

> *2 cups high grade flour*
> *1 tsp salt*
> *1 tsp baking powder*
> *220g frozen butter*
> *1/4 cup iced water*
> *(or use 500g commercial flaky pastry)*

Filling

> *1 recipe Caramelized Onions*
> *150g goat cheese, grated*

Combine flour, salt and baking powder in a bowl. Grate in the frozen butter and shake through the flour to coat. Add the water, mixing just until a soft dough is formed. Roll out pastry to a 1/2 cm thickness. Cut out rounds of about 15cm diameter. Chill for at least 10 minutes or until ready to assemble. Sprinkle a small handful of goat's cheese over the top of each pastry base, leaving a 2cm rim uncovered around the edge. Spread cooked onions on top of cheese. Sprinkle a little extra cheese over. Fold in the pastry edges in little folds (about 8) to partially cover the filling, leaving an uncovered ring of filling in the centre. Place pastry rounds on a baking tray, leaving a small gap between each. Bake at 220°C for 5 minutes then reduce heat to 180°C for a further 40-45 minutes until the tarts are crisp and golden. Makes 8.

Wild Mushroom Bruschetta

Both the filling and the bruschetta bases can be made ahead of time, ready to put together at the last minute and heat through.

To Prepare: 10 minutes

To Cook: 20 minutes

> *4 dried shiitake mushrooms*
> *1/2 cup hot water to soak*
> *2 tbsp olive oil*
> *2 cloves garlic, crushed*
> *500g flat brown or field*
> *   mushrooms thinly sliced*
> *1 tsp each chopped mint and*
> *   rosemary*
> *2 tbsp chopped parsley*
> *salt and ground black pepper*
> *juice of 1/2 lemon*
> *12-16 bruschetta bases*
> *   (see side panel)*
> *about 100g washed rind cheese,*
> *   or brie, sliced thinly*
> *Optional: handful of dried porcini*
> *   mushrooms*

Prepare bruschetta bases. If using dried mushrooms, soak in hot water while preparing other ingredients. Heat oil in a heavy pan, cook garlic a few seconds, add fresh mushrooms and chopped soaked ones (remove and discard stems of shiitakes) and cook until pan becomes dry. Season to taste and mix in herbs and lemon juice. Spoon mixture onto prepared bruschetta bases. Top with a little sliced brie and grill until cheese melts. Makes 12-16.

Other Bruschetta:
- *Sliced goat's cheese, rocket and roasted peppers.*
- *Tapenade ✪ and sliced canned artichokes, grilled with Havarti cheese.*

Bruschetta Bases

To prepare bruschetta bases, angle slice sourdough or another long country loaf or French bread. Brush with extra virgin olive oil on both sides and rub with a clove of cut garlic. Bake at 220°C for about 10 minutes until crisp and pale gold but not crumb dry. Store in an airtight container. They can be re-crisped in oven at 180°C for 5 minutes.

Onion Power

Garlic, onions and peppers have been used for centuries as natural medicines. Use them fresh to benefit from their active ingredients.

Double-baked Soufflés with Blue Cheese and Spinach

We tend to think of the soufflé as a fleeting moment of glory which sinks before you can blink. In fact, soufflés can be cooked and chilled a day or two ahead. Pouring over a little cream and baking them again in a hot oven puffs them up once more.

To Prepare: 15 minutes
To Cook: 20 minutes, then 5-7 minutes

>   60g butter, plus extra to butter
>   ramekins
>   1/2 cup plain flour
>   2 cups milk
>   pinch freshly ground nutmeg
>   salt and ground black pepper
>   5 egg yolks
>   1 cup cooked spinach, all moisture
>   squeezed out
>   150g crumbled, firm blue cheese
>   1/4 cup fresh chervil or other fresh
>   herbs, eg parsley or tarragon
>   6 egg whites

To re-heat:
>   about 1/2 cup cream
>   a little fresh parmesan, shaved with
>   a potato peeler

Pre-heat oven to 175°C. Butter 8 small ramekins and put in the fridge. Then butter again – this prevents mix from sticking. Melt butter in a large pot, add flour and stir over heat for a minute. Whisk in milk, nutmeg, salt and pepper, stirring constantly until sauce simmers and thickens. Remove from heat and beat in egg yolks, one at a time. Beat in spinach, cheese and half the herbs, reserving rest of herbs for garnish. Whip egg whites until stiff in a clean dry bowl. Add 1/4 of egg whites to sauce and fold in until thoroughly mixed. Add remainder of egg whites and fold together as lightly as possible. Fill ramekins to top. Smooth tops and run your thumb around edge of dishes so soufflés rise evenly. Set ramekins in a deep roasting dish lined with a clean tea towel, so the dishes don't crack. Pour boiling water around them to come halfway up the sides of the dishes. Place immediately into hot oven. Bake until soufflés are puffed, browned and just set in the centre, 15-20 minutes. Serve at once. For use later, take out of water bath and leave to cool – the soufflés will shrink back into the ramekins, pulling away slightly from sides. Unmould them into an ovenproof dish and keep covered in the refrigerator for up to 24 hours. To re-heat, drizzle cream over soufflés. Heat oven to 220°C. Bake soufflés until browned and slightly puffed, 5-7 minutes. Sprinkle with chervil, top with a few shavings of fresh parmesan and serve immediately. Serves 6-8.

Variation: Smoked Salmon Soufflés –
in place of spinach and blue cheese use 120g finely chopped smoked salmon and 1 cup tasty cheese

---

MENU IDEAS

Ladies for Lunch

Tio Pepe sherry served with pâté and toasted pita breads

double-baked soufflés

mixed leaf salad with favourite dressing

blueberry and macadamia coffee cake

Advance preparations

- *prepare pâté*
- *make soufflés and chill*
- *make cake*
- *prepare dressing and wash and dry salad greens*

Vegetable Samosas

This spicy mixture can be cooked in regular pastry, filo or naan bread dough. If using filo, follow the packet instructions for assembling individual pies.

To Prepare: 20 minutes, includes cooking root vegetables

To Cook: 35-40 minutes

1 tbsp olive oil

1 medium onion, diced

1 tsp each curry powder, ground cumin, ground coriander, garlic salt, fennel seed

2 tsp crushed garlic

2 tsp tomato paste

3 cups cooked cubed root vegetables, such as potato, pumpkin, kumara, carrot

1 cup peas

a pinch each of cinnamon, cloves and chilli powder

salt and ground black pepper

500g pastry, eg savoury shortcrust or filo

Heat the oil in a large heavy pan and cook the spices and onion until soft. Add the garlic and tomato paste and sizzle for a few seconds. Add the root vegetables and enough water to just cover. Simmer until just tender and the pan is dry. Remove from the heat, mix in the peas and season to taste. Allow the mixture to cool. Roll out pastry thinly and cut into 10cm rounds. Place a spoonful of filling on one half. Fold over pastry into a half moon shape. Press edges to seal and mark with a fork. Brush the top of the prepared parcels with butter or beaten egg. (They can be refrigerated for up to 24 hours or frozen.) Bake at 190°C for 20 minutes until golden. Serves 8.

Note: *Keep a stash of samosas in the freezer and bake from frozen (add 5 minutes to cooking time). Serve with Hot and Spicy Red Salsa* ✿ *and a salad of fresh tomatoes, red onions and cucumber.*

Filo Pastry

The satin-like suppleness of filo makes it wonderful to work with. Filo needs to be kept tightly wrapped as it turns brittle out in the air. Filo freezes well and will keep for several weeks in the fridge once opened.

Best results with filo are achieved by layering a stack of 5 or 6 buttered or oiled filo sheets. For a quick easy way to butter filo, simply spray between sheets with an olive oil aerosol.

Filo stacks can be cut to make individual pies. For a large pie press buttered or oiled sheets into a shallow pie dish, fill and top with another stack of buttered pastry.

Below: Vegetable Samosas served with Hot and Spicy Red Salsa

Soothing Starches

STARCHES MAY BE THE MOST BASIC OF FOODS BUT THE POWER OF STARCH GOES FURTHER,

PROVIDING SOOTHING, COMFORT AND SUSTAINING ENERGY.

Nutrition – Calories

Nutritionists tell us we should get most of our calories from starches like grains, breads, cereals and root vegetables. If you want to maintain a stable healthy weight and feel good, this is certainly the way to go. Bulky unprocessed starches — wholegrains, potatoes and other root vegetables, cereals, lentils, chickpeas, beans and brown rice tend to be high in fibre and low in fat. You feel full before you have had the chance to ingest a lot of calories.

By eating more of the starchy foods (which also provide proteins) you can decrease your calorie intake without suffering the symptoms of deprivation and hunger that are often associated with weight loss.

Pumpkin, Spinach and Goat's Cheese Lasagne

This is an ideal dish to prepare a day ahead and refrigerate. It re-heats well.

To Prepare: 30 minutes

To Cook: 30 minutes

> *2 whole bunches fresh spinach (or 480g frozen)*
> *2 tbsp pesto, basil or winter pesto*
> *3 cups pumpkin, cooked, drained and mashed*
> *2 cloves garlic, crushed*
> *100g ricotta or cottage cheese*
> *150g feta, finely crumbled*
> *½ tsp fresh grated nutmeg, grated*
> *2 eggs, beaten with a fork*
> *salt and ground black pepper*
> *2 cups pasta tomato sauce, mixed with 1 cup water*
> *3 fresh lasagne sheets, cut 25cm x 40cm (250g pack)*
> *1 cup grated tasty cheese*

Wash spinach, then drop into a pot of boiling water for 30 seconds. Drain under cold water and squeeze out all moisture. (If using frozen spinach, thaw and then squeeze dry.) Chop roughly, mix through pesto and season to taste with salt and pepper. Mix mashed pumpkin with garlic, cottage cheese, feta, nutmeg and eggs. Season to taste with salt and pepper. Spread 1 cup of pasta sauce/water mix onto the base of a 22cm x 33cm baking dish. Cover with a layer of lasagne. Spread over spinach; top with another layer of lasagne. Spread with pumpkin and cheese mixture, then a final layer of lasagne. Pour over the rest of the pasta sauce, spreading evenly. Sprinkle top with cheese. Bake uncovered at 180°C for 20 minutes. To brown top, place under grill. Serves 6.

Pasta with Spinach and Feta

This simple fresh pasta is an effortless mid-week meal. Use a good olive oil.

To Prepare: 10 minutes

To Cook: 15 minutes

> *400g dried pasta shapes*
> *2 tbsp olive oil*
> *1 large onion, finely diced*
> *2 tsp crushed garlic*
> *1 large bunch spinach, washed, stalks removed, finely chopped*
> *200g feta cheese, crumbled*
> *freshly ground black pepper*
> *good pinch nutmeg*

Cook the pasta according to manufacturer's instructions. While the pasta cooks, heat the oil in a pan and cook the onion until soft. Add the garlic and sizzle for a few seconds. Add the spinach to the pan and cook a further minute. Add the feta and season with pepper and nutmeg. Toss through the cooked pasta. Sprinkle with plenty of freshly ground black pepper and serve immediately. Serves 4.

Variation: *Use 100g crumbled blue cheese instead of feta.*

Pasta with Asian Pesto and Roasted Pumpkin

An al dente pasta tossed with a spicy pesto and sweet, densely flavoured roasted pumpkin. Try other types of pesto for a change of flavour.

To Prepare: 10 minutes

To Cook: 30 minutes

400g pumpkin, peeled, de-seeded
*   and cut into 3cm pieces*
3 tbsp olive oil
1 tsp crushed garlic
salt and ground black pepper

200g dried fusilli, or pasta tubes
¹/₂ cup Asian Pesto ✪ or
*   Winter Pesto ✪*
parmesan cheese to serve

Pre-heat oven to 220°C. Place pumpkin in a roasting dish, mix through oil and garlic, season with salt and pepper. Roast for 30 minutes until lightly golden, stirring once. Cook pasta according to manufacturer's instructions while pumpkin roasts. Drain pasta and toss through pesto and roasted pumpkin. Garnish with shavings of parmesan cheese. Serves 2.

Above: Pasta with Asian Pesto and Roasted Pumpkin

Rancid Nuts

Throw them out! Not only do rancid foods taste foul, they are also bad for you. All nuts are prone to rancidity once shelled. Check quality before buying and for best results store in the fridge or freezer. They can be used straight from the freezer. Nuts will keep 3-6 months in the fridge and a couple of years in the freezer in a sealed container.

Basic Savoury Polenta or Semolina

Polenta and semolina both cook to a thick porridge-like texture. As they cool they become firm and can be sliced and then grilled, baked or barbecued.

To prepare polenta, heat 3 cups milk with 50g butter in a big heavy pot. In a slow stream add 1 1/4 cups semolina, or 1 cup quick-cooking polenta, stirring all the time. Mix in 1 tsp salt, pinch nutmeg, and some black pepper. Stir over heat until it boils and thickens. Simmer for 3-4 minutes, or up to 20 minutes for cornmeal. Remove from heat and mix in 1/2 cup freshly grated parmesan cheese. Serve at once with a sauce (see later in this chapter for sauce ideas) or use as the basis for a range of savoury bakes, eg Corn and Spinach Polenta Slice.✪ Serves 4-6.

Roasted Walnut Blue Cheese Polenta

This easy roasted nut polenta is delicious with grilled or roast chicken or a wet mushroom sauce.

To Prepare: 10 minutes

To Cook: 10-20 minutes

> 1 cup fresh walnut pieces, or hazelnuts or almonds, chopped coarsely
> 1/4 cup oil
> 2 cloves garlic, crushed
> pinch cayenne
> 1 cup polenta, preferably instant, or medium ground cornmeal
> 3 1/2 cups water
> 1 tsp salt
> 1/2 cup finely grated parmesan cheese
> 100g blue cheese, crumbled
> freshly ground pepper

Heat oil in a pan, add garlic and nuts and cook gently for 5-8 minutes until nuts are golden. Remove from the heat and put to one side. Heat water in a heavy pot. Add salt and then pour in polenta in a steady stream, stirring constantly. Cook according to packet instructions. Cornmeal will take about 20 minutes. Once cooked stir in toasted nuts and garlic with their oil, parmesan and half the blue cheese. Season to taste. Either serve hot in spoonfuls like a purée, or spread mixture onto an oiled tray and allow to cool. Cut into triangles and grill or pan fry until golden. Serves 4.

Busy Day Dinner Idea: *Serve with slices of roasted peppers and grilled field mushrooms drizzled with olive oil, lemon juice, parsley, sea salt and pepper.*

Corn and Spinach Polenta Slice

You can use polenta or semolina to make this flavoursome, economical slice. A variety of flavour additions can be made to the cheesy base.

To Prepare: 5 minutes

To Cook: 25-35 minutes

> 1 litre milk
> 50g butter
> 1 1/4 cups quick polenta or semolina
> 3 eggs, lightly beaten
> 2 cups grated tasty cheese
> 1/4 cup parmesan cheese
> 1/2 tsp fresh grated nutmeg
> 1 cup whole kernel corn, drained and rinsed
> 1 1/2-2 cups cooked spinach, excess liquid squeezed out and diced
> salt and ground black pepper

Heat milk and butter until it just comes to boil. Add semolina and stir until the mixture boils and turns very thick. Remove from heat and quickly beat in eggs, cheese, nutmeg, corn, spinach and seasonings. Spoon mixture into a well-greased, shallow casserole dish (about 26cm). Bake at 200°C for 25-35 minutes until top is golden and crispy. To serve, spoon out of dish. Serves 4-5.

Variations:
- *Add 2 tbsp hot chilli sauce to mix before cooking.*
- *Add diced cooked bacon or ham.*
- *Add red peppers.*
- *Add 1 cup chopped walnut pieces, pinch cayenne and 1/2 cup parmesan cheese.*

Busy Day Dinner Idea: *Accompany with a Greek style salad and crusty bread.*

Péla

An exact translation of 'péla' is impossible, but a literal translation is 'pig food' – perhaps because it turns people into sighing, greedy eaters. A dish from the Grand Massif region of France where two of their best known products are potatoes and soft cheese. It's a wonderful dish to throw together for a crowd – when increasing the quantity, use a bigger dish, and enough potatoes and cheese to cover dish to a depth of 4-5cm. Again use enough water to just cover. Larger quantities may take a little longer to evaporate the water – after the first stage of cooking there is often a lot of water in the dish.

To Prepare: 10 minutes
To Cook: 1¼ hours

> 3 tbsp butter
> 750g starchy potatoes,
>   medium sliced
> salt and ground black pepper
> 250g reblochon or washed rind
>   cheese, fontina or havarti cheese,
>   thinly sliced

Pre-heat oven to 180 °C. Spread the butter to cover the base and sides of a 2 litre baking dish. Layer the potatoes and cheese into the dish, to a depth of 4-5cm, seasoning with salt and lots of ground pepper as you go. Add enough water to just cover. Cover and bake for 1 hour. Increase heat to 220°C, uncover and cook a further 40-60 minutes until golden and no longer watery. Serves 4.
Variations: Add onions or mushrooms or chopped bacon etc.
Busy Day Dinner Idea: *Serve Péla with a salad of tasty greens and an Italian dressing or lemony vinaigrette.*

Mushroom Risotto

This recipe can be made with meat stock. However, vegetarians may prefer to use a vegetable stock. In that case, the flavour won't be as dense, so add 2 tsp of crushed garlic.

To Prepare: 10 minutes plus soaking
To Cook: 25 minutes

> 50g dried porcini mushrooms
>   or dried Chinese mushrooms
> ½ cup port or red wine to soak
> 50g butter
> 1 onion, finely diced
> 400g field mushrooms, thinly sliced
> about 2 tbsp extra virgin olive oil
> 2½ cups Vialone Nano or other
>   short grain Italian rice
> 1 glass dry white wine
> about 5 cups good stock, eg meat,
>   chicken or vegetable
> salt and ground black pepper
> ½ cup grated parmesan cheese
> 2 tbsp chopped parsley

Soak the dried mushrooms in the port for about 1 hour. Strain, retaining the liquid and slice finely. Put to one side. In a pan, melt the butter and gently cook the onion until soft. Add the field mushrooms and cook until dry. Add oil and rice and stir over heat for 2-3 minutes. Add the wine, boiling stock, cooked mushrooms, soaked mushrooms and their liquid. Season to taste and cover. Lower the heat and simmer approximately 20 minutes, stirring occasionally. Before serving, sprinkle in the parmesan cheese and parsley and stir gently. Serves 4-5.
*Variation: **Duck Risotto** – Add the flesh of 1 cooked duck (if you don't want to roast your own, buy from an Asian food store) to the risotto just before serving. Garnish with crisped duck skin and parmesan.*

Pumpkin and Roast Garlic Risotto

Roasted garlic is one of my mainstay flavourings over autumn and winter. I usually make up a big batch as it keeps for over a month in the fridge (see Fridge Fixings section for method). This is a great dish to make when it seems the cupboard is bare – pumpkin and parsley are the only fresh ingredients you need.

To Prepare: 10 minutes
To Cook: 25 minutes

> *3 tbsp oil from roasted garlic or virgin olive oil*
> *2 cups short grain Italian rice, eg Carnaroli*
> *1/2 cup white wine*
> *4 cups chicken stock, hot*
> *2 cups pumpkin, diced 2cm pieces*
> *10-12 cloves Roasted Garlic* ✪
> *1/2 cup fresh parmesan, grated*
> *1/4 cup parsley, finely chopped*
> *salt and ground black pepper*

Heat oil in a heavy-based pot. Add rice and stir over heat for 2 minutes. Add wine and stir until evaporated. Add hot stock, diced pumpkin, roasted garlic and salt to taste and bring to a simmer. Press pumpkin into rice and cover pot. Once mixture boils reduce heat to a low simmer. Simmer gently for 14 minutes, stirring now and then. Rice should be sloppy. Mix in parmesan and parsley. Adjust seasonings to taste, adding plenty of black pepper. Cover and cook a further 2 minutes without stirring. Remove from heat and stand without uncovering for 3-4 minutes before serving. If risotto looks dry, add a dash more stock. Serves 4 as a stand-alone dish, or 6-8 as a side dish.

Asparagus and Fresh Rocket Risotto

Here's a simple fresh spring dinner. Creamy risotto cooked with verdant spinach and asparagus.

To Prepare: 5 minutes
To Cook: 25 minutes

> *2 tbsp olive oil*
> *1 onion, finely diced*
> *2 cups Italian short grain rice, eg Carnaroli or Arborio*
> *1/2 cup white wine*
> *4 cups chicken stock, hot*
> *finely grated rind of 1 lemon, no pith and 1 tbsp lemon juice or more, to taste*
> *400g asparagus, cut 2-3cm pieces, boiled for 2 minutes*
> *1 bunch rocket or watercress, coarse stems removed*
> *1/2 cup fresh grated parmesan*
> *salt and ground black pepper*
> Optional: *big pinch saffron threads*

Heat oil in a medium-large, heavy-based pot and cook onion over gentle heat until it is clear. Add rice and stir over heat another 1 minute. Add wine and stir until evaporated. Add hot stock, saffron threads and salt to taste. Once mix boils, reduce heat to low simmer. Simmer for exactly 14 minutes, stirring now and then. Rice should be sloppy. Mix in precooked asparagus, rocket and parmesan and adjust seasonings to taste. Cover pot and cook a further 2 minutes without stirring. Remove from heat and stand without uncovering for 1-2 minutes before serving. If risotto looks dry, add a dash more stock. Serves 4.

Variation: Add scallops or other fresh seafood in last 5 minutes of cooking.

Smart Saucery

WHEN YOU SERVE STARCHES LIKE PASTA, RICE, NOODLES POTATOES OR POLENTA, IT'S THE SAUCE THAT PROVIDES COLOUR, TEXTURE AND FLAVOUR, AND ALLOWS YOU TO CREATE A NUTRITIONALLY BALANCED MEAL.

Provençal Ratatouille

This is a fabulously versatile vegetable stew. You can vary the flavours by adding harissa, pesto, olives etc. Toss through pasta, serve with grilled polenta or with grilled or roasted meats and poultry. It freezes well.

To Prepare: 7 minutes
To Cook: 30 minutes

$^{1}/_{4}$ cup olive oil
2 large onions, thinly sliced
3 cloves garlic, crushed
1 tbsp tomato paste
10 ripe tomatoes (Italian),
    or 4 x 400g cans tomatoes in
    juice, chopped
1 tbsp dried oregano or basil
1 tsp honey or brown sugar
1 large red or yellow pepper, diced
    in 2-3cm pieces
4-5 large courgettes, cut in thin slices
1 medium eggplant, diced in
    2-3cm cubes
$^{1}/_{2}$ cup port
1 tbsp spiced vinegar
salt and ground black pepper

Heat oil in a big pot and cook onions over medium heat until tender but not browned (approximately 10 minutes). Add garlic and tomato paste and cook a further minute. Mix in all remaining ingredients, cover and simmer for 20 minutes. Adjust seasoning to taste.
Busy Day Dinner Idea: *Serve hot or at room temperature with soft or grilled polenta. Garnish each serving with shavings of parmesan cheese and a small spoon of pesto. Serves 6.*

Ratatouille Partners

- *Add 400g skinless thinly sliced chicken to ratatouille and cook 6-8 minutes*
- *Add sliced raw squid rings, diced boneless fish and prawns and cook 2-3 minutes.*
- *Serve with a roasted beef fillet*
- *For an easy vegetable chilli mix in 2-3 cans rinsed beans, 1 tbsp ground cumin and a big dollop of chilli sauce.*

Indonesian Peanut Sauce

Fragrantly spicy, this versatile sauce makes a great topping for a salad, any kind of satay, or barbecued meats.

To Prepare: 10 minutes
To Cook: 20 minutes

1 medium onion, very finely diced
4 cloves garlic, crushed
1 tbsp vegetable oil
1 cup crunchy peanut butter
1 tbsp fresh minced ginger
$^{1}/_{2}$ cup sweet hot chilli sauce (use an
    Asian brand)
$1^{1}/_{2}$ cups coconut cream
2 tbsp lemon juice
dash of salt and ground black
    pepper

To make the sauce, cook the onions and garlic in oil in a pot until soft. Add the remaining ingredients and simmer over low heat, stirring occasionally for about 15 minutes. Makes 3 cups. The sauce stores well in the refrigerator.

MENU IDEAS

Harvest Dinner

polenta with double
mushroom sauce

salad of roasted beets and carrots
with rocket and pinenuts

roasted stonefruits with
berry compote

Country-style Tomato Sauce

One mighty 'in-house' brew of tomato sauce from the Italian kitchen serves as a base for pizza, pasta, braises, soups, stews and casseroles.

To Prepare: 10 minutes
To Cook: about an hour

> 1/2 cup olive or vegetable oil
> 50g butter
> 2 medium onions, finely diced
> 4 cloves garlic, crushed
> 6 tbsp tomato paste
> 2kg peeled tomatoes (or 2kg tinned tomatoes in juice)
> 2 tbsp chopped parsley
> 1/2 cup chopped fresh basil or 1 tbsp dried basil
> 1 tbsp salt
> 2 tsp brown sugar
> 2 tsp chilli paste
> 2 tsp freshly ground peppercorns

In a large pot heat the oil and butter. Add the onion, garlic and tomato paste and cook over a low heat, stirring occasionally until the onions are soft. Add all other ingredients and simmer in a semi-covered pot for 45 minutes. Stir occasionally to prevent sticking. Remove the lid and continue cooking a further 10-15 minutes until the sauce is quite thick. Store in the fridge. Freezes or can be bottled in sterilised jars with screw-top seal lids. Makes 9 cups.
Variation: *Add a few threads of orange rind and some black olives.*

Moroccan Sauce

This is a really versatile sauce with exotic flavours of North Africa.

To Prepare: 15 minutes
To Cook: 25 minutes

> 2 tbsp olive oil
> 1 onion, finely diced
> 2 cloves garlic, crushed
> 1 tsp fine black pepper
> 1/2 tsp cayenne pepper
> 2 tsp cardamom seeds ground
> 4cm piece of fresh ginger, peeled
> 2 tsp each ground cumin, coriander and cinnamon
> 2 x 400g cans tomatoes, chopped
> 2 tbsp brown sugar
> salt to taste

To make sauce, fry onion and all flavourings in oil until softened. Add tomatoes and sugar and simmer 15 minutes. Season to taste. Sauce will keep in the fridge for several days. Makes about 4 cups.

Double Mushroom Sauce

Dried mushrooms give this sauce an intense rich flavour.

To Prepare: 10 minutes, plus soaking
To Cook: 10-12 minutes

> 4 dried Chinese mushrooms, soaked in 1/2 cup port or red wine
> 1 tbsp oil
> 400g sliced fresh field mushrooms
> 1 tsp crushed garlic
> 1 1/2 cups chicken stock
> 1 tsp cornflour, mixed with a little water
> 2 tbsp lemon juice
> salt and ground black pepper

Soak the dried mushrooms for at least 30 minutes, or for 6 minutes on defrost power in the microwave. Cut mushrooms into fine dice, discarding the stalks. Reserve with their liquid. Heat the oil and cook the fresh mushrooms until the pan is dry and the mushrooms start to brown. Add garlic and cook for a few seconds, then add the stock, dried mushrooms and their liquid and simmer for 5 minutes. Thicken with cornflour paste and adjust seasonings. Serves 4 with polenta, or pasta. Makes about 3 cups.

Other Useful Sauces

- *Caramelized Onions*
- *Slow-roasted Tomatoes puréed with stock*
- *Country-style Tomato Sauce*
- *Moroccan Sauce*
- *Cumin Chilli Tomato Sauce*
- *Cashew Sauce*

Boosting Your Nutrition Intake

Virtually all plant foods are nutritionally dense, but in the vitamin stakes certain fruits and vegetables come up trumps. There is strong medical evidence that the nutrients provided by fresh foods offer the body better protection than their bottled counterparts.

Spice It Up

THE SIMPLE ADDITION OF EXOTIC SPICES SUCH AS CARDAMOM, MUSTARD SEEDS AND GARAM MASALA TRANSFORMS A MEAL OF BASIC INGREDIENTS.

Above: Avial

Nutrition – Especially for Smokers

Vitamins A, C and E are known as the ACE vitamins for their protective benefits. Beta carotene, which the body converts to Vitamin A, is found in a number of vegetables including green leafy vegetables, sweet potatoes, pumpkin and carrots. If you smoke, you need to eat lots of these foods as carotene is associated with reducing the risk of lung cancer.

Avial
(Mixed Vegetable Curry)

This dry, richly flavoured curry comes from Southern India. It can be made with any seasonal vegetables, as available.

To Prepare: 20-25 minutes
To Cook: 20 minutes

2 tbsp oil
5 green chillies, chopped
1 tsp cumin seeds
1 tsp mustard seeds
1 cup desiccated coconut
pinch of turmeric
1 large potato, cut in 2cm pieces
1 large carrot, cut in 2cm pieces
2 eggplants, cut into small pieces
1 cup each coconut cream and water
5 beans, thinly sliced
2 courgettes, diced
1 unripe banana, peeled and sliced

¹/₂ cup natural yoghurt
2 tsp garam masala
salt and fine black pepper
chopped coriander leaves to garnish
Optional: *1 tbsp curry leaves*

Heat the oil in a large heavy-based saucepan and fry the chillies, coconut, cumin seeds, mustard seeds, turmeric and optional curry leaves over a low heat for 1-2 minutes. Add the potatoes, carrots, eggplant, water and coconut cream. Cover and cook gently for 10 minutes. Add beans, courgettes and banana and cook uncovered for another 5-10 minutes until pan is dryish and vegetables are tender. Add a little water if needed. Mix the garam marsala with yoghurt. Stir into curry and season to taste. Garnish with the coriander. Serves 4.

Busy Day Dinner Idea: *Serve on a bed of rice and accompany with poppadoms.*

Potato and Pea Curry

Poppadoms, rice, Indian pickles and yoghurt mixed with cucumber and mint turn this simple curry into a substantial vegetarian meal.

To Prepare: 5 minutes

To Cook: 25 minutes

> 6 large potatoes, washed and
>   peeled
> 3 tbsp vegetable oil
> 1 tsp each of black mustard seeds
>   and fennel seeds
> 1 tbsp cumin seeds
> 2 onions, thinly sliced
> 1/2 tsp chilli powder and black
>   pepper and turmeric
> 2 tsp garam masala
> 2 cups peas (fresh or frozen)
> juice of 1/2 lemon
> 2 tbsp chopped coriander

Boil potatoes in lightly salted water until just tender. Drain thoroughly and cool. Meanwhile, heat the oil in a saucepan and fry the mustard, fennel and cumin seeds until they start to pop. Add the onions and remaining spices and cook until the onion softens (about 10 minutes). Cut the potatoes into chunks about 2cm thick. Add to the pan and cook over high heat until they start to brown. Mix in the peas, lemon juice and coriander and serve at once. Serves 4.

Indian Spicy Dhal

The combination of the Indian pulse dish dhal with rice is the foundation of peasant Indian cuisine. Lentils or split peas can be used – neither require soaking. Leave out the cream if you prefer.

To Prepare: 15 minutes

To Cook: 40 minutes

> 2 tbsp oil
> 1 medium onion, finely chopped
> 1 tsp each chilli powder and
> ground cumin
> 1 tsp smoked paprika
> 1 cup brown lentils, washed
> 400g can tomatoes in juice
> 310g can red kidney beans, rinsed
> 1/2 cup cream
> salt and fine black pepper
> 1/4 cup chopped fresh coriander

Heat oil in a large heavy pot and gently fry onion with all spices until onion is clear. Add washed lentils, tomatoes and juice. Simmer for about 40 minutes until lentils are tender. Mix in rinsed canned beans and cream, lightly mashing to make a rough semi-thick purée. Season to taste and mix in coriander. Serves 2-3.

MENU ⚔ IDEAS

A Vegetarian Indian Feast

little samosas with kasundi
dipping sauce

poppadoms with mint yoghurt
dipping sauce

avial

spinach frittata

plain rice and naan bread

salad of rocket and cucumber

orange and almond syrup cake

Advance preparations

- *make samosas and freeze*

- *prepare avial and frittata
  and refrigerate*

- *make dough for naan
  bread and freeze or chill*

- *make cake*

- *wash and dry salad greens*

---

*Nutrition –
Potato Power*

A calorie is the amount of energy required to heat 1litre water by 1°C. Calories and kilojoules are the units used to measure the amount of energy the body gets from food. An average adult expends between 1,800 and 3,000 calories per day. 100g of potato (a medium-sized one) contains only about 100 calories, but when you add a tablespoon of fat you add another 145 calories. Gram for gram fats contain more than double the calories of protein or starch. So fill up on the spuds and go easy on the fat on top.

Sri Lankan Egg Curry (Bitter Hoddie)

The curries of Ceylon are mild and wonderfully aromatic.

To Prepare: 5 minutes
To Cook: 10-15 minutes

> 6 eggs, hard boiled
> 3 potatoes, cooked, diced in 2cm pieces
> 2 onions, peeled
> 2 tbsp oil
> 1½ tsp turmeric
> 2 tsp cumin powder
> 1 tbsp coriander powder
> ¾ tsp fennel powder
> 1 cinnamon quills
> 400mls coconut cream
> 1 scant tbsp salt

Peel the hard-boiled eggs, rinse in cold water to get off any extra shell, drain, cut in half and put into a bowl with the diced potatoes. Cut onion finely, heat the oil gently in a big pot, and add the onion and all the spices. Cook for a few minutes, stirring occasionally, until onion is soft. Add the salt, eggs and potatoes and bring back to a simmer. Cook for another 2 minutes. Serve 2-3 egg halves and some sauce on top of cooked rice. Serves 4-6.

Mexican-style Chickpeas

Serve this as a quick main course with pita bread and sour cream or as part of a buffet with grilled meats and salads. Use a commercial Cajun spice mix, or make your own.✿

To Prepare: 10 minutes
To Cook: 10 minutes

> 2 tbsp cooking oil
> 2 tsp crushed garlic
> 1-2 tbsp Cajun spice mix, to taste
> 2 cans chickpeas, drained, or 3 cups cooked chickpeas
> 2 carrots, cut in matchsticks
> ½ red pepper, cut in thin strips
> ½ cup toasted pumpkin or sunflower seeds
> 2 tbsp chopped coriander
> salt and pepper

Heat the oil in a large pan and cook the garlic and spice mix for 30 seconds. Add all other ingredients, except coriander and salt and pepper, and cook over medium heat for 10 minutes, stirring frequently. Season to taste with salt and pepper and mix in the coriander. Serves 4.

Soaking and Cooking Beans

Age and the hardness of water add to the time of soaking and cooking dried beans. They will swell 2½-3 times their original volume when soaked. Cover beans with 4 times their volume of water and soak for 4-12 hours. When time is at a premium you can fast soak beans by covering with 4 times the amount of water in a big pot. Bring to a boil, boil for 10 minutes, then stand for 40 minutes before using. After they have soaked, drain off all the soaking water. Cover them with fresh water and boil hard for 5-10 minutes, then reduce heat to a low simmer until beans are tender. Don't add salt, it prevents the beans from softening. So do highly acidic ingredients such as tomatoes and citrus juice. Boil beans uncovered – most varieties take about 1-1½ hours to fully cook. Old beans or hard water take longer to cook. Adding a piece of seaweed, such as kombu, to the pot, seems to reduce their flatulent effects. Always fully cook beans as uncooked beans are indigestible.

PROTEIN COMPLEMENTS

For those who don't eat a lot of meat, nuts provide an excellent source of protein. Because plant foods contain incomplete proteins (they are relatively deficient in one or two essential amino acids), two or more complementary plant foods need to be eaten at the same meal (or within about 2 hours) in order for the human body to make full use of all the protein available in the plant food.

Combine any legume with any grain, nut or seed and you have it covered. Alternatively, you can combine any grain, nut, legume or seed with a dairy food. So something as simple as a peanut butter sandwich provides the same quality of protein as a steak.

Meat-free Salad Meals

IT'S TRUE THAT A VEGETARIAN DIET REQUIRES CARE TO ACHIEVE NUTRITIONAL BALANCE. THESE COMBINATIONS OF NUTS, GRAINS AND VEGETABLES SOLVE THE PROBLEM WITH GREAT TASTE.

Vegetable Platter with Green Goddess Dressing

A platter of lightly cooked vegetables served with a rich garlicky dressing makes a good first course, or served as part of a buffet. Vary the vegetables according to preference and availability, allowing a about 4-6 different vegetables for each person.

To Prepare: 20 minutes

To Cook: 5-10 minutes

> *baby potatoes and kumara (cut in chunks) – boil until just tender*
> *beetroot – boil for 20 minutes, cool and remove skins*
> *beans, carrots and angle sliced courgette – blanch in boiling water for 2 minutes then refresh in cold water*
> *pepper – roast until skins blister, then peel, de-seed under running water and cut into pieces*
> *radishes, cherry tomatoes – serve raw*

Green Goddess Dressing

> *1 bunch parsley, stems removed*
> *2 egg yolks*
> *1-2 tsp garlic, crushed*
> *1 tsp prepared mustard*
> *salt and pepper*
> *2 tsp lemon juice*
> *about 1 cup virgin olive oil*

Above: Vegetable Platter with Green Goddess Dressing

Prepare all the vegetables and arrange on a large platter. To make the sauce, blend the parsley in food processor or blender until finely chopped. Add the egg yolks, garlic, mustard, salt and pepper and lemon juice. With the motor running, slowly drizzle in the oil until the sauce thickens. Dressing will keep for about 1 week in the fridge. Makes 1¼ cups.

Harvest Salad of Roasted Beets, Walnuts & Onions with Goat's Cheese Croûtons

In the autumn and winter, I love to roast vegetables like beets, onions, carrots and pumpkin as well as pears for use in warm salads. Here's a mouth-watering meal-in-one combination.

To Prepare: 15 minutes
To Cook: 40-50 minutes

> 4 large beetroot, peeled and cut in batons 2cm thick x 5cm long
> 3 large red onions, peeled and cut in thin wedges, 8-10 per onion
> 3 large pears, peeled and cored, each cut in 8 wedges
> 1/4 cup olive oil
> 2 tbsp brown sugar
> 2 tbsp balsamic vinegar
> salt and freshly ground pepper
> 1-1 1/2 cups walnut halves
> 4-6 handfuls of mixed salad greens, washed and dried
> 1 quantity pesto dressing

Goat's Cheese Croûtons

> 10-12 slices rustic bread or French bread
> 150g goat's cheese, to spread

Pre-heat oven to 220°C. Place cut up beetroot in a shallow roasting dish. In a separate dish, place onions and pears. Divide sugar, vinegar and oil evenly between the two dishes and mix through. Spread out evenly in a single layer in each dish. Bake for 40-50 minutes, stirring a couple of times until vegetables are tender and all liquid has evaporated. Bake walnuts in a separate dish for 12-15 minutes. Allow all to cool separately.

To assemble salad, combine pesto dressing ingredients and toss through salad greens. Add beets, onions, pears and walnuts and mix through. Garnish with croûtons spread with goat's cheese. Serve at once. Serves 4 as a main course and 6 as a starter.

Variation: Add 2 rashers bacon, diced and cooked until crisp.

Salad of Roasted Carrots and Beets with Rocket and Pinenuts

This is a great winter salad. It makes a delicious partner to roast chicken or served with the potato Péla.✪

To Prepare: 10 minutes
To Cook: 45-50 minutes

> 4 large beetroot, peeled and cut in batons
> 4 large carrots, peeled and cut in batons
> 2 tbsp olive oil
> 1 tbsp brown sugar
> 2 tbsp balsamic or red wine vinegar
> 2 handfuls of rocket leaves
> 1/2 cup toasted pinenuts

Place beetroot and carrots in a roasting dish. Mix through oil, brown sugar, balsamic vinegar, and season with salt and ground black pepper. Spread out in dish and roast at 180°C for 45-50 minutes until starting to shrivel. Cool and toss through with rocket leaves and pinenuts. Serves 4.

Nutrition – Potassium

There is research to suggest that potassium helps keep blood pressure in check and reduces the risk of strokes. It also works with other nutrients to keep body functions going. Excellent sources of potassium include dried beans, bananas, pumpkin, tomatoes (fresh and canned), yoghurt and spinach.

Pesto Dressing

Combine 1 tbsp pesto with 2 tbsp lemon juice and 3 tbsp extra virgin olive oil. Season with salt and ground black pepper.

Opposite: Harvest Salad of Roasted Beets, Walnuts and Onions with Goat's Cheese Croûtons

Right: Asian Deli Noodles

Dressing Noodle and Pasta Salads

These absorb all the dressing you can give them. Tossing the noodles with oil before dressing makes them less sticky.

Asian Deli Noodles

The dressing for this great little salad is likely to become a kitchen staple – it's just so useful and delicious, and it keeps for weeks in the fridge. Drizzle it over barbecued or grilled meats, mix it through stir-fries, use as a marinade for pork ribs and chicken, or use it as an accompaniment for a barbecue.

To Prepare: 5 minutes

To Cook: 5-10 minutes for noodles

Asian Deli Sauce

> *3 cloves garlic, peeled and chopped*
> *2cm piece root ginger, minced or grated*
> *2 tbsp soy sauce*
> *1-2 tbsp sweet Thai chilli sauce, to taste*
> *1 tbsp fish sauce*
> *2 tbsp peanut butter*
> *2 spring onions, chopped*
> *handful of coriander leaves*
> *1/2 cup water*

Salad

> *500g Chinese noodles, eg udon noodles, rice noodles or spaghetti*
> *1/2 cup peanuts, roasted*

Salad Garnish

> *2 spring onions, finely chopped*
> *1/4 cup fresh coriander or mint, chopped*
> *1 pkt mung bean sprouts*
> *1/2 cucumber, cut in small batons*
> *1 red pepper, diced*

To make the Asian Deli Sauce, purée all sauce flavourings, peanut butter and herbs until semi-smooth. Prepare noodles according to manufacturer's instructions. Drain and cool. Place cooked noodles in a large bowl. Mix through sauce to combine. Mix through garnish ingredients. Serve at room temperature. If planning to prepare it ahead, add a little extra oil to dressing to stop noodles sticking. Serves 6.

Variations: *Cooked chicken or shrimps can also be added to this salad.*

Greens, Pears, Spicy Pecans and Blue Cheese

The combination of blue cheese and pears is classic. Here, wedges of juicy ripe pears combine with salad greens, spicy roasted pecan nuts and some crisp croûtons spread with soft blue cheese. The result is easy, elegant and delicious.

To Prepare: 5 minutes
To Cook: 12-15 minutes

1 tbsp oil
1/2 tsp each curry powder and
    ground cumin
1 cup pecans or fresh walnut halves
8-12 French bread croûtons
2 large or 3 medium juicy pears,
    cored, each half cut in 6 wedges
1/2 cup favourite dressing or
    vinaigrette
6-8 handfuls mixed salad greens,
    washed and dried
120-150g soft blue cheese

Preheat oven to 200°C. Mix oil and spices through nuts in a baking dish. Bake for 10 minutes until lightly golden, taking care not to over cook. Alternatively, microwave on half power for 3-4 minutes, stirring every minute. Reserve to one side. Place pear wedges in a mixing bowl and mix with dressing or vinaigrette. Toss through salad greens and toasted nuts. Divide between 4 serving plates. Spread bread croûtons with cheese and serve 2 atop each salad. Serves 4 as a meal or 6 as a first course.

Variations:
- Lightly grill croûtons to melt cheese before garnishing salads.
- Use goat's cheese in place of blue cheese.

Raw Energy Salad

This salad makes a delicious fresh lunch or summer meal. Add protein with tuna, boiled eggs, marinated tofu, or cooked chicken.

To Prepare: 10 minutes

1 bunch fresh spinach, leaves
    washed and stems removed
1/4 cup vinaigrette dressing
2 tbsp chopped fresh herbs
1 large red pepper, cut in thin strips
1 crisp carrot, peeled and shredded
1 pkt snow pea shoots (about
    2 handfuls)
1 small red onion, thinly sliced
1/4 paw paw or rock melon, peeled,
    seeded and cut into segments
1 bunch radishes, sliced thinly
1/2 cup toasted almonds
juice of 1/2 lemon
1/2 tsp sugar
ground black pepper
Green Goddess Dressing ✿

Toss the spinach leaves with the vinaigrette dressing. Arrange on a big platter and sprinkle over the chopped herbs. Toss the other vegetables with lemon juice, salt and pepper and pile on top. Serve each salad with a spoonful of Green Goddess Dressing on top. Serves 2 as a meal or 4 as a starter.

Vegetable Protection

In countries such as New Zealand and Australia, the incidence of melanoma is very high. Interesting research suggests that the vegetables grown in these harsh sun environments develop their own defences against the sun and these benefits are passed on by eating them.

Free Radicals

Free radicals have been likened to delinquent teenagers. They charge around the body causing havoc and destruction. Free radicals are thought to cause cell damage and are precursors to a number of diseases such as artheriosclerosis and some types of cancer. We all produce them, but stress, smoking and other pollutants cause them to increase. Fresh fruits and vegetables contain anti-oxidants which bond with free radicals and neutralise them before they can do any damage. Kiwifruit, pumpkin, kumaras, red peppers, broccoli and other cruciferous vegetables are particularly potent sources of anti-oxidants.

CHICKEN

Grilled Chicken Salad with Citrus Chilli Dressing

Thai Chicken and Noodle Salad

Syrian Chicken Salad

Smoked Chicken, Strawberries, Peaches and Summer Herbs

Chicken Salad with Pesto Dressing

All Dressed Up

Chinese Chicken Salad

Pesto, Corn and Chicken Salad

Oriental Poached Chicken

Chicken Noodle Salad

Grilled Chicken Caesar Salad

Beijing Duck Salad Pancakes

Moroccan Duck Salad

Italian Grilled Chicken with Lemon and Herbs

Pesto Chicken Breasts with Eggplant and Red Pepper

Whole BBQ Chicken

Chicken Fajitas

Moroccan Grilled or Barbecued Chicken

Thai Chicken Skewers

Marinades

Vietnamese Ginger Chilli Chicken

Burmese Chicken and Spinach

Thai Chicken Curry

Cantonese Chicken

Chicken Yakitori

Asian Chicken, Peppers and Noodles

Provençal Chicken with Prunes, Apricots and Olives

Spicy Moroccan Chicken Tagine

Balsamic Chicken Breasts with Crispy Mint and Pinenuts

Fragrant Portuguese Chicken

Chicken with Dijon Mustard

Coq Au Vin

Tex Mex Chicken Wraps

Chicken Pasta with Garlic, Rosemary and Spinach

Pasta, Chicken, Bacon and Asparagus

Mango Glazed Poussin

Lemon Roast Chicken with Pumpkin and Onions

Twice-roasted Duck with Lemon Pepper

Celebration Roast Turkey with Country Ham and Fig Stuffing

Country Fig Stuffing

Chicken Salads

THE ENORMOUS ADAPTABILITY OF CHICKEN LENDS ITSELF TO ALL MANNER OF WONDERFUL SALAD COMBINATIONS AND DRESSINGS. NO MATTER WHAT THE INGREDIENTS, OR THE DRESSING, THE METHOD IS USUALLY THE SAME – IN THE BIGGEST BOWL YOU CAN FIND, TOSS THE SALAD GREENS WITH DRESSING TO COAT, THEN ADD OTHER INGREDIENTS AND TOSS GENTLY TOGETHER BEFORE SERVING.

Cooking Chicken for Salads

Tender, always moist chicken for salads is best achieved by poaching. Place chicken pieces, breasts or thighs in a single layer in a pan or pot. Cover with cold water, add a couple of bay leaves, parsley stems and peppercorns to flavour. Bring slowly to a simmer. Simmer for 5 minutes then let cool in the cooking liquid.

Tossing Salads

In Italy they say you are old enough to marry when you can toss a salad without losing some over the sides. I say get a big bowl. It's so much easier to combine ingredients and prevents fragile things like avocados from getting mashed.

Previous page: Lemon Roast Chicken with Pumpkin and Onions

Grilled Chicken Salad with Citrus Chilli Dressing

The divine dressing for this salad is best prepared at least 6 hours in advance. It's wonderful on all types of chicken, as well as seafood and meat.

To Prepare: 15 minutes

To Cook: 2-3 minutes

Citrus Chilli Dressing
> *juice of 1 orange*
> *juice of 2 limes or lemons*
> *3 tbsp rice wine vinegar*
> *2 tbsp fish sauce*
> *1/2 tsp hot chilli sauce*
> *1 clove garlic, crushed*
> *1 tbsp sugar*
> *salt and ground black pepper*
> *2 tbsp each of minced coriander and mint*

Salad
> *4 boneless chicken breasts, sliced thinly*
> *2 tbsp olive oil*
> *salt and ground black pepper*
> *8 handfuls of fresh mixed salad greens, washed and dried*
> *1/2 red onion, finely cut*
> *3 oranges, peeled and segmented*
> *1 large avocado, cut into wedges*

Combine all dressing ingredients and refrigerate at least 12 hours (up to 1 week in the fridge). Mix oil through chicken and season with salt and pepper. Cook on a pre-heated grill or hot fry-pan. Mix dressing with any cooking juices. Spoon a little dressing over cooked chicken. Toss the rest of the dressing through salad greens with chicken. Gently toss through red onion, orange segments and avocado. Divide between plates. Serves 6.

Thai Chicken and Noodle Salad

Cooked chicken with crisp salad vegetables and silky noodles is a perfect combination.

To Prepare: 25 minutes (includes 20 minutes soaking time)
> *80g (1/3 packet) vermicelli rice noodles*
> *1 crisp lettuce, finely shredded*
> *2 carrots, grated and mixed with 1 tsp sugar*
> *2 spring onions, sliced thinly*
> *1/2 cup roasted peanuts, chopped*
> *1/2 cup chopped coriander or mint*
> *flesh of 1 cooked chicken, shredded in bite-sized pieces*

Thai Dressing
> *2 tbsp fish sauce*
> *1 tsp sugar*
> *2 tbsp lime or lemon juice*
> *1/4 cup Thai sweet chilli sauce*

Soak the vermicelli noodles in warm water for about 20 minutes until clear and soft. Drain thoroughly. Combine the noodles with the salad ingredients in a large bowl. Mix the chicken and dressing ingredients and toss through salad. Pile onto a large flat serving plate. Serves 4.

Syrian Chicken Salad

Here, a wonderful fresh lemon and parsley chicken salad is served atop a vegetarian salad of roasted carrots, beets and pinenuts. The chicken mixture is also delicious as a filling for pita breads.

To Prepare: 15 minutes

To Cook: 15 minutes

> 1 recipe *Salad of Roasted Carrots and Beets with Rocket and Pinenuts* ✺
>
> 4 *cooked chicken breasts, finely diced*
>
> *¹/₂ cup Winter Pesto* ✺
>
> 2 *handfuls spinach, watercress or rocket, very finely shredded*
>
> *juice of ¹/₂ lemon*
>
> *salt and ground black pepper*
>
> Optional: 2 *tbsp mayonnaise*

Prepare Roasted Carrot and Beet Salad. Combine finely chopped chicken with all other ingredients. Season to taste. Divide Roasted Carrot and Beet Salad between serving plates and serve a mound of chicken on top. Serves 4.

Cashew or Orange Walnut Dressing

Puréeing toasted nuts with fresh juice gives a wonderful creamy dressing for chicken and seafoods. Walnuts, pecans and pistachios provide Mediterranean flavours, while peanuts and cashews create dressings with tropical Asian overtones. Purée together until smooth 1 cup fresh orange juice and ¹/₂ cup toasted nuts.

Home-smoking Chicken

Tastes wonderful and no chemicals used. If you don't own a fish smoker, find an old deep roasting dish and a rack that will fit inside it. Line the dish with tinfoil. Sprinkle with a handful of untreated sawdust. Place rack in dish and arrange chicken on rack, leaving a gap between pieces for smoke to get through. Sprinkle chicken breasts with a little salt and brown sugar. Cover roasting dish tightly with foil and place on a hot element or BBQ grill. Cook for 6-7 minutes then transfer to a 200°C oven for 10 minutes. Allow to cool before uncovering. Chicken should be perfectly cooked. If it is not ready simply return to the oven for a few minutes to cook through.

Opposite: Chicken Salad with Pesto Dressing

Smoked Chicken, Strawberries, Peaches and Summer Herbs

Here's one of those great spur-of-the-moment meals you can throw together if people arrive unexpectedly and you want to feed them something fresh and yummy fast. Any stone fruit, paw paw or melon can be used.

To Prepare: 15 minutes

To Cook: 1 minute

> *2-3 handfuls snow peas or 2 stalks celery, sliced thinly*
> *4 smoked chicken breasts, sliced, or flesh of 1 smoked chicken, skin removed, meat shredded*
> *1 punnet strawberries, hulled and halved if large*
> *2-3 peaches, halved, stones removed, sliced in wedges*
> *2-3 tbsp fresh mint or tarragon or basil, chopped*
> *1 recipe Orange Walnut Dressing or Pesto Dressing* ✿

Pour boiling water over snowpeas or celery and stand 1 minute, then drain and cool under cold running water. Drain and put in a large mixing bowl. Add all other salad ingredients. Mix dressing ingredients together and gently toss through the salad. Divide salad between plates and serve at once. Serves 4 as a main, 6 as a starter.

Variation: *Mix chicken with wedges of rockmelon, sliced celery and spring onions and a can of drained lychees or mangoes, sliced.*

Chicken Salad with Pesto Dressing

Go behind the scenes in a small café or restaurant and you'll see wonderful salads being prepared in a flash. From various bowls, ready cooked ingredients are quickly combined and deftly tossed together. The secret is having a very large mixing bowl and all the ingredients ready to assemble. Vary the ingredients according to what's on hand.

To Prepare: 5 minutes

> *4 cooked chicken breasts*
> *flesh of 2-3 roasted red peppers, sliced*
> *2 handfuls fresh asparagus, tough ends snapped, or halved beans, boiled 2 minutes and cooled in cold water*
> *2 potatoes or sweet potatoes, boiled and sliced*
> *flesh of 1 paw paw, cut in thin slices*
> *6 handfuls salad greens washed and dried*

Pesto Dressing
> *¹/₂ cup Favourite Vinaigrette* ✿
> *2 tbsp pesto*

Have all ingredients prepared ahead of time. When ready to serve, put greens into a very big bowl and toss with combined dressing. Add all other ingredients and toss lightly to combine. Serves 6.

ALL DRESSED UP

Main course chicken salads are a mix and match affair. Have all ingredients prepared ready to put together and serve. Use commercial dressings as a base or start from scratch with all your own flavours.

- Cashew Orange Dressing with chicken, celery, grapes, red peppers and salad greens
- Citrus Chilli Dressing with smoked chicken, avocado, spinach and orange slices
- Watercress or Rocket Mayonnaise with potatoes, chicken, walnuts, celery, spinach and spring onions
- Green Goddess Dressing with chicken, asparagus and avocado

- Tapenade Dressing with chicken, tomatoes, olives, capers, cucumber and peppers
- Caesar Dressing with chicken, bacon, romaine lettuce and croûtons
- Pesto Dressing with chicken, roasted pears, roasted onions, beets and salad greens
- Moroccan Dressing with chicken, olives, capers and greens

Above: Chinese Chicken Salad

Chinese Chicken Salad

Here's a wonderful crisp fresh salad made in a flash. It is photographed served in a crisp tortilla basket but is wonderful served just on its own.

To Prepare: 10 minutes

> *2 cups cooked diced chicken (can use Oriental Poached Chicken* ⊙*)*
> *2-3 spring onions, slivered*
> *1 large carrot, cut into matchstick strips*
> *2 stalks celery, thinly sliced*
> *1 red or green pepper, finely diced*
> *½ cup toasted sesame seeds*

Ginger Sesame Dressing

> *2 tsp minced fresh ginger*
> *1 tbsp sesame oil*
> *2 tbsp rice vinegar*

Optional: 1 pkt crispy noodles
> *2-3 handfuls beansprouts*
> *6 tortilla baskets to serve*

Combine chicken with all vegetables and sesame seeds in a mixing bowl. Stir together dressing ingredients and mix through. When ready to serve, toss through optional crispy noodles and beansprouts. If desired serve salad in Crisp Tortilla Baskets. Serves 6.

Tortilla – crisp baskets

Pre-heat oven to 200°C. Place a fresh tortilla in a pudding bowl, folding it to follow bowl shape. Stack another bowl on top to secure. Place on a baking tray and bake for 10 minutes, then remove from bowls, reduce heat to 180°C and bake for another 10-15 minutes until crisp.

Pesto, Corn and Chicken Salad

This salad sings of summer. Make it when corn and basil are at their peak.

To Prepare: 15 minutes

400g fresh green beans
1 medium-sized cooked chicken (or 1 smoked chicken), remove skin, bones and fat, dice flesh
1 cup cooked whole kernel corn off the cob
diced flesh of 1 large avocado
3 tomatoes, cored and quartered
2 spring onions, finely sliced

Dressing
1/2 cup vinaigrette dressing
2 tbsp pesto, eg basil or parsley

Drop beans into a pot of boiling water for 2 minutes, drain and cool under cold water. Place with chicken and other salad ingredients in a bowl. Combine dressing ingredients and toss through the salad. Pile onto a serving platter. Accompany with fresh bread or Bruschetta.✪ Serves 4.

Oriental Poached Chicken

This simple preparation has a wonderful flavour. It can be served simply sliced as an hors d'oeuvre, as a luncheon salad platter with fresh vegetables, and in wonderful Chinese Chicken Salad.✪

To Prepare: 2 minutes
To Cook: 5 minutes plus cooling time

Oriental Cooking Broth
1/2 cup soy sauce
1/2 cup orange juice
1 1/2 cups water
3 x 2.5cm thick slices fresh ginger, smashed with the back of a knife
1/2 tsp five-spice powder or 2 whole star anise

4 boneless, skinless chicken breasts

Sunday Lunch

martinis
Jilly's roasted pepper soup
Beijing duck salad pancakes
surprise chocolate cake

Advance preparations

- *make cake*
- *make Beijing pancakes (or buy fresh flour tortillas)*
- *make soup*

In a pot, bring to the boil all the liquids and spices for the broth. Reduce the heat to a simmer and add the chicken breasts. Cover the pot and simmer on very low for 2 minutes, then turn chicken over and simmer for 2 minutes. Cool in the liquid. When cool, remove and slice each breast diagonally into about 5 pieces. Reserve liquid. Serves 6.

Note: This may be made one day in advance if desired – the breasts are left in the broth and refrigerated.

Variation: Chicken Noodle Salad – *Prepare Oriental Poached Chicken. While it cools, fry 2 thinly sliced red peppers in 1 tbsp sesame oil until soft. Remove from heat and add 1/2 cup cooking liquid from chicken, 300g cooked noodles, 2 sliced spring onions and the sliced cooked Oriental Chicken. Toss together to combine and garnish with 2 tbsp toasted sesame seeds. Great hot or cold. Serves 4.*

Corn Kernels from the Cob

Use a heavy knife to cut kernels from fresh corn cobs. Heat a little olive oil or butter and panfry for 2-3 minutes to cook.

To Core Tomatoes

Always cut cores out of tomatoes before using. Remove core in a plug with a small sharp pointed knife before slicing.

Star Anise

One of the few spices used in Chinese cooking and popular in Europe since the 1600s. Is said to be a mild sedative. Star Anise has a licorice or aniseed flavour. It can be used like cinnamon and is one of the 6 or 7 components of five-spice powder. Store in an airtight container well away from light and heat and it will keep for months.

Grilled Chicken Caesar Salad

Leave the chicken out for a classic Caesar or add lightly poached eggs.

To Prepare: 10-15 minutes
To Cook: 10 minutes

> 4 boneless chicken thighs, skin removed
> finely grated rind of $1/2$ lemon
> salt and ground black pepper
> about 1 tbsp oil
> 1 large head romaine or other crisp lettuce, leaves washed and dried
> 1 quantity Caesar dressing (see side panel)
> 12 Croûtons ✪
> $1/4$ cup parmesan cheese, shaved with a potato peeler
> ground black pepper
> *Optional:* 4 eggs, preferably free range
> 1 tbsp each salt and vinegar

Mix chicken with lemon rind, salt and pepper. Heat a fry-pan with a little oil. Pan fry chicken about 6-8 minutes until cooked through. Remove and stand while preparing salad. If using eggs break into a pot of simmering water to which 1 tbsp each of salt and vinegar has been added. Simmer gently for about 1 minute until egg whites are set, remove with a slotted spoon and put to one side. Place lettuce leaves in a large salad bowl. Toss dressing through lettuce. Slice and add chicken pieces. Throw on Croûtons, sprinkle with parmesan and grind over black pepper. Toss it all together. Divide between 4 serving plates and, if desired, top each with a poached egg.

Beijing Duck Salad Pancakes

In the middle of the table place a stack of fresh chewy Chinese pancakes and 4 bowls containing shredded cooked duck or chicken, hoisin sauce, spring onions and crispy lettuce. It's a simple formula which makes for thoroughly convivial dining. If you can't be bothered making the pancakes, improvise using soft flatbreads, like warmed fresh flour tortillas brushed with a little sesame oil to give them a more Oriental flavour.

To Prepare: 5 minutes

> 2 cups shredded cooked duck meat or chicken, no fat or bones, crisp skin optional
> $1/2$ cup hoisin sauce
> 3 spring onions, halved lengthwise, cut into 4cm lengths
> $1/2$ crisp iceberg lettuce, finely shredded
> 1 batch Chinese Grilled Pancakes ✪ or 4 fresh flour tortillas cooked, brushed sparsely with sesame oil and cut into small rectangles

Place everything in separate bowls or dishes. Split Chinese Grilled Pancakes, smear thinly with hoisin sauce (don't overdo it) and fill with a little duck or chicken, a length of spring onion and a little shredded lettuce. Roll up and eat. Makes enough for 4 people.

Moroccan Duck Salad

Here's one for a special occasion like Christmas. Shred the duck flesh and toss with capers, olives, pickled lemons, salad greens and a delicious creamy dressing.

To Prepare: 15 minutes

Moroccan Dressing

> 1 cup cream
> $^1/_2$ cup lemon juice
> $^1/_2$ cup Moroccan Sauce ✪
>   or $^1/_2$ cup tomato pasta sauce
>   and 2 tsp Moroccan spice mix
> 6-8 handfuls washed and dried
>   mixed salad greens
> flesh of 1 large cooked duck, fat,
>   skin and bones removed, flesh
>   shredded

$^1/_4$ cup of thinly sliced Pickled
    Lemon Rind ✪
$^1/_4$ cup capers
1 cup black Calamata olives
freshly ground black pepper

Combine all the dressing ingredients and toss with salad greens in a large bowl. Add all other ingredients and gently toss to combine. Serve at once. Serves 6.

To Roast Ducks: *Place ducks on a rack in a roasting dish and season with salt and ground black pepper. Pour 1$^1/_2$ cups water or wine into the dish. Bake at 220°C for $^1/_2$ hour to release fat, then reduce heat to 180°C and cook a further 1$^1/_4$-1$^1/_2$ hours until tender.*

Above: Moroccan Duck Salad

Instant Roast Duck

Chinese food stores do a great line in roasted duck. Delicious in salads, soups and risottos.

BBQ Chicken

JUST THE SMELL OF A BARBECUE WAKENS THE APPETITE AND INSPIRES LENGTHY SUMMER LUNCHES AND OUTDOOR DINNERS. FRESH AIR, SUCCULENT FLAVOURS AND EASY INFORMALITY ARE A SEDUCTIVE COMBINATION.

Right: Italian Grilled Chicken with Lemon and Herbs on Orzo Salad

Marinades for Tenderness

Marinades carry flavour and impart tenderness via acid elements such as wine, fruit juice and yoghurt. The enzymes found in kiwifruit and paw paw do more than tenderize – they actually break down proteins to mush. Don't use these fruits for marinating meats, fish or poultry.

Italian Grilled Chicken with Lemon and Herbs

Flattened boneless chicken breasts or thighs take just a few minutes to cook over high heat. A range of marinades can be used. This one is light and aromatic with flavours of lemon, garlic, rosemary and oregano.

To Prepare: 10 minutes, plus marinating
To Cook: 5-7 minutes

> *5 boneless chicken thighs, or 4 single boneless chicken breasts*
> *¹⁄₄ cup lemon juice*
> *2 cloves garlic, crushed*
> *1 tsp chopped rosemary*
> *1 tsp chopped oregano*
> *salt and ground black pepper*

Place each breast or thigh between plastic wrap and flatten to a thin schnitzel using a rolling pin or a heavy, flat implement. Combine all the remaining ingredients, except salt, and mix through the chicken. Marinate for at least 15 minutes or up to 4 hours in the fridge. Season with salt. Barbecue, pan fry or grill for 5-7 minutes until chicken is golden and cooked. Serves 4.

Busy Day Dinner Idea: *Serve with flatbread and a selection of sliced vegetables grilled on the barbecue.*

Pesto Chicken Breasts with Eggplant and Red Pepper

Vegetables and chicken combine deliciously in this mixed grill. Other seasonal vegetables can be used as they become available, such as courgettes, leeks and kumara. Play around with various types of pesto – for example, mint or coriander are also delicious.

To Prepare: 10 minutes
To Cook: 8-10 minutes

> 2 skinless, boneless chicken breasts,
>   or 4 boneless thighs
> juice of ¹/₂ lemon
> 3 tbsp olive oil
> 2 tbsp prepared pesto
> salt and ground black pepper
> 1 eggplant, sliced into 1cm rounds
> 1 red pepper, cut into wide wedges

Place chicken breasts between 2 sheets of plastic wrap. Lightly pound to flatten to about 1.5cm. Combine lemon juice, oil, pesto, salt and pepper and brush over chicken, eggplant and pepper slices. Pre-heat a barbecue grill plate or large fry-pan and lightly oil. Cook chicken, eggplant and pepper until all are cooked through. Eggplant will take the longest. Serves 2.
Busy Day Dinner Idea: *Serve with Aïoli,* oven fries and a crisp green salad.

Chicken Fajitas

Pronounced 'far heetas', these tasty Mexican treats can be prepared successfully using any type of thinly sliced meat, poultry or seafood. Make up your own Cajun spice mix or buy one of the commercially produced ones.

To Prepare: 5 minutes, and
5-10 minutes to marinate
To Cook: 10 minutes

> 400g boneless chicken breasts,
>   or thighs, cut in thin strips
> 1 tbsp oil
> 1 tsp crushed garlic
> 2-3 tsp Cajun Spice Mix
> 1 red pepper, sliced in thin strips
> 1 red onion, sliced in thin wedges
> salt and ground black pepper
> 8 pita bread halves

Mix chicken with all other ingredients and stand for 5-10 minutes before cooking. Pre-heat a barbecue hot plate or fry-pan. Cook large handfuls of chicken and vegetables for 10 minutes over a medium-high heat – about 5 minutes on each side, turning frequently until chicken is cooked through. Do not over crowd hot plate. Remove from heat. Fill toasted pita bread halves, mountain bread or warmed tortillas. Garnish with a dollop of guacamole and lettuce leaves. Makes 8 pockets.

Whole BBQ Chicken

Cut out the backbone from a whole chicken. Open out bird and place on a board with the inside facing down. Flatten bird, using the weight of your hand, to give a flat butterfly shape. Mix with marinade of your choice. Marinate for at least 1 hour, or up to 24 hours in the fridge. Lift out of marinade and season. Cook first in the microwave on a covered plate for 6 minutes at 100% power and then grill for 10-15 minutes until cooked through.
If chicken is not microwaved first, allow about 45-60 minutes barbecue time to cook through.

Chillies

The hotness of chillies comes from the alkaloid capsaicin. This is concentrated in the white membrane which attaches the seeds inside. If you want more chilli flavour and less heat, take out this membrane. Capsaicin is an irritant and can 'burn' the skin (don't ever rub your eyes). The body's response comes in the form of watery eyes, a runny nose and sometimes a sweat, and wait for it – endorphins. So instead of that run around the block, lie back on the sofa with a big bowl of fiery food and wait for the euphoria to set in.

- Dense cuts of chicken greatly benefit from brief cooking before barbecuing, as the long cooking time required to cook chicken right through may cause excessive charring.
- Wooden skewers or metal skewers can be used to thread kebabs and satays etc. Wooden skewers have the advantage of being disposable and easy to handle, but they require at least 15 minutes soaking in cold water to prevent them from burning through.
- Meat should always be marinated in a non-corrosive container – a clean plastic bag makes the ideal marinade container as it is easy to handle and allows the meat to marinate evenly.
- When marinating in a plastic bag, press out the air before sealing the bag with a twist tie. Place the bag into a bowl and refrigerate, turning the bag occasionally to distribute the marinade evenly.
- If marinating cuts of meat, fish or chicken for more than 1 hour, they should be refrigerated to prevent bacterial action.

Opposite: Moroccan Grilled Chicken, Chilli Lemon Cous Cous with Nuts and Grapes

Moroccan Grilled or Barbecued Chicken

You can also use Moroccan Rub ✿ mixed with yoghurt to marinate this tender tasty chicken.

To Prepare: 10 minutes, plus marinating
To Cook: 10-15 minutes

> *6 single chicken breasts*
>
> **Marinade**
> *4 cloves garlic*
> *1 tbsp cumin seeds, toasted*
> *1 fresh chilli, chopped*
> *½ tsp freshly ground cardamom seeds*
> *2 tsp paprika*
> *150mls plain yoghurt*

Purée marinade ingredients well in the food processor. Pour marinade over the chicken and marinate in the fridge 2-8 hours. Shake off excess marinade and grill or BBQ until cooked, 10-15 minutes. Serves 6.

MENU IDEAS

Moroccan Summer Barbecue

corn and feta fritters

Moroccan grilled chicken

chilli lemon cous cous
with nuts and grapes

hot flour tortillas

Moroccan tomato sauce

cucumber and sprout salad with
yoghurt dressing

berries and syllabub

Advance preparations

- *marinate chicken*
- *make Moroccan sauce*
- *prepare fritter batter*

Thai Chicken Skewers

Any kind of marinade can be used for this dish. Vegetables, such as peppers, courgettes and onions, can be threaded in between the chicken.

To Prepare: 5 minutes
To Cook: 6 minutes

> *600g boneless chicken thighs, trimmed of any fat and cut into 2cm pieces*
> *2 tbsp fish sauce*
> *1 tbsp Thai green or red curry paste*
> *1 tsp brown sugar*
> *2 tbsp lemon or lime juice*
> *wooden skewers, cut in half and soaked in cold water for at least 10 minutes*

Combine all the ingredients and leave to marinate in the fridge for at least 2 hours (or up to 6 hours). Thread onto skewers, allowing about 3 pieces of chicken per skewer. Place on an oven tray and press down gently to flatten the chicken. Grill for 3 minutes each side, until cooked through. Serve with a peanut sauce made by heating peanut butter, crushed garlic and chilli sauce with enough water or coconut cream to form a dipping consistency. Makes 40 skewers.

Other Ideas: *Marinade is also good with other chicken cuts, fish and lamb.*

Busy Day Dinner Idea: *Serve on a bed of rice with a bowl of peanut sauce.*

MARINADES

Marinades add flavour, colour and sometimes tenderness to poultry and other meats and seafood. The sweeter the marinade the more quickly it will char. Pepper can be added with the marinade, but add salt at cooking time.

Tarragon, Honey and Mustard Marinade
Combine 1 tsp crushed garlic, 2 tbsp olive oil, 1 tbsp French mustard, 3 tbsp chopped fresh tarragon or mint, 1 tsp honey and some freshly ground black pepper. Makes enough for 1kg chicken pieces.

Moroccan Marinade
Mix 3 tbsp Moroccan Rub ✪ with 1 cup plain unsweetened yoghurt and juice of ½ lemon. Good with chicken, fish and lamb.

Pesto Marinade
Mix 2 tbsp pesto of your choice with 2 tbsp olive oil. Great with chicken, fish and lamb.

Mango Glaze ✪
Ideal for any poultry or pork cut.

Red Pepper Sauce ✪
Ideal for any poultry or pork cut.

Black Bean and Chilli Marinade
Great for chicken, pork or beef.
½ cup black bean sauce, 2 tbsp sweet Thai chilli sauce, juice of 1 orange, 1 tbsp honey, 1 tsp sesame oil.

Tandoori Marinade
Especially good for chicken and fish.
½ cup unsweetened yoghurt, 1 small onion grated, 1 tbsp tandoori paste.

Asian Flavours

THROUGHOUT ASIA THE ANCIENT TRADITIONS OF PREPARING AND COOKING POULTRY HAVE

PRODUCED SOME OF THE BEST FLAVOURS IN THE WORLD.

Above: Vietnamese Ginger
Chilli Chicken

Vietnamese Ginger Chilli Chicken

Thin strips of chicken meat are combined with some of the essential flavours of Asia in this flavoursome pan dinner.

To Prepare: 5 minutes
To Cook: 10 minutes

> *3 tbsp vegetable oil*
> *finely grated rind of 1 lemon*
> *2 tbsp minced fresh ginger*
> *1 small red chilli, finely chopped*
> *2 cloves garlic, crushed*
> *600g boneless chicken, cut in*
>   *thin strips*
> *1 tsp sugar*
> *2 tbsp fish sauce*
> *2 tbsp lime or lemon juice*
> *2 tbsp water*

> *2 tsp cornflour*
> *2 handfuls bean sprouts,*
> *2 spring onions, thinly sliced*
> Optional: *snow peas, cabbage, carrots,*
>   *peppers, etc*

Heat oil and fry lemon rind, ginger, chilli and garlic for about 1 minute until garlic starts to brown. Add chicken and stir-fry for 5 minutes, until lightly browned. Add sugar, fish sauce, lime juice and water mixed with cornflour and simmer for 2-3 minutes. Mix in sprouts and spring onions and any other vegetables for 1 minute to heat through. Serve over rice or noodles. Serves 4.

Busy Day Dinner Idea: *Serve on rice noodles with fried peppers and green beans.*

Mincing Ginger

A ginger grater is a very useful tool, producing a fine paste with just a few rubs over its raised ceramic surface. Buy at an Asian foodstore.

Burmese Chicken and Spinach

Great for a quick, healthy meal-in-one, this curry uses frozen spinach to make the preparation even easier.

To Prepare: 5 minutes

To Cook: 8-10 minutes

> 1 large onion, finely diced
> 1 tbsp salad oil
> 2 tsp crushed garlic
> 1 tbsp green curry paste, to taste
> 1 cinnamon quill
> pinch of ground cloves
> 1/2 pkt frozen spinach, thawed or a
>   large bunch spinach, blanched
>   and squeezed dry
> 1 cup chicken stock
> 400-500g boneless chicken thighs,
>   sliced into thin strips
> 1/2 cup cream or yoghurt
> salt and ground black pepper

Cook the onion in the oil in a large pan over a medium heat until clear. Add the garlic and curry paste and sizzle a few more seconds. Mix in the cinnamon quill, cloves, spinach and stock and bring to a simmer. Add the chicken and cream and simmer for 6-8 minutes, until the chicken is cooked through. Lift out the cinnamon quill and discard. Season to taste. Serves 4-5.

Note: If using yoghurt, stir into the sauce just before serving, so it does not separate.

Busy Day Dinner Idea: Serve with fragrant Thai rice and a sweet mango chutney.

Thai Chicken Curry

Here's a great recipe for a cook-ahead dinner. Green curry paste keeps in the fridge. The fragrant sauce can be prepared well ahead of time, ready to simmer chicken.

To Prepare: 10 minutes

To Cook: 15-18 minutes

> 2 tbsp green curry paste
> 1 tbsp vegetable oil
> 1 1/2 cups chicken stock or water
> 400ml can coconut cream
> 2 tbsp fish sauce
> finely grated rind of 1/2 lemon
> salt and ground black pepper
> 1kg boneless chicken thighs, thinly
>   sliced
> sliced spring onions
> 1/2 cup toasted cashew nuts
> *Optional:* 6-8 dried curry leaves or fresh
>   lime leaves

In a large heavy saucepan heat oil and fry curry paste for about a minute. Add coconut cream, stock or water, fish sauce, lemon rind and optional curry leaves and simmer for 10 minutes (sauce can be prepared ahead to this point and stored in the fridge). When ready to serve, add the sliced chicken. Reduce heat to low, cover tightly and leave to cook on lowest possible heat for 5-6 minutes without uncovering until the chicken is cooked and has turned opaque. Do not over cook. Season to taste and garnish with spring onion and cashew nuts. Serves 6-8 as a main course.

Busy Day Dinner Idea: Serve with rice, poppadoms and a salad of spinach, red pepper, caramelized onions, toasted nuts and crunchy sprouts.

Cooking Poppadoms

You don't need to fry poppadoms, they can be cooked very easily in the microwave – which requires no fat. Cook two at a time on 100% power for about 1 minute until pale gold and crisp.

No Thai Curry Paste?

Curry pastes are available in a range of styles and flavours. Once opened they should be kept in the fridge. If you don't have any, improvise by mixing together 2 tsp garlic, 1 tsp fresh minced ginger, 2 tbsp sweet Thai chilli sauce, and the finely grated rind of 1 lemon or lime.

Seasoning

Seasoning

The two most important condiments in cooking are salt and pepper. When marinating foods, leave out the salt until cooking time as it will draw moisture. I prefer to season my food gently at the start of cooking and then check for seasoning right at the end. Over salting is a problem – you can try adding starches such as potatoes and rice which will absorb some salt, or extend the dish by increasing the volume of sauce – with liquid such as stock or tomatoes. White pepper is much hotter than black. For everyday cooking use freshly ground black pepper. Fine white pepper is good for sauces and mashed potato.

Mirin

Mirin is a sweet rice wine (sake) used in Japanese cooking to add mild sweetness and in glazes and marinades. It is a thin golden syrup with an alcohol content of 13-14 percent and is used solely for cooking, not for drinking. Only a few tablespoons are needed to prepare most dishes. It is stocked in Japanese and Asian food stores. If you cannot find mirin, substitute 1 tsp sugar, mixed with 1 tbsp white wine for 1 tbsp of mirin.

Cantonese Chicken

Chicken, seafood or pork can be used for this quick stir-fry. Remember to slice the meat thinly across the grain for maximum tenderness. Use seasonal vegetables as available.

To Prepare: 10 minutes
To Cook: 17 minutes, includes sauce

> 2 large onions, cut into thin
>   segments
> 1 tbsp oil
> 1 tbsp each crushed garlic and
>   fresh root ginger, grated
> 1/2 cup oyster sauce
> 1/2 cup water
> 500g boneless chicken, cut into
>   very thin strips
> 500g assorted fresh vegetables,
>   sliced, eg carrots, broccoli,
>   beans, courgettes
> 2 spring onions, sliced
> 1 handful beansprouts
> 1-2 tbsp chilli sauce

Cook onions in oil in a large pan or wok until soft. Add garlic, ginger, oyster sauce, water and chicken and simmer for 5 minutes. While the chicken cooks, steam or microwave the sliced vegetables until crisp/tender (approx 4 minutes). Add vegetables to the chicken with beansprouts and spring onions and toss over a high heat for 30 seconds. Serve immediately. Serves 4.
Busy Day Dinner Idea: *Serve with rice or noodles.*

Chicken Yakitori

If you don't have sake, you can use a medium sherry.

To Prepare: 10 minutes, plus marinating
To Cook: 6-8 minutes

> 1/2 cup sake
> 1/4 cup soy sauce
> 1 tbsp fresh grated ginger root
> 1 tbsp sugar
> 800g boneless chicken thighs or
>   breasts, diced in 2cm pieces
> 6 spring onions cut in 2cm lengths
>   or 1 green pepper cut in wedges

Dipping Sauce
> 1/2 cup sweet sherry or mirin
> 1/2 cup soy sauce
> 1 tsp wasabi powder or 1/2 tsp
>   wasabi paste

Combine the sake, soy sauce, ginger and sugar in a bowl or clean plastic bag and mix through the diced chicken. Marinate in the fridge for at least 6 hours and up to 24 hours. Remove chicken from marinade and thread 3-4 pieces onto soaked wooden skewers, alternating with pieces of spring onion. Heat the mirin or sherry and then remove from heat and ignite. When the flames have died down, stir in the soy sauce and bring to a boil. Simmer for 5 minutes. Grill the skewers over high heat, for about 2 minutes, on each side, basting once or twice with dipping sauce during cooking. Transfer cooked skewers to a serving plate and accompany with dipping sauce in a small bowl. Makes 16 skewers.
Variation: *Prepare yakitori using chicken livers. Thread the marinated chicken livers onto the skewers; or alternate livers with pieces of chicken.*

Asian Chicken, Peppers and Noodles

Here's a tasty easy noodle dish. Cook the chicken in a chilli sauce, toss sauce through cooked noodles, then add sliced chicken, peppers and spring onions. Great for a quick meal-in-one dinner.

To Prepare: 10 minutes

To Cook: 10 minutes

> 2 tbsp vegetable oil
> 4 chicken breasts or 6 boneless
>   thighs
> salt and ground black pepper
> 1/2 cup sweet Thai chilli sauce
> 2 tbsp soy sauce
> 2 tbsp fish sauce
> 1 tbsp minced fresh ginger
> about 1/2 cup water
> 400g cooked noodles,
>   eg udon noodles

> 1 tbsp sesame oil
> 2 red peppers, thinly sliced
> 2 chopped spring onions
> 2 tbsp sesame seeds

Heat a fry-pan with a little oil. Season chicken and brown on either side. Add chilli sauce, soy sauce, fish sauce and ginger to pan, plus about 1/2 cup water. Cover and cook chicken over low heat for about 6 minutes each side. While chicken simmers, cook noodles or, if using fresh noodles, rinse under hot water. Heat sesame oil, fry peppers until softened. Lift out and slice cooked chicken. Mix cooking liquid from chicken through cooked noodles, toss through the chicken, peppers and spring onions. Sprinkle with sesame seeds. Serves 4.

Asian Chicken, Peppers and Noodles

Ginger

Ginger is an incredibly medicinal aromatic. Its soothing properties are used for upset stomachs, colicky babies and motion sickness. Slices of fresh ginger in hot water with lemon and honey make a refreshing and fortifying winter drink.

Saucy Chicken

DRAWING ON FLAVOURS FROM AROUND THE GLOBE, THESE DISHES MELD AROMATIC FLAVOURS TO CREATE MEALS THAT ARE DEEPLY SATISFYING.

Provençal Chicken with Prunes, Apricots and Olives

The master method used for this delicious chicken casserole – first browning the chicken pieces and then aromatics, adding ingredients for the sauce and baking the dish in the oven – can be adapted by using a range of different flavours.

To Prepare: 10 minutes
To Cook: 30 minutes for pieces, 20 for boneless

> 12-16 dried pitted prunes and apricots
> 1 cup water to soak
> 1 tbsp olive oil
> 6 chicken pieces or 10-12 boneless thighs
> 1 tsp crushed garlic and fresh thyme leaves
> 1 tbsp tomato paste
> 1 cup white wine
> 2 tbsp sherry or port
> 1½ cups chicken stock
> 1 cup green olives

Soak dried fruits in water for 1 hour or microwave for 5 minutes. Put to one side. Pre-heat oven to 180°C. Season 8-10 chicken pieces and brown in batches in olive oil just until lightly browned. Place in a casserole dish. Cook garlic, thyme and tomato paste for a few seconds. Add white wine, sherry, chicken stock and dried fruits and their liquid. Bring to a boil. Pour over the chicken. Cover with a lid and bake for 40 minutes. Add olives, and if desired thicken with 1 tbsp corn-flour mixed with a little water. Serves 6.

Spicy Moroccan Chicken Tagine

A tagine is the name given to the vessel used to cook North African stews. Over time it has come to mean the style of dish – a fragrant stew slowly simmered with spices and dried fruits.

To Prepare: 10-15 minutes
To Cook: 25-30 minutes

> 18 chicken drumsticks, or 14-16 chicken pieces
> 1 tbsp Moroccan Spice Rub ❂
> 2 tbsp olive oil
> salt and ground black pepper
> 2 onions, thinly sliced
> 2 cloves garlic, chopped
> 2 chillies, minced
> 1 tsp each ground cumin, coriander and ginger
> 4 cardamom pods, crushed
> 400g can pulped tomatoes
> 2 cups water
> 1 cup dried apricots
> ½ cup fruit chutney, eg peach or mango
> Optional: pinch of saffron

Sprinkle chicken with Moroccan Rub and massage in to coat. Heat oil in a large heavy ovenproof pan or pot. Brown chicken pieces well all over in batches. Put to one side. Add onions, garlic and all spices to pan and cook gently for 5-6 minutes. Mix in tomatoes, water, optional saffron and apricots, and simmer for 15 minutes. Add chicken back into pan and bake covered at 180°C for 1 hour. Add chutney and season to taste.
Serves 8-10.

No ovenproof dish?

If you don't own a dish which can be used to cook on the stove top as well as the oven, you will need to brown chicken in a fry-pan, then transfer to a casserole dish. Make the rest of the sauce in the pan and when it boils pour it over the chicken before covering and baking in the oven.

Opposite: Provençal Chicken with Prunes, Apricots and Olives

Balsamic Chicken Breasts with Crispy Mint and Pinenuts

A quick roast in a hot oven, then into a delicious, sweet-sour, Italian-styled sauce to finish cooking. This easy chicken dish is ideal for rush hour entertaining.

To Prepare: 10 minutes plus marinating
To Cook: 25 minutes

> *6 single chicken breasts, skin on*
> *¼ cup balsamic vinegar*
> *3 tbsp brown sugar*

Sauce

> *1 tbsp olive oil*
> *2 cloves garlic, crushed*
> *3 cups chicken stock*
> *1 cup white wine*
> *2 whole sprigs mint*
> *salt and ground black pepper*
> *1 tsp grated fresh ginger*
> *½ cup whole mint leaves, fried*
> *½ cup pinenuts, toasted*

Mix chicken with balsamic vinegar and brown sugar. Leave to marinate in the fridge for at least ½ hour, or up to 12 hours. To make sauce, heat oil in a large heavy fry-pan and gently cook garlic for a few seconds. Add stock, wine and whole mint sprigs. Simmer for 10 minutes, or until reduced to ⅓ of the volume. Add ginger. Remove from heat and discard mint. Sauce can be made well ahead of time and refrigerated. To cook chicken, pre-heat oven to 220°C. Season marinated chicken with salt and place skin side up on a shallow baking tray and bake for 15 minutes until golden. At the end of cooking, brush any cooking juices over the skin to give it a great colour. Heat sauce and add marinade from the chicken. Remove chicken from oven, add to hot sauce, simmer very gently on lowest heat for 5-10 minutes. Place chicken on hot dinner plates, spoon over sauce and top with fried mint leaves and toasted pinenuts. Serves 6.

Fragrant Portuguese Chicken

This spicy pan-cooked chicken is a blend of sweet and hot flavours.

To Prepare: 10 minutes, plus marinating
To Cook: 15 minutes

> *4 single boneless, skinless chicken breasts or 6 thighs*
> *salt and ground black pepper*
> *1 tbsp crushed garlic*
> *1 tbsp olive oil*
> *2 red or yellow peppers, thinly sliced*
> *2 tsp ground coriander*
> *1 cup prepared pasta sauce*
> *½ cup water*
> *2 tbsp marsala or port*
> *1-2 tsp Tabasco, or other hot pepper sauce*

Optional: *pinch of saffron threads*

Season the chicken with pepper and mix with the garlic. Leave to marinate for at least 10 minutes. Heat the oil, season chicken with salt and fry until lightly browned all over. Remove and reserve. Add the peppers and coriander to the pan and cook until starting to soften. Add the pasta sauce, water, optional saffron, marsala and chicken, pressing it into the sauce. Simmer for about 15 minutes, turning the chicken after 10 minutes, until cooked through. Serves 4.

Variation: *Add green beans and fresh diced tomatoes to sauce in last 10 minutes of cooking.*

Busy Day Dinner Idea: *Serve with rice and lightly cooked vegetables.*

Nutrition – Nuts

Nuts are an excellent source of B vitamins, vitamin E and minerals such as iron, calcium, magnesium and potassium. All nuts, except chestnuts, are high in fat, which means more calories. A handful – about 30g – equals between 107 calories and 200 calories depending on the variety. Peanuts have the lowest calorie count and macadamias the highest.

Fried Mint Leaves

Frying mint leaves renders them crisp. Heat 2-3cm of oil in a deep pot, drop in a handful of fresh leaves, fry for about a minute until crisp. Drain on paper towels. These can be prepared ahead of time and kept in an airtight container.

Opposite: Balsamic Chicken Breasts with Crispy Mint and Pinenuts served with potato gratin, roasted onions and green beans

Here's another great variation on the casserole theme.

To Prepare: 20 minutes
To Cook: 1 hour

> 8-10 chicken pieces
> olive oil to brown
> 2 medium onions, sliced
> 2 sticks celery, thinly sliced
> 1 whole bulb garlic, cloves peeled
> 2 tsp fresh thyme leaves
> 1 bay leaf
> salt and ground black pepper
> 3 cups dry white wine
> ⅓ cup Dijon mustard
> *Optional:* 2 tbsp port mixed with 1 tbsp cornflour

Pre-heat oven to 180°C. Season chicken pieces and brown in batches in oil just until lightly browned. Place in casserole. Cook onions and celery for 8-10 minutes until softened. Add garlic, thyme leaves and bay leaves. Add white wine and Dijon mustard and bring back to boil. Stir well to combine. Pour over the chicken. Cover with a lid and bake for 40 minutes. Thicken with 1 tbsp cornflour mixed with 2 tbsp port and adjust seasonings to taste. Serves 6.

Variation: Mediterranean Chicken Casserole – Make the sauce with 2 sliced onions, 3 cloves crushed garlic, 2 sliced green peppers, 2 x 400g cans of tomatoes in juice, 1 cup white wine and ½ cup black olives.

Busy Day Dinner Idea: Accompany Chicken with Dijon Mustard with mashed potatoes and green beans.

Coq au Vin

Based on a classic French coq au vin, this delicious dish never dates.

To Prepare: 15 minutes
To Cook : 40-45 minutes

> 2 tbsp olive oil
> 400g button mushrooms
> 3 rashers bacon, diced
> 8-10 baby onions, peeled and halved
> 12 cloves garlic, peeled and halved
> 2 x 400g cans tomatoes in juice, chopped
> 1½ cups red wine
> 3 cups chicken stock
> 3 bay leaves
> 1 tsp fresh rosemary, chopped
> 2 tsp fresh thyme, chopped
> salt and ground black pepper
> 12 chicken pieces
> 2 tbsp cornflour
> 2 tbsp port or sherry

Heat oil in a large heavy pot. Add mushrooms and bacon. Brown well, then remove and put to one side. Add onions and garlic to pot and cook gently for 8-10 minutes until onion is softened and starting to brown. Add tomatoes and juice, wine, stock, herbs and seasonings, and browned mushrooms and bacon to the pot. Simmer gently for 20 minutes. Sauce can be prepared ahead of time to this point. Pre-heat oven to 200°C. Brown chicken pieces in a little hot oil, place in a casserole dish and pour over hot sauce. Cover and bake for 40 minutes. Combine cornflour and port or sherry and mix into sauce, stirring over heat until lightly thickened. Adjust seasonings to taste. Serves 6.

Variation: Coq au Vin Pie – Use 1kg boneless chicken thighs, halved. Mix into hot cooked sauce, place in a pie dish, cover with flaky pastry and bake for 10 minutes at 220°C then 40 minutes at 200°C.

Using the Whole Chicken

If you buy whole chickens and cut them up you can use the frames to make stock. Use a heavy knife or cleaver to portion the chicken – take off the legs and remove breasts with wing on to leave a bare carcass. This can then be used to make stock.

Creative Left-overs

Left-overs provide a whole new realm of improvisation. A creamy risotto gets spread into a tray and chilled ready for slicing and grilling as a tasty finger food or base for some quick toppings; left-over potato is fried in a pan with diced bacon and left-over vegetables to a crisp hash; left-over rice becomes stir-fried Chinese rice, or an easy rice pudding baked with milk, an egg, sugar and vanilla. However you treat them, the leftovers from one meal can be put to great use for another.

Tex Mex Chicken Wraps

This easy chicken pan-fry makes a great filler for tortillas, tacos or pita bread.

To Prepare: 10 minutes

To Cook: 15 minutes

>   2 tbsp oil
>   400g boneless chicken, thinly sliced
>   1 medium onion, finely diced
>   2 tbsp tomato paste
>   1 tsp crushed garlic
>   1 tbsp ground cumin
>   1/4 cup sweet chilli sauce
>   1/2 cup water
>   1 cup prepared pasta sauce
>   310g can red kidney beans, rinsed
>   salt and ground black pepper
>   150g sour cream
>   2-3 tbsp chopped coriander to
>   garnish
>   4-6 flour tortillas, warmed, to serve

Heat the oil and brown the chicken in batches. Reserve. Add the onion and tomato paste and cook over a medium heat until the onion is soft. Add the garlic and cumin and cook a further minute. Mix in the chilli sauce, water, pasta sauce and kidney beans. Season to taste and return the chicken to the pan to simmer for 5 minutes. Remove from the heat and mix in the sour cream. Garnish with coriander. Accompany with tortillas. Serves 4.

Above: Tex Mex Chicken Wraps

Wrap Fillings

- lettuce greens
- spinach
- sprouts
- peppers
- tomatoes
- avocado
- onions
- salsa
- sour cream
- coriander

Other Chicken Pasta Combinations

- chicken, tomato pasta sauce, olives, capers and anchovies
- chicken, tomato pasta sauce, red peppers and pesto
- chicken, cooked bacon and onion, tomato pasta sauce and parsley
- chicken, cream, beans, garlic and parmesan
- chicken, mushrooms, garlic, bacon, capers and lemon rind

Hot Plates

Hot dinner plates are one of the best ways to keep dinners hot. Simply wetting plates under the tap, then stacking and microwaving on 100% power for 1-2 minutes gets them hot. Dry off with a tea towel. Or fill a sink with hot water and soak plates for a couple of minutes before draining and drying.

Chicken Pasta with Garlic, Rosemary and Spinach

Here's a light fresh pasta great for spring or autumn when spinach is in full season.

To Prepare: 8-10 minutes
To Cook: 12 minutes

400g dried pasta
2 tbsp olive oil
large bunch spinach, washed and
    thinly sliced
3 cloves garlic, crushed
1 tbsp fresh rosemary leaves,
    chopped
400g boneless chicken, thinly sliced
salt and ground black pepper
finely grated rind and juice of
    1 lemon

Cook pasta according to manufacturer's instructions. Heat half the oil in a large pan, add spinach, cover pan and cook just until wilted. Remove from pan and put to one side. Add rest of oil to pan and heat, add garlic and rosemary and cook gently for about a minute. Add chicken and simmer for about 5 minutes until cooked through. Drain pasta and toss through lemon rind and juice, then spinach, then cooked chicken. Adjust seasonings to taste. Serve at once. Serves 4.

Note: Stir boiling water while adding pasta to keep it free flowing and stop it sticking together.

Pasta, Chicken, Bacon and Asparagus

A great tasting pasta that has a 'dry' sauce with a terrific combination of textures.

To Prepare: 8 minutes
To Cook: 5-8 minutes

500g dried pasta
2 tbsp olive oil
4 rashers bacon, diced
2-3 cloves garlic, crushed
400g boneless chicken, thinly sliced
3/4-1 cup cream
1-2 bunches asparagus, tough ends
    snapped off, cut in 2-3cm pieces,
    or 2 handfuls of green beans,
    sliced
1/2 cup grated parmesan
salt and freshly ground pepper

Cook pasta according to manufacturer's instructions adding asparagus or beans in last 2 minutes of cooking. While it cooks, heat oil and fry bacon until it starts to crisp. Add garlic and chicken and cook about 5 minutes over medium heat until chicken is cooked. Add cream and bring just to a boil and season to taste. Drain pasta and asparagus and toss through chicken and bacon sauce. Serve at once. Accompany with freshly grated parmesan. Serves 4-5.

Variations:
- *Add 250g sliced mushrooms with bacon.*
- *Add 2 tbsp pesto.*

KEEPING CHICKEN SAFE

- Keep raw chicken cold at all times.
- Store on a plate or somewhere there is no risk of meat juice dripping and contaminating other foods in the fridge.
- Cool cooked chicken quickly.
- When re-heating, ensure chicken gets fully hot and any sauce boils.

- Wash knives and chopping board thoroughly after cutting raw chicken and do not use the same knife or board to cut raw and cooked chicken.
- Do not freeze more than once.
- Always cook chicken well. It should never be rare. To test, skewer in the thickest part. When the juices run clear the chicken is cooked.

Roast Me Tender

The smell of roasting chicken takes us back to childhood birthdays and Christmas.

For sheer appetite appeal, it's hard to beat.

Mango Glazed Poussin

This is one of those effortless and wonderfully impressive dishes that's great for a crowd. The glaze serves also as a marinade, and is terrific with all kinds of poultry as well as pork.

To Prepare: 5 minutes plus marinating

To Cook: 25-30 minutes poussin, 15-20 minutes for quail, 30-45 minutes for chicken quarters

Mango Glaze

> *1 cup mango chutney*
>
> *1/4 cup tamarind concentrate (from Asian foodstores)*
>
> *2 cloves garlic, crushed*
>
> *1/2 cup sake or white rum*
>
> *3 poussins halved, or 6-8 quails halved, or 6 chicken quarters*

To make marinade/glaze, combine chutney, tamarind, garlic and sake. Mix through birds; chill for up to 4 hours. To cook birds, pre-heat oven to 220°C. Lift birds from marinade, reserving it for sauce, and place them in a roasting dish. Roast quail for 15-20 minutes (it can be served rare). Other birds need to be fully cooked, so allow 25-30 minutes for poussin, 30-35 minutes for chicken quarters. While the birds cook, bring marinade to the boil and simmer for 5 minutes. Serve with boiled marinade poured over as a glaze. Serves 6.

Variation: *Use 1/2 cup Red Pepper Sauce ✿ in place of Mango Glaze.*

Above: Mango Glazed Poussin

Other Uses for Mango Glaze

- *Spread Mango Glaze over a lamb rack before roasting.*
- *Mix Mango Glaze through sliced pumpkin or kumara before roasting.*
- *Marinate a whole chicken with Mango Glaze before roasting, and serve as a hot sauce on the side.*
- *Mix Mango Glaze through spare ribs before baking in a covered dish at 180°C for 1 1/2 hours.*

One Easy Roast

Cut a lemon in half. Cut one half in small pieces and place inside chicken cavity. Put chicken in a roasting dish. Tie drumsticks together and tuck wings under. Squeeze other half of lemon over chicken. Season with salt and pepper. Roast at 220°C for 20 minutes then reduce heat to 200°C and cook another 40-60 minutes until juices run clear when a skewer is inserted into the thickest part of the thigh. When roasting an unstuffed chicken it is even easier to check if it is done – just check the juices inside the cavity by the tail bone. Once they are no longer bright red the chicken is cooked.

Gravy

The brownings that form in the bottom of the roasting pan are laden with flavour and make a great base for an easy pan gravy. Drain off fat and place dish on stove top. Add 1 tsp sugar, sizzle for a minute, add a splash of wine or brandy and water from boiled vegetables. Simmer, stirring to remove brownings from bottom of pan. Season well with salt and pepper. Thicken lightly with a tablespoon of cornflour mixed until smooth with a little cold water. If tasteless, add a spoonful of miso, Vegemite or soy sauce. Finish with a splash of balsamic vinegar or rice vinegar.

Lemon Roast Chicken with Pumpkin and Onions

An initial roast at a high temperature browns and crisps the skin and releases the fat of this tender moist chicken. The surrounding vegetables bulk out the meal and add rich flavour to the sauce.

To Prepare: 10-15 minutes

To Cook: 1 hour 15 minutes

> *1 medium-sized fresh chicken,*
> *visible fat removed*
> *olive oil and salt, to rub*
> *400-600g pumpkin, peeled and cut*
> *into 4cm wedges*
> *3-4 cloves garlic, sliced in half*
> *4-6 small-medium onions,*
> *unpeeled, washed, cut in half*
> *finely grated rind and juice of*
> *½ lemon, no pith*
> *1½ cups chicken stock or*
> *1 x 375ml carton*
> *1 tsp fresh rosemary, chopped*
> *salt and ground black pepper*

Pre-heat oven to 220°C. Rub chicken all over with olive oil, sprinkle with salt and set on a rack in a deepish roasting dish. Roast at 220°C for 20 minutes until browned. Take out of oven, remove rack and drain fat from dish, and place bird in bottom of dish. Reduce oven temperature to 200°C. Arrange pumpkin, garlic and onions cut-side down around chicken. (Leaving skins on protects onions and they can be popped out of their skins to eat.) Mix lemon rind and juice with ½ cup of stock and pour over chicken. Sprinkle over rosemary. Bake at 180-200°C for 45-55 minutes, until juices run clear, basting chicken 2-3 times with pan juices during cooking. Lift chicken out of pan onto a serving platter with vegetables. Place pan on heat, add remaining stock, adjust seasonings to taste and simmer. If desired, thicken sauce with 2 tsp cornflour mixed with a dash of water. Serves 4.

Twice Roasted Duck with Lemon Pepper

All too often duck can be greasy and stringy. This method of double cooking the duck is the most successful I have come across, counteracting both of these problems. Allow half a duck per serving (unless it's a really big duck when everyone gets a quarter).

To Prepare: 10 minutes plus overnight marinating (optional)

To Cook: 1 hour 40 minutes

> *4 medium ducks (size 7 or 8) or*
> *2 very large ducks (over size 11)*
> *grated rind of 2 lemons, no pith*
> *salt and ground black pepper*
> *1 cup orange juice*
> *3 cups stock or water*
> *2 tbsp balsamic vinegar mixed with*
> *1 tbsp cornflour*

Cut ducks in half through backbone. If large, cut in quarters. Prick skin all over with a sharp skewer or pin (to release fat during cooking). Rub in ½ the lemon rind. Season well with pepper and leave to marinate in fridge for up to 24 hours. Pre-heat oven to 220°C. Season birds with salt, place on a roasting rack and bake for 40 minutes. Remove from oven and drain off fat. Reduce oven heat to 170°C. Remove roasting rack, return ducks to roasting pan or casserole dish, pour over juice and 1 cup of stock or water. Sprinkle with rest of lemon rind and cook uncovered for a further 50 minutes to 1 hour. To finish sauce, lift ducks out of pan and keep warm. Remove any fat that has accumulated on top of cooking liquid. Add about 2 more cups of stock or use cooking water from vegetables. Bring to a simmer, mix in balsamic and cornflour mixture. Stir over heat until lightly thickened, adjust seasonings to taste. Serves 8.

Celebration Roast Turkey with Country Ham and Fig Stuffing

For Christmas or midwinter Christmas or a special feast or birthday, there is nothing more celebratory than a great golden-brown roast turkey.

To Prepare: 30 minutes
To Cook: 4-4½ hours

Stuffing

> *1 recipe Country Fig Stuffing*
> *or other stuffing of your choice*
> *6.5kg whole turkey, cleaned*
> *and dried*
> *3 stalks celery, cut in half crosswise*
> *2 onions, peeled and cut in sixths*
> *2 large carrots, peeled and*
> *quartered*
> *1 cup white wine*
> *3 cups water*
> *¼ cup flour*
> *½ cup port*
> *finely grated rind of ½ orange*
> *pinch of allspice*
> *salt and white pepper*

Rinse the turkey and pat dry inside and out. Fill the cavity with two-thirds of the stuffing and close securely. Stuff the neck area with the remaining third and secure the flap under the turkey. Put any extra stuffing in a small roasting dish. Arrange the celery, onion and carrot on the bottom of a large roasting pan and put the turkey on top. Place the neck, gizzard and liver alongside. Pour the wine and water into the pan. Cover with a tight-fitting lid or butter a piece of tinfoil and cover the dish tightly. Bake at 170°C for 4½ hours (for smaller birds use the 50-minutes-per-kilo-method). Cook extra stuffing in roasting dish or stuffing roll for last hour. Remove the cover, strain all the liquid into a pot (discarding the vegetables and neck and giblets) and skim off any fat. Brush the bird with melted butter. Increase the heat to 220°C and cook a further 20-30 minutes until golden and juices run clear when bird is skewered deep into the thigh, brushing with butter every 5-10 minutes. Remove the turkey from the oven dish, cover with foil and stand for 10-15 minutes before carving. To make the gravy, heat the strained liquid to a simmer. Mix the flour to a paste with the port, whisk into the juices and bring to a boil, stirring until lightly thickened. Simmer for about 5 minutes, season with orange rind, a little allspice and salt and pepper. Serve in a jug. Serves 14-16.

Country Fig Stuffing

This richly flavoured stuffing can also be cooked separately and served as a stuffing roll. Form into a mound on a sheet of baking paper or oiled tinfoil and roll up into a tight cylinder. Twist ends to secure. Bake for 1 hour at 180°C.

To Prepare: 10-15 minutes
To Cook: 5 minutes

> *4 tbsp butter*
> *2 large onions, finely diced*
> *400g smoked ham, diced finely*
> *1 cup finely chopped fresh parsley*
> *2 tsp dried sage*
> *(or 1 tbsp minced fresh sage)*
> *2 tsp dried thyme*
> *(or 1 tbsp fresh thyme leaves)*
> *12 dried figs or apricots, chopped*
> *8 cups fresh breadcrumbs*
> *pinch each of mixed spice, salt*
> *and pepper*
> *3 eggs*

Melt the butter and cook the onion until clear. Remove from the heat and mix with the stuffing ingredients, adding the eggs at the end to bind. Allow to cool – it will keep in the fridge for two days. Stuffing makes 4½ cups.

MEAT

Steaks with Green Peppercorn
Sauce

Lamb Steaks with Tomatoes,
Olives and Rosemary

Steaks with Tapenade, Beans
and Peppers

Pork Fillets with a Red Wine
Vinegar Sauce

A Great Berry Sauce for All Red
Meats

Port and Onion Sauce

Smart Sauces for Steaks and
Snarlers

China Coast Black Bean Beef
and Noodles

Orange and Sesame Beef
Stir-fry

Beef Teppanyaki

Mexican Tomato Salsa

Peach and Mint Salsa

Chunky Guacamole Salsa

Kiwifruit and Paw Paw Salsa

Fresh Banana Salsa

Corn and Pepper Salsa

Mango Salsa

Pico de Gallo

Mango Pork Ribs

Mexican Lamb or Beef Fajitas

Thai Pork Sticks

Beautiful Burgers

Ginger and Black Bean Pork

Pesto Barbecue Lamb

Mediterranean Summer Grill
Plate

Lamb Chwarma Pockets

Louise's Thai Beef Salad

Chinese Hot and Spicy Pork
Salad Cups

Roasted Walnut, Orange and
Lamb Salad

Beef Fillet with Ratatouille

Slow Cooked Pork

The Perfect Roast

Spiced Seared Lamb
with Chickpea Purée
and Eggplant

Spiced Lamb with Date and
Pinenut Stuffing and
Moroccan Sauce

Braised Oxtails with Asian Spices

Thai Beef Stew

Braised Lamb Shanks with Black
Beans and Chilli

Steak, Mushroom and
Kidney Pie

Sue Story's Lamb Tagine

Saag Goshi
(Lamb Curry with Spinach)

Useful Side Dishes

Saucy Steaks

FOR A QUICK DINNER FOR MEAT LOVERS BRING OUT THE STEAK. MAKE SURE IT'S BEEN
WELL-AGED AND COMES FROM A GOOD CUT, LIKE FILLET, SIRLOIN OR PORTERHOUSE. TRIM OFF THE FAT
AND BROWN FIRST IN A PAN, THEN POP INTO A VERY HOT OVEN FOR A FEW MINUTES.

Cooking the Perfect Steak

- *Choose lean, well-aged steak, cut 3-4cm thick*
- *Season and cook in a hot pan with a little oil or butter*
- *For rare steaks allow about 40-50 seconds per side*
- *For medium-rare steaks allow 1-1½ minutes per side*
- *For well-done allow 2-3 minutes per side*
- *Always stand for 2-3 minutes before serving*
- *If cooking steaks thicker than 2cm, brown first in a pan then finish in a 220°C oven for 3-5 minutes. Stand for 5 minutes before serving.*

Shallots

These small brown skinned members of the onion family have a mild flavour. Use them in sauces or dressings, or roast whole. If unavailable use a little onion diced very finely.

Previous page: Steak and Kidney Pie

Steaks with Green Peppercorn Sauce

Argentina is famous for its beef. Finishing steak in a sauce is a technique often used there and makes the meat very juicy and tender.

To Prepare: 10 minutes
To Cook: 20 minutes

> 1 tbsp butter
> 1 tbsp shallots, finely diced
> ¾ cup red wine
> 4 cups good beef stock
> 3 tbsp green peppercorns
> 1 tsp finely grated lemon rind
> 2 tsp wine vinegar
> 2 tsp cornflour mixed with
>   ¼ cup port
> 6 beef or venison steaks, cut in
>   4cm cubes
> salt and ground black pepper
> a little olive oil, to cook

To prepare the sauce, heat the butter in a large fry-pan and gently cook the shallots until softened. Add the wine and stock and boil hard until the mixture has reduced to about 2 cups total (about 15 minutes). Add the peppercorns, lemon rind and wine vinegar and simmer for 5 minutes. Mix in the cornflour and port paste until lightly thickened. Adjust the seasonings to taste. When ready to serve, season the steaks and brown well in a lightly oiled pre-heated pan for about 2 minutes. Return prepared sauce to the meat pan and simmer at the lowest possible heat for 2-3 minutes, turning the steaks once, just until the meat is medium-rare. Lift the steaks from the sauce and slice thinly. Serve with a little sauce. Serves 6.
Variation: *Use mushrooms instead of peppercorns and cook with shallots.*
Busy Day Dinner Idea: *Serve with potato gratin and green vegetables.*

Lamb Steaks with Tomatoes, Olives and Rosemary

The flavours of the Mediterranean come to the fore in this simple pan dinner.

To Prepare: 5 minutes
To Cook: 20 minutes

> 4 lamb steaks, fat trimmed off
> salt and freshly ground pepper
> a little oil, to brown
> 1 onion, diced finely
> 2 cloves garlic, crushed
> 400g can tomatoes in juice, pulped
> 1 tsp chopped fresh rosemary
> ½ cup Calamata olives
> 1 tsp sugar
> 2-3 tsp white or red wine vinegar

Season steaks. Heat heavy pan with a little oil and brown steaks well on each side. Remove from pan and put to one side. Add onions to pan and cook gently for 5 minutes. Add garlic, tomatoes, rosemary, olives, sugar and vinegar. Season with salt and pepper to taste and simmer gently for 15 minutes. Return browned steaks to pan and cook gently for 5 minutes. Serves 4.
Busy Day Dinner Idea: *Serve with mashed potato and green beans.*

Steaks with Tapenade, Beans and Peppers

Here's a dinner that looks really smart and yet is so easy. Great for a dinner á deux.

To Prepare: 5 minutes
To Cook: 6 minutes

> 1 tbsp olive oil
> 6 beef steaks, cut 2-4cm thick
> freshly ground black pepper
> 1 red pepper, cut in thin strips
> 1 bunch beans, halved
> 1/4 cup prepared Tapenade ✿
>   or olive paste

Pre-heat oven to 220°C. Boil the beans for 2 minutes. Drain. Season the steaks and pan fry over a high heat for about 1 minute each side. Transfer to hot oven for 3-4 minutes. Rest for 2-3 minutes before serving. While meat cooks in the oven stir-fry peppers and boiled beans for 3-4 minutes in a little olive oil. Place a pile of vegetables onto each serving plate and top with a steak. Put 2 tsp of Tapenade on top of each steak. Serves 6.

Pan Gravy: If you wish to make a pan gravy, add 1/4 cup water, a splash of port or Marsala and 1 tsp balsamic vinegar to the meat pan and boil hard for 1-2 minutes.

Busy Day Dinner Idea: Serve with Rosemary and Garlic Roast Potatoes.✿

Above: Steaks with Tapenade, Beans and Peppers

Arrowroot or Cornflour

While arrowroot gives a very clear sauce, it does tend to have a very gluey texture if too much is used. Arrowroot also breaks down and loses thickening power when boiled so you need to add it right at the end of cooking.

Pork Fillets with a Red Wine Vinegar Sauce

This is one great sauce. Infinitely useful with all types and cuts of pan-fried steaks, roasts or as the base for a casserole. Make the sauce ahead of time – it will keep in the fridge for several days.

To Prepare: 10 minutes
To Cook: 20 minutes

Sauce

2 tbsp olive oil
2 red peppers, seeds and pith removed, flesh cut in 2cm dice
³/₄ cup sugar
2 cups red wine
1 cup red wine vinegar
2 tsp mustard seeds
3 tbsp currants

4 pork fillets or steaks
salt and ground black pepper

Pre-heat oven to 220°C. To make sauce, heat a little oil in a heavy pot or pan and cook peppers for a minute or two until softened. Add sugar, wine, vinegar, mustard seeds and currants and bring to a fast boil. Boil 15 minutes until it is reduced by about a third. (Sauce can be prepared to this point up to two days ahead and chilled.) To cook meat, season with salt and pepper. Heat a little oil in a pan and brown meat for 2-3 minutes each side. Remove from heat and transfer to oven and roast 5-6 minutes. While meat cooks, heat sauce. Stand meat for 5 minutes before slicing on angle. Serve meat on a pool of sauce. Serves 6.

Pink Pork

Pork is a meat that once needed to be served well cooked to avoid trichinosis. This disease is no longer found in pigs and so tender pork cuts such as steaks and fillets can be served slightly pink – the texture is not particularly appealing if the meat is rare.

Love Your Butcher

Buy meat from someone who cares to take the time to buy good meat and age it properly. The difference is pure tenderness. You'll also find there's usually less waste and less fat to pay for.

Cut Off the Fat

Wherever possible cut off all visible fat from meat before cooking. Gram for gram fat has more than 2 times the calories of either protein or starch, and the saturated fats of red meats, unlike unsaturated oils from products such as olives or fish, are not beneficial for your body.

Opposite: Pork Fillets with a Red Wine Vinegar Sauce on Kumara Mash with Chinese Greens

A Great Berry Sauce for All Red Meats

In a saucepan, heat 3 tbsp brown sugar and ¼ cup malt vinegar for about 2 minutes until they form a pale caramel. Add 2 cups frozen raspberries or blackberries and simmer over low heat for about 15 minutes. Strain through a fine sieve to remove the pips. Mix 2 tsp cornflour with 1 tbsp port and stir until the sauce is lightly thickened. Season to taste with salt and lots of freshly ground black pepper. Makes about 2 cups.

Port and Onion Sauce

Prepare Caramelised Onions.° Add 1½ cups beef stock and 2 tbsp port mixed with 1 tsp cornflour and simmer. Season to taste. Terrific with steaks, sausages and as a casserole base.

MENU IDEAS

Mid-week Dinner à Deux

fresh oysters with brown bread, ground black pepper, lemon wedges

steak with tapenade, beans and peppers

rosemary and garlic roasted potatoes

roasted peaches with macaroon topping

Advance preparations

- *prepare macaroon topping for peaches*
- *prepare rosemary roast vegetables*
- *uncork a good bottle of red wine*

SMART SAUCES
FOR STEAKS AND SNARLERS

Steak loves potatoes – mash, oven-roasted with rosemary and garlic, crisp oven chips, or in a creamy garlicky gratin. It also enjoys a good sauce. Most sauces can be made ahead of time and re-heated to serve. I often like to heat the sauce and once it simmers add the browned steak to it to infuse over very low heat for a few minutes. The meat cooks through gently without the worry of over cooking and the flavours of the sauce blend with any meat juices.

- Vegetable Chilli
- Green Peppercorn Sauce
- Double Mushroom Sauce
- A Quick Onion Sauce

- Country-style Tomato Sauce
- Moroccan Tomato Sauce
- Provençal Ratatouille
- Indonesian Peanut Sauce

A Flash In the Pan

WHEN YOU ARE HUNGRY AND TIRED THE QUICK ONE PAN DINNER APPROACH IS HARD TO BEAT.

COOK THE STARCH FIRST – PASTA OR RICE TAKE LONGER THAN A STIR-FRY

OR SIMPLE PASTA SAUCE.

Preparing Stir-fries

Regardless of the flavours you choose for a stir-fry the principles of preparation remain the same. Stir-fries cook so quickly you need to have everything sliced and ready to go before you begin cooking.

Half cook (microwave or steam) dense vegetables such as beans or carrots in advance so they can be added in at the same time as the other light vegetables.

Oodles of Noodles

When using egg noodles, allow about 60-75g per person. Cook in plenty of boiling salted water according to manufacturer's instructions.

Maximising Tenderness

If you are carving cooked meat always cut across the grain for maximum tenderness.

China Coast Black Bean Beef and Noodles

Other Asian sauces can also be used in this quick stir-fry.

To Prepare: 10 minutes
To Cook: 15 minutes

> *2 large onions, cut in thin segments*
> *1 tbsp sesame oil*
> *1 tsp crushed garlic*
> *1/2 cup water*
> *1/2 cup black bean sauce*
> *1 tsp hot chilli sauce*
> *salt and ground black pepper*
> *1 tbsp oil*
> *400g rump or sirloin steak,*
> *   or schnitzel, thinly sliced*
> *300-400g sliced vegetables,*
> *   eg red or green peppers, beans,*
> *   courgettes, carrots and snowpeas*
> *400g cooked noodles*
> *2 thinly sliced spring onions*

In a wok or large pan, cook the onions in the oil until clear. Add the garlic and cook for another minute. Add the water, black bean and chilli sauces and simmer for 5 minutes. Season to taste. Remove and reserve until ready to use. Slice the meat thinly across the grain. Drop the vegetables into boiling water for 1 minute or microwave for 2 minutes in a covered dish. Drain and cool in cold water. Pre-heat clean wok or pan with a little oil and cook handfuls of beef over a high heat for about 40 seconds on each side to seal. Return all the meat back to the pan, add the hot sauce, the vegetables and the noodles. Stir to combine over heat. Serves 4-5.

Orange and Sesame Beef Stir-fry

Cervena (farm raised venison) or pork can also be used for this easy wok cooked combination.

To Prepare: 10 minutes
To Cook: 6-8 minutes

> *2 bunches asparagus, trimmed*
> *2 carrots, cut in small batons*
> *200g mushrooms, thinly sliced*
> *1 tbsp fresh ginger, minced*
> *2 cloves garlic, crushed*
> *finely grated rind of 1/2 orange*
> *400g lean beef steak or Cervena*
> *   venison thinly sliced*
> *1 tbsp vegetable oil*
> *2 tsp sesame oil*
> *2 tbsp oyster sauce*
> *juice of 1 orange*
> *dash chilli sauce*
> *2-3 tbsp sesame seeds, toasted,*
> *   1 spring onion, chopped and/or*
> *   2-3 tbsp fresh coriander,*
> *   chopped, for garnish*

Boil, steam or microwave vegetables until almost tender. Cool under cold water, drain and reserve. Mix ginger, garlic and orange rind through sliced meat. Heat both oils in a wok or heavy pan, add half meat and stir-fry 2-3 minutes over high heat until just browned – do not over cook. Remove. Re-heat pan with a little oil and cook other half. Mix in cooked vegetables and all other ingredients including meat and, using a big spoon, toss over heat until heated through. Pile onto a heated serving plate and sprinkle over garnish. Serve at once. Serves 4.

Left: Beef Teppanyaki

Beef Teppanyaki

This is an easy stir-fry with a Japanese twist. Take care not to over cook the beef. Once added, the meat should only be cooked for about 3 minutes.

To Prepare: 5 minutes and 10 minutes standing beef

To Cook: 5 minutes

Marinade

> *2 tbsp soy sauce*
> *1-2 tsp hot chilli sauce, to taste*
> *1 tbsp sesame oil*
> *2 tbsp root ginger, grated*
> *¼ cup sake, mirin or sherry*
> *1 tbsp rice wine vinegar or wine vinegar*
> *1 tbsp sugar*
>
> *200-250g lean beef steak, eg rump, sliced in very thin strips*
> *2 tbsp vegetable oil*
> *200g mushrooms, thinly sliced*
> *1 red pepper, cut in thin strips*
> *2 spring onions, peeled and thinly sliced*
> Optional: *¼ cup pickled ginger, finely sliced, as garnish*

Combine all marinade ingredients in a clean bowl or plastic bag. Mix sliced meat through marinade. Leave for 10-15 minutes. Heat oil in a large wok or fry-pan and cook mushrooms and pepper for 2-3 minutes stirring or shaking pan frequently. Remove from pan and put to one side. Lift meat from marinade and drain, reserving marinade. Add meat to pan with spring onions and cook over very high heat for 2-3 minutes until cooked. Add reserved marinade into pan with onion and mushroom mixture and heat through. Sprinkle over pickled ginger and serve at once. Serves 2.

Busy Day Dinner Idea: *Accompany with rice noodles and poppadoms.*

Which Vinegar

'Vin aigre' means literally sour wine, but vinegar is made from a wide range of products – beer hops (malt vinegar), apples (cider vinegar), grain (white vinegar), even honey. Rice vinegar is a sweetish mild vinegar, almost fruity in flavour, while white vinegar tastes like diluted acid. The list of essential vinegars includes rice vinegar, red and white wine vinegar, malt and balsamic vinegar. Add a splash of vinegar into soups and sauces to balance flavours. A spoonful of rice or white wine vinegar is delicious beaten into mashed potatoes and can help if a dish is over-salted. And if you happen to choke on a fish bone take a slurp of vinegar. It's an old Chinese trick – vinegar softens bones.

Natural Poisons

Next time you reach to put the mouldy bread in the toaster – stop. Mould in bread is very toxic, as is mould in kumara and other sweet potatoes. Charred BBQ'd meats should also be avoided, as should cooking food in oil which has overheated. Both of these are carcinogens.

Fresh Salsa Partners

WHEN YOU THINK SALSA, DON'T JUST THINK OF SPICY MEXICAN TOMATO BREWS. SALSAS MAKE AN EXCELLENT PARTNER FOR A QUICK GRILL OR PAN-FRY. THEY ARE GENERALLY MADE WITH RAW OR LIGHTLY COOKED FRUIT OR VEGETABLES AND HAVE A CHUNKY SAUCE-LIKE TEXTURE. USING THESE RECIPES AS A GUIDELINE, CREATE YOUR OWN SALSA TASTES.

Commercial Sauces

Convenience products such as pesto and taco sauce are ideal for adding texture and flavour to simple, fresh salsa ingredients.

Discolouration in Salsas

Salsas made with bananas, avocados or other fruits which discolour need to be made just before serving. Other salsas will keep for 1-2 days in the fridge.

To Toast Coconut

Coconut burns quickly and is best toasted in the oven. Spread on a tray and bake at 180°C for 10-15 minutes until pale gold. Store in an airtight container.

Mexican Tomato Salsa

Blend together 4-5 large, peeled and chopped tomatoes, ½ cup commercial taco sauce, 2 tbsp chopped fresh coriander. Season to taste. Chill until required. Salsa will keep in the fridge for 2-3 days.

Peach and Mint Salsa

Finely dice 3 peaches, mix with 2 tbsp lemon juice, 2 tbsp finely chopped mint, 1 finely chopped spring onion and a little salt and pepper to taste. Serve within 2 hours or salsa will discolour.

Chunky Guacamole Salsa

Dice 1 large avocado and mix with 2 finely diced tomatoes, ½ finely chopped red onion, 1 tsp crushed garlic and the juice of ½ lemon. Season with salt and freshly ground black pepper to taste. Serve within 2 hours or salsa will discolour.

Kiwifruit and Paw Paw Salsa

Finely dice ½ a paw paw or melon and 4 kiwifruit. Combine with ¼ cup finely chopped red onion, 2 tbsp chopped coriander, the juice of 2 limes and ¼ tsp Tabasco sauce. Season to taste with salt and freshly ground black pepper. Chill until required. Salsa will keep in the fridge for 1 day.

Fresh Banana Salsa

Combine 2 small mashed bananas, 1 tbsp lemon juice, ¼ cup toasted thread coconut, pinch each of salt and freshly ground black pepper and 1 tbsp minced lemongrass (optional). Serve at once as salsa discolours quickly.

Corn and Pepper Salsa

Mix 1 cup cooked kernel corn with ½ cup finely diced red or green pepper, 2 tbsp chopped mint or coriander, ½ tsp crushed garlic, a pinch of chilli powder, salt and freshly ground black pepper to taste and 1 tbsp oil. Chill until required. Salsa will keep in the fridge for 2-3 days. Diced avocado makes a good addition at serving time.

Mango Salsa

Mix together the diced flesh of 2 mangoes, 2 tbsp sweet chilli sauce, 2 tbsp fresh lime or lemon juice and 2 tbsp chopped fresh coriander. Salsa will keep well up to 12 hours in the fridge.

Pico de Gallo

Combine 2 finely diced tomatoes, 1 small finely diced onion, 4 cloves minced garlic, 4 tbsp chopped coriander, 2 tbsp lime juice, 2 tbsp olive oil and salt and pepper to taste. Stand 30 minutes before serving. Keep in the fridge and eat the same day.

BBQ MEAT

THERE'S NOTHING QUITE LIKE THE WAFTING AROMAS OF A BARBECUE TO PUT EVERYONE INTO A

CASUAL HOLIDAY MOOD. THROW ON A POT OF NEW POTATOES AND WHIP UP A

FRESH SALAD, SOME TASTY SAUCES AND BREAK A LOAF OF CRUSTY BREAD – PERFECT PARTNERS

FOR THE FARE FROM THE GRILL.

Mango Pork Ribs

Mango Glaze ✪ is delicious not just with poultry but also with pork. Pre-cooking ribs before barbecuing makes them melt-in-the-mouth tender.

To Prepare: 5 minutes

To Cook: 1¼ hours

> 4 sets short pork spare ribs (get butcher to cut in half crosswise if ribs are long)
> 1 recipe Mango Glaze ✪
> 1 cup water

Cut ribs into groups of 2-3. Place ribs in a large pot with Mango Glaze and water. Cover and bring to a boil then reduce heat to lowest temperature and cook for 1 hour. Cool in their cooking liquid. When ready to barbecue, drain ribs, boil marinade until thick and grill ribs until golden. Pile ribs onto a platter and pour over hot marinade.

Variation: *Ribs glazed with Red Pepper Sauce.*✪

Summer BBQ Idea: *Accompany ribs with grilled asparagus and Honey Sesame Kumara.*✪

Above: Mango Pork Ribs

BBQ Cooking

- *Never cook over a direct flame.*
- *Use charcoal that has not been soaked in chemicals and avoid using kerosene or fire starters.*
- *When BBQ cooking for a large number of people pre-cook by boiling or microwaving to speed up BBQ time.*
- *Avoid charring meat by reducing the cooking heat, or raising food away from the heat source.*
- *Use sprigs of fresh herbs on the hot grill to add flavour to meats – try rosemary with lamb, thyme and sage with pork and hickory, manuka or tea tree chips with beef. Soak woodchips and herb sprigs in water for 15 minutes before using and use only a handful at a time.*

Pre-cooking and Then Barbecuing

- *Beef fillet: Microwave on high power for 5 minutes, then barbecue for 8-10 minutes per side.*
- *Butterflied leg of lamb: Microwave for 6 minutes, then barbecue for 6-8 minutes per side.*
- *Spareribs: Microwave 500g at a time on medium power for 5 minutes, then barbecue for 5-7 minutes.*

Oposite: Thai Pork Sticks with Mango Salsa

Mexican Lamb or Beef Fajitas

I have used a Cajun spice mix with the fajitas but they are also good with other rub flavours – like the Moroccan Rub.✪

To Prepare: 10 minutes, plus marinating
To Cook: 10 minutes, plus standing

> 2-3 tbsp Cajun Spice Mix ✪
> 500g lamb rumps or thick beef steaks
> 2 medium onions, halved and cut in thin wedges
> 1 tbsp oil
> 1-2 green or red peppers, cut into thin strips
> 4 potatoes, cut in thin wedges
> 2 tbsp oil
> 1-2 tbsp sweet chilli sauce
> 2 tbsp chopped coriander or mint

Combine the spice mix and oil and rub all over the meat. Leave to marinate for at least 1 hour (or up to 24 hours in the fridge). Lightly oil a barbecue plate or heavy pan and brown the meat all over on a high heat. Mix the vegetables with the second quantity of oil and place around the meat. Reduce the heat to medium and cook until the meat is done and the vegetables are cooked and lightly browned. Stand the meat for 5 minutes before carving. Mix chilli sauce and coriander or mint through vegetables. Serves 4-5.

Busy Day BBQ: *Accompany with a salsa of your choice, tortillas, a bowl of sour cream and avocado sauce.*

Quick Avocado Sauce: *In a food processor, blend the flesh of 1 firm but ripe avocado with 1 clove crushed garlic, 2 tbsp lemon juice, 1/4 cup vegetable oil and 1 tsp hot pepper sauce. Season with salt and pepper, and serve at once.*

Thai Pork Sticks

Good with beef, pork or chicken. Don't use meat which has been frozen, it is too wet. Pre-boil sticks ahead of time ready for a quick flick on the BBQ.

To Prepare: 20 minutes
To Cook: 10 minutes

> 1 spring onion, roughly chopped
> 2 cloves garlic, chopped
> 2 tbsp fresh ginger, chopped
> 1 tsp finely grated lemon rind
> 1/4 cup fresh coriander, chopped
> 2 tbsp fish sauce
> 1/2-1 tsp salt
> 2 tbsp sweet Thai chilli sauce
> 1 egg white
> 600g lean pork mince (beef or chicken mince can also be used)

Purée together the spring onions, garlic, ginger, rind, fresh coriander, fish sauce, salt, chilli sauce, salt and egg white. Mix the mince through by hand until well combined. With wet hands, mould about 1 tbsp of mixture onto disposable wooden chopsticks (or barbecue skewers), to evenly cover 3-4cm length of the top of each stick. Boil a large saucepan of water. Drop 4-5 prepared sticks into boiling water for 2 minutes until just set. Remove and repeat to pre-cook all skewers. Leave to cool. The skewers can be prepared ahead of time to this point and refrigerated for up to 48 hours. Brush with oil. Grill or barbecue until brown for about 4-5 minutes. Serves 6-8.

Busy Day Dinner Idea: *Accompany with Asian Deli Noodles ✪ and Mango Salsa.✪*

Cajun Spice Mix

Into a jar place 5 tbsp paprika, 5 tbsp ground cumin, 3 tbsp garlic powder, 1½ tbsp each of chilli powder, brown sugar and salt and 2½ tsp chopped dry rosemary. Seal the jar and shake to combine. It makes enough for 2kg of meat or chicken. Allow 3 tbsp per 500g meat. Store in an airtight jar.

Moroccan Rub

Combine together 2 tbsp ground cumin, 1 tsp each ground cardamom seeds, cinnamon, cayenne pepper, fine black pepper and brown sugar, finely grated rind of 1 lemon, ¼ cup olive oil, ¼ cup lemon juice, 3 tbsp minced fresh ginger. Rub will keep in the fridge for a few weeks or can be frozen. Makes enough for 3 large roasts.

Thai Shrimp Marinade

Don't be put off by the fishy smell of shrimp paste – it loses all its smell when cooked and imparts incredible flavour. Heat 2 tbsp vegetable oil in a fry-pan and sizzle 1 tsp shrimp paste, stirring to break it up. Remove from heat and add 2 tbsp fresh minced ginger, 1 tbsp minced lemon grass, 2 tbsp fish sauce, 3 tbsp brown sugar, finely grated rind of 1 lime or lemon and 2 minced chillies. Marinade keeps in the fridge for a couple of weeks.

Beautiful Burgers

It's hard to beat the old fashioned pleasures of barbecue burgers. Make them with lean steak mince shaped into fat patties, seasoned with salt, pepper and any other flavours you fancy and cook till juicy and pink in the middle over a barbecue grill. You can zap up the flavours in the patty with cajun spice, pesto, harissa, olive paste or a tasty marinade. Put cooked patties into split toasted buns, focaccia, panini or pita, spread with mayonnaise or guacamole, then layer tomato, spinach or lettuce, and roasted red peppers. Top the lot off with spicy sauce – a fresh tomato salsa or the tried and true Tomato Kasundi ✪ make a great change from regular ketchup.

Great burger combinations:
- *Old fashioned burgers – fried egg, pickled beetroot, lettuce, sliced red onion and tomato.*
- *Thai burgers – make burgers using flavours for Thai Pork Sticks (see this chapter). Make into burgers with coriander-flavoured mayonnaise, sliced avocado, tomatoes, shredded lettuce, carrots, cucumber and spring onions.*
- *Italian Burgers – flavour patties with garlic and pesto, serve in burgers with olive-flavoured mayonnaise, sliced tomatoes, rocket and roasted peppers.*

Ginger and Black Bean Pork

Mix 500g thinly sliced lean pork with with 2 tbsp oyster sauce or black bean sauce, 1 tsp sesame oil and 1 tbsp fresh minced ginger. Barbecue or pan fry until cooked. Serves 4.

Pesto Barbecue Lamb

Mixing meat with a flavour base such as pesto, a prepared Asian sauce, or a dry spice rub is a really quick way to impart exciting flavours to grills or barbecues. Use just enough to lightly coat meat – 1-2 tbsp per 500g.

To Prepare: 5 minutes
To Cook: 5-8 minutes

> *3-4 lamb cutlets*
> *salt and ground black pepper*
> *2 tbsp pesto of your choice*

Season lamb fillets with salt and pepper. Rub in pesto. Barbecue or pan fry lamb until cooked. Serves 2.

Busy Day Dinner Idea: *Slice and serve on Quick Pesto Cous Cous ✪ and toasted flatbreads.*

MENU IDEAS

Summer Barbecue

Thai prawn fritters

Thai pork sticks

Asian deli noodle salad

mango salsa

Bella's berry trifle

summer sangria

Advance preparations

- *make and pre-cook pork sticks and chill*
- *prepare dressing for noodle salad*
- *make trifle and chill*
- *prepare fritter batter*

Mediterranean Summer Grill Plate

This recipe is perfect for a summer barbecue or terrace dinner with friends. The meat cooks in a whole piece for about 40-45 minutes with the vegetables added in the last 30 minutes. A variety of beef, lamb or venison cuts can be used. The thicker the cut, the longer the cook time – a sirloin of beef will take 10-15 minutes longer than the thinner Cervena venison rump.

To Prepare: 15 minutes

To Cook: about 20 minutes

> 1-1.2kg beef fillet, sirloin, flank
>   steak, boned leg of lamb or
>   Cervena venison, 5-6cm thick
> 1/2 cup olive oil
> 2 large cloves garlic, crushed
> 1/2 tsp finely grated lemon rind
> 2 tbsp lemon juice
> 1 tbsp chopped fresh rosemary
> black pepper
> vegetables – use any combination
>   allowing 4-5 per person

Trim the meat to an even-sized piece, folding in any thin edges. Place in a clean plastic bag or dish. Combine the oil and garlic and pour half over the meat. Sprinkle over lemon rind and juice and rosemary and marinate for at least 30 minutes or up to 12 hours in the fridge. Reserve the rest of the garlic-flavoured oil for the vegetables.

When ready to cook, pre-heat a barbecue plate or grill. Lift the meat from its marinade and place onto the grill. Cook over high heat for about 5 minutes each side, then turn heat down to its medium-low setting (for a charcoal cooker, lift the cooking rack until you can hold your hand at the same level over the heat source for 5 seconds before it feels too hot). Cook for 15-20 minutes. Grill the vegetables, brushing well with garlic oil. They will take about 10 minutes to cook.

Stand the meat for 5 minutes before carving. Serves 8-10. Accompany with Garlic, Basil and Anchovy Dipping Sauce.

Lamb Chwarma Pockets

No need to call for takeaways next time you fancy a Middle Eastern feast. These pita pockets filled with Middle Eastern-style lamb are really good. This marinade is ideal for summer lamb barbecues.

To Prepare: 5-10 minutes

To Cook: 10 minutes

> 500g lean lamb, cut into tiny slivers
> 1 tsp each of ground cumin, dried
>   oregano, allspice
> 1/4 tsp cinnamon
> 1 medium onion, finely diced
> 2 tsp crushed garlic
> 1 tbsp olive oil
> salt and ground black pepper
> juice of 1 lemon
> pita breads
> Parsley and Sprout Salad ⊙
> Garlic and Chive Sour Cream
>   (see side panel)
> tomato relish or Tomato Kasundi ⊙

Combine the lamb with the spices, onion, garlic and oil. Leave for at least 15 minutes before cooking, or up to 6 hours refrigerated. Pre-heat a pan or barbecue hotplate to medium-high and oil lightly. Cook the lamb, tossing over heat for 3-4 minutes, until it is just browned. Season to taste with salt and pepper. Place the meat in a serving dish and keep warm. To prepare warmed pita pockets, slice the pita breads in half. Stack one half on top of the other and wrap in tinfoil. Place on a hot barbecue or oven and turn the tin-foiled stack frequently, until warmed through (5-10 minutes). Squeeze the lemon juice over the meat and serve with warmed pita pockets, Garlic and Chive Sour Cream and relish or Kasundi.⊙ Serves 4-6.

Garlic and Chive Sour Cream

Mix 1/2 cup sour cream with 1 cup yoghurt, 1 tsp crushed garlic and 2 tbsp chopped chives.

Garlic, Basil and Anchovy Dipping Sauce

This delicious sauce is a great accompaniment with the meat and vegetable platter. Purée 1 1/2 cups home-made mayonnaise, 1 egg yolk, 4 mashed anchovy fillets, 15-20 basil leaves or 2 tsp basil pesto, 1 tbsp capers and 2 cloves crushed garlic until smooth. Makes 1 3/4 cups.

Chopsticks

Using chopsticks as skewers looks really effective. Pre-cook skewers by boiling for a couple of minutes. This sets the protein and stops the meat mixture from falling off the skewers.

Stopping Meat from Sticking

If you are preparing minced meat for hamburgers or skewers, wet your hands slightly to stop the mixture from sticking.

Main Course Salads

THIN SLIVERS OF MEAT TOSSED WITH A FRESH FLAVOURSOME DRESSING, VEGETABLES
AND SALAD GREENS MAKES A LIGHT, FRESH WAY TO EAT WHEN THE WEATHER IS HOT.
VARY THE DRESSING FOR A RANGE OF DELICIOUS MAIN COURSE SALADS.

*Right: Louise's Thai Beef
Salad*

Tamarind

*The pulp of the seed pod of
a tropical tree, tamarind has
a unique sweet sour flavour –
a bit like dates mixed with
lime. It is commonly used in
Asian, Indian and sometimes
Latin American cooking to
give a sour flavour. If you buy
it in a block with the seeds in
it, cover with very hot water
(about ¼ cup per walnut-
sized ball), soak for 15
minutes, then with your
fingers work it with the
soaking liquid into a purée,
discarding the seeds. In
the block or as a
concentrate tamarind will
keep indefinitely.*

Louise's Thai Beef Salad

Here's a wonderful Thai beef salad that
takes very little effort. If there's no
tamarind, substitute equal amounts of
lime juice.

To Prepare: 10 minutes
To Cook : 5 minutes

> *600g beef fillet or sirloin cut in 4*
> *   thick beef steaks*
> *3 spring onions, thinly sliced*
> *1 large red onion, thinly sliced*
> *1½ telegraph cucumbers, cut in*
> *   small finger batons*
> *2 tomatoes, diced*
> *¾ cup mint leaves*
> *½ cup coriander leaves*
> *Dressing:*
> *2 tbsp lime or lemon juice*
> *2 tbsp fish sauce*
> *½ tsp minced red chilli*
> *1 tsp sugar*
> *¼ cup sweet Thai chilli sauce*
> *finely grated rind of 1 lime*
> *   or lemon*
> *2 tbsp tamarind concentrate*
> *Optional: cooked noodles, bean sprouts,*
> *   sliced red pepper*

Grill or pan fry beef to medium rare. Cut
into fine diagonal strips while hot. Mix
through combined dressing ingredients.
Allow to cool. When ready to serve, toss
with other ingredients. Pile onto a serving
platter. Serves 4.

Busy Day Dinner Idea: *Mix through
400g cooked noodles and 2 sliced red
peppers.*

Chinese Hot and Spicy Pork Salad Cups

The printer I often work with in Hong Kong is a self-confessed foodie who always knows the best place to eat everything – from pigeon to abalone, he knows where to go. He introduced me to this popular lunch combination of stir-fried pork with crispy noodles rolled up in crunchy lettuce leaves.

To Prepare: 5 minutes
To Cook: 8 minutes

> 200-250g pork mince or chicken
>   mince
> 1 tbsp sweet Thai chilli sauce
> 1 tbsp sesame oil
> 1 tbsp fresh ginger, minced
> 1/4 cup oyster sauce
> 1 x 320g can water chestnuts,
>   rinsed and thinly sliced
> 2 spring onions, sliced thinly
> 1/4 cup peanuts or cashews, roasted
> 1 carrot, peeled, shredded or grated
> 2 tbsp coriander or mint, chopped
> 2 large handfuls crispy noodles
> 10-12 crunchy green lettuce leaves,
>   carefully separated and washed

Combine mince with chilli sauce, sesame oil and root ginger. Stand for 5 minutes or up to 8 hours in the fridge. Heat a wok or large fry-pan and fry pork over a high heat until browned and cooked through, about 5-8 minutes. Mix in oyster sauce and remove from heat. Mix water chestnuts, spring onion, nuts, carrot, coriander and crispy noodles through meat. Use 5-6 lettuce leaves to make a basket in each bowl. Spoon mixture into lettuce cups. Serve at once. Eat by rolling up the stir-fry mix in lettuce leaves. Serves 2.

Roasted Walnut, Orange and Lamb Salad

Toasted walnuts, fresh beets, oranges and tender pink lamb fillets combine in this easy summer salad.

To Prepare: 10 minutes
To Cook: 6-8 minutes

> 2 tbsp vegetable oil
> 3/4 cup walnuts
> 8 handfuls mixed salad greens,
>   washed and dried
> 2 oranges, peeled and flesh cut in
>   segments
> 1 beetroot, peeled and cut in
>   matchstick strips
> 1/2 cup Favourite Dressing,✪ with
>   finely grated rind of 1/2 orange
> 4-6 lamb fillets
> salt and ground black pepper

Heat a fry-pan with the oil. Season 4-6 lamb fillets with salt and freshly ground black pepper. Cook over medium-high heat for 3-4 minutes, until medium rare. Stand 3-5 minutes, then slice fillets on an angle, 2cm thick. Roast walnuts in a 200°C oven in a shallow dish for 6-8 minutes, or gently fry in a little oil for 2-3 minutes. While meat rests, prepare salad ingredients. Toss greens with dressing in a big bowl then toss through with all other salad ingredients. Serves 4.

Cous Cous

Cous cous is unbelievably easy to prepare. The cous cous we buy today has been pre-cooked and only requires a brief soaking in hot water to fluff up. The rule of thumb is 1 1/4 cups boiling liquid per 1 cup cous cous. Add flavourings such as lemon rind, pesto, saffron, chilli sauce, etc and some salt (1/2 tsp per cup of cous cous) to the boiling liquid before mixing in the cous cous. After about 10 minutes all the liquid will have been absorbed. Fluff up the cous cous with a fork and add other ingredients of your choice –

- *roasted red peppers, chick peas, coriander and mint*
- *saffron, dates, toasted walnut, orange rind and orange segments and mint*
- *see also the Useful Sides Section for more cous cous ideas.*

DELICIOUS MEAT SALAD MEALS

Adding protein to a salad converts it from a side dish to a main. Cool cooked meats to room temperature before slicing thinly across the grain. For maximum flavour, mix through some of the dressing as soon as the meat is sliced. Combine with the other salad ingredients or serve on top.

Roasts

THERE'S A WONDERFUL SENSE OF NOSTALGIA IN A GOOD ROAST, AND IT'S SUCH AN EASY MEAL TO

COOK. EXTEND THE MEAT WITH LOTS OF DIFFERENT VEGETABLES —

YAMS, KUMARA, POTATO AND PUMPKIN CAN ROAST WITH THE MEAT. COOK GREENS ON THE

STOVE TOP JUST BEFORE SERVING.

Beef Fillet with Ratatouille

Here's a great dish for a crowd. Tender, perfectly cooked beef and fresh tasty ratatouille. All you need as an accompaniment is some fresh bread.

To Prepare: 15 minutes

To Cook: 40 minutes for ratatouille,

20-25 minutes for beef

> 1 beef fillet or scotch fillet
> a little mustard and soy sauce
> 1 tbsp olive oil
> ground black pepper

Ratatouille

> 6 large onions, chopped
> 1/4 cup oil
> 2 tbsp tomato paste
> 1 1/2kg tomatoes, or 2 x 820g cans
> 6 cloves garlic, crushed
> 2 large eggplants, diced
> 10 courgettes, sliced
> 3 peppers (red, green and/or
>   yellow), chopped into chunks
> 1 tbsp dried oregano
> 1 tbsp dried basil
> 1 tbsp sugar
> 1 tbsp salt
> 1 tsp coarse black pepper
> 1/2 cup port
> 2 tbsp spiced vinegar

Cook the onions slowly in oil until translucent. Add the tomato paste and cook a further minute or two. Add the tomatoes (and their juice if canned) and cook for 20 minutes over low heat. Add the rest of the vegetables and seasonings,

plus the port and vinegar and simmer for about 15 minutes, stirring occasionally until the vegetables are tender. Allow to cool. Meanwhile, pre-heat oven to 220°C. Rub the meat all over with mustard and soy sauce. Place in roasting dish. Drizzle with olive oil and sprinkle over black pepper. Place in hot oven and cook for between 20-30 minutes until meat feels slightly springy in the thickest part. Remove from oven and allow to rest for at least 10 minutes before carving. Meat is also good served at room temperature. Serve Ratatouille at room temperature. Makes one very large (about 3 litre) serving dish, enough for 18-20 people.

MENU IDEAS

Summer Holiday Dinner

crudité with feta and fennel dip
and hummus

slow cooked pork

kumara salad

red Chinese slaw

fresh fruit salad with
passionfruit syrup

Advance preparations

- *cook pork (it takes 8 hours)*
- *make salads and salsas and chill*
- *make passionfruit syrup*

When Is Meat Cooked?

Judging whether meat is rare, raw or over cooked can be unnerving, especially if you have a large piece of meat and a bunch of people expecting a delicious dinner. There's a good trick to gauge how cooked meat is, especially useful for big cuts. Use the flesh at the base of your thumb – the Mount of Venus – as a guide.

Relax your hand and press the flesh at base of your thumb – the X Spot. This is what raw meat feels like.

Rare – touch thumb and first finger and now press the X Spot.

Medium-rare – touch thumb to middle finger and press on the X Spot.

Medium – touch thumb to the 4th finger and press the X Spot.

Overdone – touch thumb and little finger and then press the X Spot.

Slow Cooked Pork

This is one of my favourite ways to cook pork – it takes nearly all day but emerges meltingly tender and moist. Go to the beach while it cooks! This technique features in American and Italian cooking – the Texan do theirs over a slow barbecue and the Italians in a cool wood oven. You can use all kinds of coatings on the pork – Cajun spices, a Moroccan rub or this simple fennel, garlic and salt mixture. Get the butcher to score the pork skin for you with cuts about ½ cm wide.

To Prepare: 10 minutes

To Cook: 8 hours!

> 1 whole pork leg or forequarter, skin scored
>
> 1 tbsp fennel seeds
>
> 5 cloves garlic, cut in thin slivers
>
> 1 tsp coarse salt eg Maldon salt
>
> or use 2 tbsp Moroccan Spice Rub ✿ or Cajun spice mix
>
> ¼ cup lemon juice

Pre-heat oven to 250°C. Combine fennel garlic and salt (or use one of the spice rubs) and rub into the slashes of the skin all over the meat. Place skin side up in a roasting dish and roast for 40 minutes until the skin starts to blister. Reduce oven temperature to 120°C, brush over lemon juice and cook for about 8 hours. Test for doneness by pushing meat with your finger – the meat should give way completely underneath the skin. Stand 10 minutes before serving. Lift off skin and break up, cut portions of the meat. Delicious with Mango Salsa.✿ Serves 6-8.

Above: Beef Fillet with Ratatouille

Seasoning a Pan

Sometimes a fry-pan loses its surface and everything you cook seems to stick. This can often happen after poaching eggs. To remedy, sprinkle a big handful of salt into dry pan and heat for 3-4 minutes. Wipe out with a dry cloth. When you buy a new fry-pan apply the same treatment.

The Perfect Roast

Many people believe roasts require a lot of fat to cook properly. They don't. What they do need is a decent standing time once cooked so the juices can disperse evenly. If you are dealing with a tougher cut, such as shoulder, cook it with some water in a covered dish for the first 1½ hours to semi-steam the meat, then finish it in a hot oven to crisp the skin. Again, don't forget to rest it before carving.

To Prepare: 20 minutes

To Cook: 40 minutes

>   800g-1kg piece lean beef or lamb,
>   eg lamb leg, beef sirloin, beef
>   fillet (or a bigger cut)
>   2 tbsp mustard
>   1 tbsp soy sauce
>   4-6 medium potatoes, scrubbed and
>   cut into 4cm cubes
>   ¼-½ pumpkin, washed and cut
>   into chunks
>   2-3 large kumara, scrubbed and cut
>   into chunks
>   4-6 peeled baby onions
>   2 tbsp olive oil
>   1 tbsp chopped fresh rosemary
> Optional: 2 red peppers, seeds and pith
>   removed, cut in quarters

Pre-heat the oven to 220°C. Trim the fat from the meat, fold under any thin edges and tie to secure. Place the meat in a roasting tray. Combine the mustard and soy sauce and spread over the top and sides of the meat. Prepare the vegetables. Drop the prepared root vegetables and baby onions into a saucepan of boiling water and boil for 5 minutes. Drain thoroughly. Roast the meat at 220°C for 10 minutes. Reduce the heat to 200°C and cook another 30 minutes. Mix the oil and rosemary through the pre-cooked root vegetables and onions and add to pan. After 15 minutes add peppers if using, and cook for the remaining 15 minutes, until all vegetables are cooked. Take out the meat and leave to rest on the bench. Increase the oven temperature to 220°C and crisp the vegetables for a further 5-10 minutes. Carve the meat in thin slices, overlap on a large platter and surround with root vegetables. Serves 4-6. Accompany with lightly cooked vegetables and gravy.

Spiced Seared Lamb with Chickpea Purée and Eggplant

Any quick cooking lamb cut, such as lamb racks, rumps or lamb fillets, works well in this great autumn combination. Remember to rest the meat for about 5 minutes before slicing.

To Prepare: 10 minutes

To Cook: 15-20 minutes

>   1-2 lamb rumps or 4 lamb fillets
>   1-2 tsp Cajun spice mix, to taste
>   salt and ground black pepper
>   2 tbsp olive oil
>   2 tsp Pesto ✪
>   1 medium eggplant, in 2cm slices
>   ¾ cup Hummus ✪ heated
> Sauce
>   1 tsp tomato paste
>   ¼ cup stock
>   1 tbsp port
>   1 tsp balsamic vinegar
>   pinch sugar
>   salt and ground black pepper

Pre-heat oven to 220°C. Rub lamb all over with spice mix. Season with salt and pepper. Heat 1 tsp of olive oil in a heavy pan and brown lamb well all over (5 minutes). Transfer to a small roasting dish. Mix rest of olive oil with pesto and brush on both sides of each slice of eggplant. Arrange slices in a single layer on a baking tray. Season with salt and pepper. Place eggplant in hot oven and cook for 10-12 minutes. Add lamb to oven and bake for 6-8 minutes until lamb is medium rare, and

How to Make Gravy

It's easy to make a delicious pan gravy using the caramelized juices of the roast meat in the pan. Remove the roast from the cooking dish. Drain off all but about 2 tbsp of oil or fat from pan. Transfer dish to the stove top on medium heat and stir in 1 tsp brown sugar and 2 tbsp flour. Cook for about a minute or two until starting to brown then slowly add water from cooked vegetables, eg potatoes or greens, or plain water. If needed for flavour, add a spoonful of miso or Vegemite or a beef stock cube. Simmer for about 5 minutes. Season well with salt and ground black pepper and a splash of red wine or balsamic vinegar. Pour into a warmed jug for each diner to help themselves.

eggplant is lightly golden. Rest lamb and eggplant for 5 minutes. While it rests, heat Hummus and make sauce. Heat pan used to brown meat. Fry tomato paste for 1 minute. Add stock, port, vinegar and sugar and simmer for 2-3 minutes. Season to taste with salt and pepper. Slice each rump in half, then each half into 4-5 slices. Fan meat onto 2 heated serving plates. Layer eggplant slices alongside, spooning a little Hummus between each. Spoon sauce over and around meat. Serves 2. Recipe doubles easily.

Spiced Lamb with Date and Pinenut Stuffing and Moroccan Sauce

This is really a feast – great for a special dinner or winter weekend lunch.

To Prepare: 20 minutes

To Cook: 1½ -2 hours

> 1 leg lamb tunnel boned (shank
>   bone cleaned and left on)
> ¼ cup Moroccan Rub ✿ – buy
>   or make

Stuffing

> 1 onion, finely diced
> 1 red pepper, finely diced
> 2 tbsp olive oil
> finely grated rind of 1 lemon
>   and 1 orange
> 1 cup chopped, pitted dates
> ½ cup toasted pinenuts
> ¼ cup finely chopped parsley
> 4 cups fresh breadcrumbs
> 1 egg
> salt and ground black pepper
> Moroccan Sauce ✿ to serve

Optional: 2 tbsp chopped capers

Spread rub all over lamb. To make stuffing, gently cook onion and garlic in oil for 5-10 minutes until softened. Remove from heat and mix ingredients. Stuff into cavity of lamb and close lamb securely with skewers. (If there is stuffing left over, form into a roll, wrap in lightly oiled tinfoil, place in a sponge tin and bake for 40-45 minutes.) Roast lamb at 180°C for 1½-2 hours or until tender. Stand for 10 minutes before carving. Roast vegetables such as beets, pumpkin, kumara and potato, and braised beans, broccoli and leeks go well with this roast. Serves 6-8. Accompany with Moroccan Sauce.

Above: Spiced Lamb with Date and Pinenut Stuffing and Moroccan Sauce

Nutrition – Iron

Women need iron more than men, as menstruation depletes iron supplies on a regular basis. Eating lean meat once or twice a week is sufficient to provide the body with the iron it requires.

Boning Out Meat

Ask the butcher to bone cuts of meat for you. They are experienced and can do the job quickly and easily.

Prepare Ahead

GOOD CASSEROLES AND OVEN BAKES NEED TIME TO TENDERIZE AND DEVELOP FLAVOURS. THEY TASTE BETTER WHEN MADE A DAY OR TWO AHEAD. THIS SORT OF FOOD IS INCREDIBLY USEFUL WHEN YOU ARE BUSY — HAUL IT OUT OF THE FRIDGE OR FREEZER FOR INSTANT COMFORT FARE.

Pickled Kumquats

Heat together 1 cup water, 2/3 cup spiced vinegar and 1/3 cup sugar. Bring to a boil and add 1 1/2 cups washed kumquats, a small handful of peppercorns and a few cloves. Simmer gently for 15-20 minutes. They will keep for months, stored in a covered jar in the fridge.

Deep-fried Leek Strips

If you wish to prepare deep-fried leek strips this can be done ahead of time and the cooked leeks drained and stored in a paper bag in the fridge. Freshen in the oven for 10-15 minutes before using.

Browning Meat

Browning meat adds caramelized flavours and gives depth to sauces. Meat can be browned in a hot, lightly oiled pan or, for oxtails or lamb shanks, in a hot oven for 30-40 minutes.

Opposite: Braised Oxtails with Asian Spices with Noodles, Pickled Kumquats and Deep-fried Leek.

Braised Oxtails with Asian Spices

Ginger, garlic, soy sauce, rice wine vinegar, star anise and chillies give the oxtails a spicy kick and a wonderfully rich, dark hue. Brown the oxtails, add all other ingredients and cook slowly for a couple of hours. Finishing the dish with Pickled Kumquats makes it very special.

To Prepare: 10 minutes

To Cook: 2 1/4 hours

> *18-22 pieces of oxtails, about 1 1/2 kg, trimmed of excess fat*
> *salt and ground black pepper*
> *2 tbsp oil*
> *500mls tomato juice*
> *500mls water*
> *1 tbsp brown sugar*
> *2 tbsp rice wine vinegar*
> *1/3 cup soy sauce*
> *4 each of whole star anise and dried chillies*
> *50g fresh ginger, thinly sliced*
> *peel of 1/2 orange cut with a potato peeler, no pith*
> *1 whole head garlic, cloves peeled and halved*
> **Optional: (for special occasions)**
> *12-18 pickled kumquats to garnish (see side panel)*
> *thin slices of deep-fried leek or onion as topping*

Pre-heat oven to 180°C. Season oxtails, heat oil in a large heat proof casserole (preferably big enough to hold all oxtails in a single layer), brown well in batches and put aside. Drain fat from pan, add all other ingredients to pan and bring to a fast boil. Add oxtails and mix through sauce. It should nearly cover. Cover the top with a piece of baking paper cut to the same size as the dish to prevent tops of oxtails from drying out. Cover tightly with a lid and bake for 2 hours. Mix in pickled kumquats. Serve on rice noodles or mashed kumara and garnish with a handful of fried leek strips. Serves 6.

Thai Beef Stew

This slow spicy simmer cooks on the stove for about an hour and a half. Make it a day or two ahead to allow flavours to develop.

To Prepare: 10 minutes

To Cook: 1 1/2 hours

> *1 tbsp oil*
> *2 tbsp Thai curry paste*
> *1 tbsp tomato paste*
> *finely grated rind 1 lime or lemon*
> *1 tsp minced fresh ginger*
> *1kg cross-cut blade or gravy beef, diced 3cm*
> *400ml can coconut cream*
> *2 tbsp fish sauce*
> *2 tbsp chopped basil*
> *1-2 finely chopped spring onions*

In a large pot, heat oil and fry curry paste, tomato paste, lemon or lime rind and ginger for about a minute. Add beef, coconut cream and fish sauce. Cover and simmer over lowest heat for about 1 1/2 hours until tender, or pressure cook for 15 minutes. Mix in basil and spring onions, adjust seasonings to taste and serve. Serves 6.

Right: Braised Lamb Shanks
with Black Beans and Chilli

Tender Dumplings

Place 1 cup plain flour in a basin and mix in ¹/₄ tsp salt, 2 tsp chopped fresh rosemary, 2 tsp chopped fresh thyme and 2 tsp baking powder. Mix in about ³/₄ cup milk or enough to form a soft dough. Drop spoonfuls onto the simmering (thickened) stew. Cover tightly and cook a further 20 minutes until dumplings have risen and cooked through.

Pressure Cooker Comfort

If you have a pressure cooker it makes things really fast. Slow-cooking meats like steak and kidney require only about 15 minutes until tender, compared to well over an hour in a pot. Always make sure there is enough liquid to fully cover the base of the pressure cooker when using, otherwise food may catch and burn.

Braised Lamb Shanks with Black Beans and Chilli

These are so simple yet have a wonderful flavour and melt in the mouth texture. I like to roast the shanks in a hot oven first to get them brown and get rid of any fat that I have not been able to trim. They then get mixed with spicy flavourings for a final bake.

To Prepare: 5 minutes

To Cook: about 2 hours

> 8 large lamb shanks, cut in half
> 2 tbsp minced fresh ginger
> 3 cloves garlic, crushed
> 1 tsp sesame oil
> 1 cup black bean sauce
> ¹/₂ cup Thai sweet chilli sauce
> 1 cup water

Pre-heat oven to 220°C. Trim visible fat from shanks, season with salt and pepper and place into hot oven for 40 minutes to release fat and brown. Drain off fat and put shanks in a deep casserole or pot. Add all other ingredients. Mix through. Cover and bake for about 1 hour at 170°C or simmer at lowest heat for about ³/₄-1 hour until very tender. Serves 6.

Busy Day Dinner Idea: Accompany with Kumara Mash ✿ and greens.

Steak, Mushroom and Kidney Pie

This recipe is comfort food just like Gran used to make. The steak and kidney mixture can also be topped with dumplings instead of pastry.

To Prepare: 20 minutes

To Cook: up to 2 hours

> 800g blade or chuck steak, diced in 2cm chunks
> 4-6 lamb kidneys, cut into pieces
> 1 large onion, thinly sliced
> 200g dark mushrooms, sliced
> 1 bay leaf
> 2 tsp miso or Vegemite or a stock cube
> 1½ cups water
> 200g baby carrots, washed
> 1 tsp salt and plenty of ground black pepper
> 2 tbsp cornflour, mixed with ¼ cup port or water
> 2 tbsp chopped parsley
> about 350g shortcrust or puff pastry
> Optional: 2 leeks, thin angle cut

Place the meat, onions, mushrooms, bay leaf, miso and water in a pot or pressure cooker. Cover tightly and simmer on lowest heat for 1¼ hours adding carrots and optional leeks after ¾ hour, or pressure cook everything for 15 minutes. Stir in cornflour paste to thicken. Season well to taste and mix in parsley. Cool filling. Place in a pie dish. Cover with pastry and bake at 200°C for about 35 minutes until pastry is golden and cooked through. Serves 4-5.

Busy Day Dinner Idea: *Serve with mashed potato and greens.*

Sue Story's Lamb Tagine

Made in a pot or baked in the oven, this wonderful Moroccan stew makes great fare for a crowd. Or freeze in batches for an impromptu mid-week dinner.

To Prepare: 10 minutes

To Cook: 1 hour 15 minutes

> 1kg lean lamb, cubed 3-4cm pieces
> 2 tsp ground cumin
> 2 tsp ground coriander
> 1 tsp cinnamon
> 1 tsp ground ginger
> 1 tsp dried oregano
> ½ tsp cayenne, to taste
> 2 tbsp oil
> 1 large onion, chopped
> 1 cup dried apricots
> 1½ cups chicken stock or 1 x 375ml carton
> salt and ground black pepper
> 1-2 tsp harissa to taste
> Optional: 1 can chickpeas, rinsed and drained

Mix all dry spices and herbs through the meat. Heat half the oil in a large fry-pan over high heat. Add half the meat, spread out and brown on one side only. Remove to a plate. Repeat, heating other half of oil to brown only one side of meat. Place browned meat in a medium casserole dish or saucepan. Add onion to the fry-pan to soften slightly, then add apricots, stock and optional chickpeas, stirring to incorporate all flavours and tasty bits in the pan. Tip this into browned meat, stir and simmer gently for one hour. If using the oven, cook covered for 1 hour at 160°C or until the meat is tender. Season to taste with salt, pepper and Harissa.⊙

Serves 5-6. Freezes well.

Busy Day Dinner Idea: *Serve with cous cous and green beans.*

Cook A Day Ahead

When making a meat stew or slow oven bake prepare it a day ahead and chill so you can take off any of the hardened fat that has set on the top. Cooking ahead of time also allows the flavours in the dish to develop and mingle.

Flouring Meat

Flouring meats before they are browned helps seal the meat and lightly thickens a stew or casserole. The easiest and least messy way to flour meat (or fish) is to put the flour and seasoning – salt and ground pepper – in a brown paper or plastic bag. Shake to mix and then add meat pieces a few at a time, hold the top of the bag closed tightly and shake a few times to coat the meat pieces. Shake excess flour off meat and throw out any flour not used.

Right: Saag Goshi

Saag Goshi
(Lamb Curry with Spinach)

Traditionally, the spinach is cooked with the meat for a long period, but if you want a greener fresher colour add it near the end of cooking.

To Prepare: 15 minutes
To Cook: 40-45 minutes

1.5cm 'thumb' fresh ginger, peeled
6 cloves garlic, peeled
3 onions, peeled
2 dry red chillies
500g spinach, washed and trimmed
3 tbsp olive oil
2 bay leaves
3 whole cardamoms
6 whole cloves
2cm piece of cinnamon stick
800g lean lamb, cubed
2 tsp salt
500ml water
1/2 cup unsweetened yoghurt

In a food processor, purée the ginger, garlic, onions and chillies to form a paste. Steam or pan fry the spinach in a large saucepan for about 6 minutes until liquid has evaporated. Drain, squeeze dry and purée until smooth. Heat the oil in a large heavy-based saucepan. Brown the meat in batches and put to one side. Add the bay leaves, cardamoms, cloves and cinnamon stick. Cook for 2 minutes. Mix in the onion paste and cook for 5 minutes. Stir in the spinach purée, water and browned meat. Cover and cook over lowest heat for 1½ hours until the meat is tender and a thick, dark green gravy has formed. Stir occasionally. Stir in the yoghurt. Remove the bay leaves and cinnamon stick. Serves 4 as a main course or 6 as a buffet dish. Freezes well.

Useful Side Dishes

WHETHER YOU SERVE YOUR VEGETABLES WITH MEAT OR FISH OR ON THEIR OWN, THEY DESERVE AS MUCH CARE AND THOUGHT AS THE MAIN DISH. HERE ARE PERENNIAL FAVOURITES AND NEW INTERPRETATIONS.

Mashed Potato

You need a good, starchy, boiling potato here, nothing waxy. Place 6 large mashing potatoes peeled and cut in half or quarters in a pot with cold water to cover. Season with a good teaspoon of salt. Bring to a boil and simmer until tender. Drain, then return to heat and cook at lowest temperature for 1-2 minutes to dry off potatoes. Push through a sieve or mash until fine. (Don't blend in a food processor – you'll end up with glue.) Add a big knob of butter or a splash of extra virgin olive oil, season with salt and pepper. Add 1-2 tbsp lemon juice or white wine vinegar to taste (optional) and mash until light and fluffy. Serves 4-6.

Roasted Garlic Mash

Mash the flesh of 1 head of roasted garlic to a paste, heat to warm through, then mash into potatoes to combine evenly.

Parsnip and Rocket Purée

Place 6 peeled and chopped parsnips in a roasting dish with 2-3 tbsp butter and ¼ cup of water and salt and pepper. Cover and bake at 220°C for 10 minutes, then 170°C for about 1 hour or until tender. Steam or microwave a bunch of rocket or watercress, drain off any excess water. Place in a blender with cooked parsnip and its juices and purée until smooth. Purée can be quickly re-heated in the microwave – long re-heating will cause colour loss. Serves 6.

Kumara Mash

Make mash as for mashed potatoes but using 50-50 potatoes and kumara or sweet potatoes.

Honey Sesame Kumara

Scrub 3-4 kumara and slice thinly (about 1cm). Boil for 5 minutes, then drain. Heat ½ cup orange juice and ¼ cup honey and mix through the kumara with 2 tbsp olive oil. Spread in a roasting dish, sprinkle with 2 tbsp sesame seeds and bake at 220°C for about 25 minutes, turning occasionally until crispy.

Whole Baked Kumara

Kumara baked in their skins develop a wonderful caramelized sweetness. Choose smallish kumara, preferably organically grown. Scrub skins and bake whole at 180°C for about 45-60 minutes until they start to smell aromatic and feel soft when squeezed.

Caramel Roast Pumpkin

Place pumpkin wedges in a roasting dish. Drizzle with olive oil and golden syrup. Season with salt and pepper. Cover and microwave for 5 minutes. Transfer to a hot (220°C) oven to roast for 20 minutes till golden and tender.

Kumara Salad

In a large bowl combine 1kg diced cooked kumara, 1 cup chopped dates, 2 stalks sliced celery, 2 sliced spring onions, flesh of 2 sliced oranges, 1 cup mayonnaise and ¼ cup orange juice mixed with 1 tsp curry powder. Season to taste.

Slow-roasted Tomatoes

Cut 8-10 tomatoes in half, removing cores. Place in a shallow roasting dish. Sprinkle with 1 tbsp brown sugar, 1 tbsp balsamic vinegar and 2 tbsp olive oil. Season with salt and pepper. Roast at 170°C for 1½-2 hours until slightly shrivelled.

Rosemary and Garlic Roast Potatoes

Cut 6 peeled or scrubbed potatoes into smallish pieces, about 3cm. Place in a roasting dish with 2 tbsp olive oil, a sprinkle of fresh chopped rosemary and a little salt. Spread out in a single layer in roasting dish and bake at 220°C for 30 minutes. Add whole garlic cloves and cook another 20-30 minutes until golden and crisp. A little lemon peel is also a good addition with rosemary.

Shirley's Oven Fries

My friend Shirley makes these great crunchy oven fries. They use just a skerrick of oil. Cut 6 potatoes into chips or wedges and place in a large shallow roasting dish. Mix through 1-2 tbsp olive oil and about ¼ cup flour until evenly coated. Spread out and season with salt. Roast at 220°C for about 35 minutes until golden and crisp.

Potato Gratin

Thinly slice 6 big potatoes and layer about 4cm thick in a buttered baking dish. Season with salt and pepper between the layers. Pour over about 3 cups milk to which you have added 2 cloves crushed garlic and a good pinch nutmeg. Use enough milk to almost cover the top layer of potatoes. Dot the top with butter, cover and microwave 10 minutes then uncover and bake 45-50 minutes at 200°C until golden and tender. If you have no microwave, bake for about 1¼ hours.

Quick Pesto Cous Cous

Mix 2½ cups boiling water with 1 tsp salt and 1 tsp crushed garlic. Add 2 cups cous cous – leave to absorb for 10 minutes. Fluff up with a fork and add 3 tbsp pesto, 2 diced tomatoes, 1 finely diced cucumber and ½ cup chopped mint leaves.

Black Bean Salad

In a big pot heat ¾ cup rice vinegar, 2 tbsp sugar, 1 tbsp ground cumin, 3 tbsp Thai sweet chilli sauce, 4 cloves crushed garlic, 1½ tsp each salt and fine black pepper. Mix through 6 cups hot cooked black beans. Add 2 diced red peppers, 3 tomatoes, 5 sliced spring onions, 2 cups cooked corn kernels and ½ cup Asian Pesto ○ or chopped coriander or mint.

Roasted Onions

Cut 2 large red or brown onions in wedges. Leave skins on if organic. Place in a microwave bowl with 2 tbsp olive oil. Cover and cook on 100% power for 8 minutes. Mix in 1 tbsp each brown sugar and rice vinegar. Spread into a roasting dish, season with salt and pepper and roast for 30-40 minutes at 200°C until starting to caramelize.

Red Chinese Slaw

Mix ½ cup very finely sliced Chinese cabbage, 1 grated carrot, 3 sliced spring onions, 1 cup currants or raisins, 2 diced kiwifruit, ½ cup toasted sesame seeds with ¼ cup fresh orange juice, 2 tbsp sesame oil and 2 tsp minced fresh ginger. Season to taste with salt and pepper.

Orzo Salad

Cook a packet of orzo or another dried pasta according to manufacturer's instructions. Drain and toss through ½ cup pesto or Salsa Verde,○ ¼ cup olive oil, 2 tbsp lemon juice. When cool add ½ cup grated parmesan, 1 diced red or yellow pepper, a handful of sliced cooked green beans, and if desired 1-2 sliced spring onions.

Chilli Lemon Cous Cous with Nuts and Grapes

Here's a great side dish for roast or grilled meats or stews. This cous cous can be prepared in advance and served hot or cold. Mix 2½ cups boiling water with the finely grated rind of 1 lemon, 2 tsp Thai sweet chilli sauce and 1 tsp salt. Add 2 cups cous cous and leave to absorb for about 10 minutes. Fluff up with a fork and mix in ½ cup of toasted nuts, eg pistachios, almonds or pinenuts, ½ cup chopped mint or coriander (or a mix of both) and 1 cup chopped grapes. To heat, cover and microwave for 3-4 minutes just before serving.

Speedy Spinach

Wash 2 big bunches of spinach, strip off and discard stems. Heat 2 tbsp olive oil in a large heavy fry-pan, add spinach, season with salt and pepper, cover and cook for 3 minutes until wilted.

Chinese Greens

Cut baby bok choy into quarters lengthwise and wash well. Heat 1 tbsp sesame oil in a wok or pan. Add wet vegetables and a grating of fresh ginger, cover and cook over high heat 2-3 minutes until wilted, stirring occasionally.

Roast Beets and Carrots

Cut 4 peeled beetroot and 5 large peeled carrots into batons the size of a small finger. Place in a roasting dish with 2 tbsp olive oil, 1 tbsp brown sugar, 1 tbsp vinegar, eg balsamic or red wine, and $\frac{1}{2}$ cup fresh orange juice. Season with salt and pepper. Mix to combine evenly and spread out in dish. Roast at 180°C for about 50-60 minutes until tender. Serve hot or cold. Serves 6.

Rocket and Cucumber Salad

Cut a telegraph cucumber into batons the size of a little finger and mix with a couple of handfuls of rocket leaves. Drizzle with a little extra virgin olive oil and the juice of $\frac{1}{2}$ lemon and grind over black pepper.

Pan-fried Beans

Boil trimmed green beans for 2-3 minutes. Drain and cool. When ready to serve place in a fry-pan with 2 tbsp extra virgin olive oil, season with ground black pepper and a little finely grated lemon rind. Fry for 2-3 minutes until starting to brown.

Avocado, Bacon and Banana Salad

This combination of bacon, avocado, banana and spinach is easy to put together and is always popular.

Strip the leaves from a large bunch of washed spinach and break into bite-sized pieces. Toss with $\frac{1}{2}$ cup Favourite Vinaigrette,⊙ then add 3 rashers diced, cooked bacon, 2 firm bananas, thinly sliced and 1 large firm but ripe avocado, cut into wedges. Toss to combine. Serve at once. Serves 4.

Courgette, Mushroom and Olive Salad

This marinated vegetable salad improves over a couple of days in the fridge. Add the tomatoes just before serving. Combine 5 small sliced courgettes, about 20 button mushrooms, wiped, and 1 cup black olives. Mix in 2 tbsp Salsa Verde,⊙ $\frac{1}{4}$ cup olive oil and 2 tbsp red wine vinegar. Leave in the fridge for up to 24 hours. Add a punnet of cherry tomatoes just before serving and season to taste. Serves 6.

Braised Beans, Broccoli and Leeks

Cook individually, or make a combination. Vary quantities to suit. Cut up vegetables into serving sized pieces. Place in a pot with $\frac{1}{2}$ cup water and $\frac{1}{4}$ cup best quality extra virgin olive oil. Season with salt and pepper. Cover and cook gently until vegetables are tender and water has evaporated.

Rice

For every cup of long grain rice add 1$\frac{1}{2}$ cups cold water and $\frac{1}{2}$ tsp salt. Bring to a boil, stir and cover. Reduce heat to lowest level and cook for 12 minutes. Remove from heat and stand another 12 minutes without lifting lid. Rice will still be hot after 20-30 minutes.

A Quick Green Salad

Choose a mixture of salad greens. Wash and dry (if not using at once refrigerate; they will keep for about a week). To serve, place greens in a large bowl, drizzle with a little olive oil, a splash of lemon juice or balsamic vinegar, salt, good pepper and a pinch of sugar. Toss to combine and serve.

DESSERTS

Tiramisu

Strawberry Fool

Fantasy Pavlova

Bella's Berry Trifle

Frozen Chantilly Coconut Cake
with Berry Compote

A Sauce for All Occasions

Panna Cotta

Macadamia and
Apricot Ice Cream

Syllabub

Lemon Mascarpone

3-Bowl Ice Cream

Sweet Feijoa and Ginger Sauce

Spiked Caramel Sauce

Three Great Syrups for Fruit Salad

Dark Rich Chocolate Sauce

Hot Jaffa Sauce

Mother's Old Fashioned
Chocolate Sauce

Berry Coulis

Butterscotch Sauce

The Art of Delicious Fruit Salad

Roasted Pears in Pink Ginger
Syrup

Peaches with
Ginger Crumble

Roasted Peaches with Macaroon
Topping

Baked Bananas with Maple Syrup
and Coconut Cream

Roasted Figs with Raspberries

Slow-baked Apricots with
Cardamoms

Roasted Stonefruits with Berry
Compote

Fruit Crumble with Ginger,
Cardamom and Cashews

Old Fashioned Apple Pie

Rhubarb and Raspberry Pie

Creamy Rice Pudding

Fruit Sponge

Ginger and Pineapple Upside-
down Cake

Tamarillo Clafoutis

Apricot and Orange Soufflés

Orange and Almond Syrup Cake

French Plum Cake

Blueberry and Macadamia Coffee
Cake

Almost Fudgy Chocolate Cake

Surprise Chocolate Cake

Chocolate Truffle Fudge Cake

Spice Trail Biscotti

Panforte

Polenta Cardamom Christmas
Star Biscuits

Chocolate Brownies

Apricot Coconut Slice

Berry Compote

Kish Mish

Classic Chocolate Chip
Cookies

Kisses

Chocolate Truffles

Truffle Variations

Louise Cake

Cool and Creamy

IT'S DIFFICULT TO THINK ABOUT PUDDINGS WITHOUT THINKING ABOUT CREAM. THAT SILKY COOL

SMOOTHNESS MAKES SUCH A SATISFYING FINISH TO THE MEAL.

Mastering Meringues

For best results with meringue, egg whites should be at least 7 days old and at room temperature. Too fresh and the meringue will 'bleed' in syrupy threads. Before you start make sure there is absolutely no yolk in meringue – it won't work if there is.

Meringue Recipe

Using an electric beater, beat together 2 egg whites, 1 cup sugar, 1 tsp malt vinegar and 11/2 tbsp boiling water until the mixture is glossy and very stiff (this will take about 15 minutes). Mix in 1 tsp baking powder. Drop small spoonfuls of the mixture, or pipe it, onto a tray covered with baking paper. Bake at 150°C for about 1 hour, until crisp. Makes 2 dozen meringues.

Previous page: Roasted Peaches with Macaroon Topping

Tiramisu

Be warned, this version is more than mor-eish. Tiramisu is usually made with mascarpone cheese, but for a lighter effect use whipped cream. It benefits from being made a day or two in advance.

To Prepare: 10 minutes plus chilling

> *2 cups cream*
> *1 tbsp icing sugar*
> *1 tsp vanilla essence*
> *100g dark chocolate, chopped*
> *2 tbsp sugar*
> *1 large cup very strong black coffee*
> *¼ cup brandy or cognac*
> *1 chocolate sponge, cut in half horizontally, then sliced into 4cm-thick strips*

Whip the cream to soft peaks with the icing sugar and vanilla. Fold in the chocolate. Dissolve the sugar in the coffee and mix in the brandy. Have a shallow serving dish ready. Quickly pass the sponge fingers one at a time through the coffee mix (don't let them sit in it) and place in a single layer in the base of the dish. Spoon over a third of the cream mixture. Dunk remaining sponge pieces in the coffee mix one at a time, forming another layer on top of the cream mixture. Repeat until the sponge is all used. Top with the rest of the cream mix, spreading it evenly. Sprinkle with sifted cocoa or coffee powder. Refrigerate for at least 1 hour (or up to 12 hours, covered) before serving. Serves 6.

Strawberry Fool

Delicious fruit fools are simple to pre-pare. Choose fruit that purées well and has a good acidity, such as stewed plums apricots or gooseberries; or fresh puréed berries. Allow about 1-1½ cups of fruit purée per 300mls cream.

To Prepare: 10 minutes

> *1 punnet strawberries, hulled*
> *2 tbsp icing sugar*
> *1 tbsp lemon juice*
> *300ml cream, whipped*

Blend the strawberries to a purée with the icing sugar and lemon juice. Fold into the whipped cream. Serves 4.
Variation: Use 50/50 custard and whipped cream.

Fantasy Pavlova

To make a pavlova you really need an electric beater and egg whites that are not too fresh. If they are the pavlova will weep.

To Prepare: 15 minutes

To Cook: 1 hour and 5 minutes

> *6 egg whites, preferably free range, at room temperature*
> *pinch of salt*
> *1½ cups castor sugar*
> *2 tsp cornflour*
> *1 tsp vinegar*

Topping

> *1 cup Berry Compote ✿*
> *3 punnets fresh mixed berries, eg raspberries, strawberries (hulled and halved) and blueberries*

Above: Fantasy Pavlova

Heat the oven to 180°C. Line a baking tray with baking paper and mark a circle about 16cm diameter with a plate. Place the egg whites into the clean bowl of an electric beater. Add the salt and beat until stiff. Slowly add the sugar with the beater running. Beat for about 10 minutes at high speed until the meringue is thick and glossy – it should be thick enough not to fall from the beater. Last of all, whisk in the cornflour and vinegar. Use a big spoon to drop dollops of meringue into the circled area of baking paper. Form into a circle of meringue, making swirls with the spoon on the top rather than flattening to a neat tidy disc. Bake at 180°C (not fan bake) for 5 minutes then reduce oven temperature to 130°C and cook a further hour. Turn off oven and leave pavlova to cool in the oven. Pavlova can be cooked ahead a couple of days and stored in an airtight container, or frozen. To serve, spoon Berry Compote over pavlova and scatter over mixed berries. Serves 8-10.

Bella's Berry Trifle

Another wonderful chilled dessert to make ahead. Mix 250g mascarpone into the cream if you like it richer. Packaged custard and sponge make for a speedy assembly.

To Prepare: 5 minutes
To Cook: 15 minutes

> *250g each frozen blackcurrants and boysenberries*
> *1/2 cup sugar*
> *1/2 cup water*
> *1/2 cup strawberry jam*
> *1/4 cup kirsch or sherry*
> *1 layer of sponge cake*
> *500mls custard*
> *300mls cream*
> *a little sugar and vanilla to sweeten*
> *1 punnet strawberries hulled and sliced and 1 cup canned peach slices*

Optional: 250g mascarpone

Simmer berries with sugar and water for about 15 minutes. Take off the heat and add grog. Strain off fruit and mix with the jam, and put to one side. Get out the serving bowl or dish. Cut sponge into cubes. Quickly dunk each piece, one at a time, into berry liquid, enough to make a single layer in the bottom of the serving dish. If using mascarpone, beat with cream until thick. Otherwise just whip the cream. Fold together the custard and the cream and drizzle about 1/2 over the soaked sponge. Top with about 1/3 sliced berries and peaches, and a little of the cooked jam and berry mix. Repeat with another layer of soaked sponge, more custard cream and more fruit. Chill. When ready to serve, drizzle the last of the jam and fruit mix over the top and scatter with last of the sliced strawberries and if desired some toasted flaked almonds. Serves 6-8.

Frozen Chantilly Coconut Cake with Berry Compote

This is a really easy make-ahead dessert which always wins rave reviews. Once you have made it a few times, think about varying the filling and adding other flavours into the frozen meringue, eg ground toasted hazelnuts, or Christmas fruit mince. You need a springform cake tin with a removable bottom.

To Prepare: 15 minutes
To Freeze: 3-4 hours

> *3 egg whites, at room temperature*
> *pinch salt*
> *1/4 cup sugar*
> *300mls cream*
> *1 tsp vanilla essence*
> *6 meringues, crumbled, or 10-12 crumbled Amaretti biscuits*
> *1/2 cup lightly toasted thread coconut*
> *1 recipe Berry Compote ✿*

Optional: 2 tbsp liqueur of your choice, eg kirsch

Whip egg whites in a very clean bowl with salt until they form soft peaks. Slowly add the sugar and beat until very stiff. Whip cream and vanilla until it holds its shape. Fold in crumbled meringues and coconut. Add some liquer if desired. Spoon mixture into a 20cm cake tin with removable bottom, lined with plastic wrap. Cover and freeze 3-4 hours or until firm. Unmould onto a serving plate and serve in slices. Accompany with Berry Compote. Serves 6-8.
Variations: Layer 1 1/2 cups of boozy Christmas mince or 1 1/2 cups Lemon Curd into the centre of the cake.

A SAUCE FOR ALL OCCASIONS

Berry Compote is a wonderful sauce that will keep in the fridge for several days. You'll find the recipe on page 209. Here are some terrific ways to use it.

- Serve Berry Compote with Lemon Mascarpone and Star Shortbread Biscuits
- Roast peaches or nectarines and pour hot Berry Compote over them
- Serve with ice cream and fresh peaches
- Partner with Fudgy Chocolate Cake

- For special occasions, make Frozen Chantilly Coconut Cake and serve with Berry Compote
- Fold through ice cream and re-freeze
- Spoon chilled Compote over pavlova and scatter with fresh berries
- Mix through fresh fruit salad

Above: Panna Cotta

Using Gelatine

To dissolve gelatine, first soak in a little cold water. Sheets of gelatine can be dissolved in hot liquid without soaking and seem to give a smoother texture. One sheet usually equals 8 grams.

1 tsp powder gelatine equals 5 grams and will set 250mls of liquid to a soft jelly.

Panna Cotta

This silky chilled cream can be flavoured with ginger, vanilla, almond oil or rosewater. Don't overflavour or you will lose its delicate creaminess. This dessert needs at least 4 hours to set.

To Prepare: 5 minutes
To Cook: 5 minutes, including infusing

> *1½ cups cream*
> *1½ cups milk*
> *1 vanilla pod, split, or 1 tsp vanilla essence*
> *⅓ cup castor sugar*
> *3 tsp gelatine, soaked in 2 tbsp warm water*

Bring the cream, milk, vanilla and sugar slowly to the boil so that the vanilla has time to infuse its flavour into the cream. Remove from the heat and take out vanilla pod. Whisk in the soaked gelatine and make sure it has dissolved. Oil six half-cup pudding moulds, or small cups with a flavourless oil or sweet almond oil. Pour mixture into oiled moulds. Cool and refrigerate until set. Serve in moulds or turn out. To remove Panna Cotta from moulds, run a knife around the edge of each mould and dip the base into hot water for a minute before turning out onto serving plates. Serves 6.
Serving Suggestions: *With berries and coulis or fruit compote, with Kish Mish.*⊙

Macadamia and Apricot Ice Cream

This easy ice cream can be adapted with a range of wonderful flavour variants. Favourite combos include macadamia and marmalade and chocolate and raspberry. And it's certainly the easiest ice cream recipe I know of.

To Prepare: 10 minutes

> 1 litre cream, chilled
> 1½ cups sweetened condensed milk
> rind of 1 lemon and 1 orange,
>   finely grated
> 1 tbsp lemon juice
> 1 tsp vanilla essence
> ½ cup apricot jam, melted
> 1 cup toasted macadamia nuts, salt
>   wiped off, roughly chopped

Whip cream until a pourable custard consistency. Using a wooden spoon, fold in condensed milk, then all other ingredients. Place in individual moulds or large mould/container. Freeze. Makes 8-10 small moulds or about 1½ litres.

Syllabub

One of the oldest desserts in the world, originally made by whipping sweetened milk or cream with wine.

To Prepare: 5 minutes

> 1¾ cups icing sugar
> 2 cups cream
> ⅓ cup high quality dry sherry or
>   brandy, etc
> ½ cup lemon juice
> grated rind of 1 lemon

Beat the sugar and cream until it forms soft peaks. Add sherry or brandy and lemon juice and beat just to incorporate. Fold through the rind. Refrigerate and serve very cold. It will keep for 3-4 days. Makes a large bowlful. Delicious with berries and Christmas tart.

Lemon Mascarpone

A very useful, quick and elegant dessert that's great with the Berry Compote and Biscotti or crisp Cardamom Star Biscuits. Make it up a day or two ahead of time.

To Prepare: 10 minutes and 1 hour to marinate

To Cook: 2-3 minutes

> 300g mascarpone
> ¼ cup icing sugar
> 2 tbsp raspberry liqueur or other
>   alcohol of your choice
> 2 tbsp finely chopped mixed peel

Optional: juice of ½ lemon

Whip all ingredients together with a beater until fluffy and well combined. Store in the fridge in a covered container. Flavour improves after 1 day. Mixture will keep for up to 1 week in the fridge. To serve, spoon about 1-2 tbsp of the mixture into a loose pyramid form on individual plates, spoon around berry compote, top with fresh berries and dust with icing sugar. Makes enough for 6-8 servings.

Variations:
Add 2 tbsp finely chopped glacé ginger to mascarpone mix.

3-Bowl Ice Cream

Here's the ice cream we grew up on. In one bowl beat 4 egg whites with 2 tbsp sugar until peaky. In the next, beat 4 yolks with 2 tbsp boiling water and ½ cup sugar until pale, thick and ribbony. In the third bowl, whip 600mls cream until it forms peaks. Fold all three mixtures together with 2 tsp vanilla and up to 1 cup of puréed sweetened fruit, eg stewed feijoa, or plums, or fresh kiwifruit, or other flavours of your choice.

Parfait Perfect

Whipped cream or yoghurt, layered or folded with fresh or dried fruits, nuts, crumbled biscuits or chocolate make heavenly desserts that are easy to assemble. Whipped cream folded with boysenberries, chopped marshmallows and chunks of white chocolate is always popular. If you prefer a lower fat option, use yoghurt or 50:50 yoghurt and cream in place of full cream.

Boysenberry Ginger Parfait

Mix 2 cups fresh or frozen boysenberries (or other berries) with 2 cups fruit yoghurt or 1 cup cream whipped, and 3 crumbled brandy snaps. Sweeten if desired with 2 tbsp runny honey. Serve chilled.

Dessert Sauces

WHEN IT COMES TO DESSERTS, SAUCES DISH UP THE GLAMOUR. KEEP ONE OR TWO ON

HAND IN THE FRIDGE FOR ANYTIME USE.

Greek Yoghurt

Mix 2 cups of plain low-fat yoghurt, 1 cup crème fraîche or sour cream and 2-3 tbsp runny honey to taste. Store in the fridge. It will keep for about a week.

Raspberry Cream Cheese

This makes yummy soft spread or filling to use like lemon honey or custard. Blend 250g cream cheese with ½ cup raspberry jam, ½ cup fresh chopped berries and the juice of ½ lemon. Keep covered in the fridge for a few days.

Ice Cream & Liqueurs

- *Vanilla ice cream with Baileys Irish Cream, grated chocolate and macadamia nuts*
- *Vanilla ice cream with frozen blueberries macerated in cassis and honey*
- *Chocolate ice cream with Crème de Cacao and roasted chocolate-coated coffee beans*
- *Chocolate ice cream and raisins that have been soaked in whisky for an hour or two*
- *Peach or apricot ice cream with poached dried apricots and Amaretto.*

Sweet Feijoa and Ginger Sauce

Try this delicious sauce with ice cream or mix through a fresh fruit salad. If feijoas are not available, then pears can be substituted.

To Prepare: 10 minutes
To Cook: 8 minutes

> *500g feijoas, peeled and diced*
> *¼-½ cup sugar to taste*
> *2 tbsp water*
> *50g crystallised ginger, chopped*
> *2 tsp cornflour mixed with 2 tbsp dry sherry or fruity wine*

Place feijoas, sugar, water and ginger in a microwave container or pot. Cover and cook for 5 minutes, stirring well after 3 minutes. Thicken with cornflour and sherry mixture and cook a further minute. Keeps for about a week in the fridge. Freezes. Makes 2 cups.

Spiked Caramel Sauce

This sauce is delicious with ice cream or as a sauce for baked desserts.

To Prepare: 1 minute
To Cook: 3 minutes

> *150g Caramello chocolate*
> *300ml cream*

Optional: *3 tbsp Irish cream liqueur*

Break up chocolate and place in a microwave bowl with cream. Cook for 3 minutes on medium (60% power), stirring well after 2 minutes. Stir until smooth, then mix in liqueur. Keeps for about a week. Makes 2 cups.

Three Great Syrups for Fruit Salad

- *Lemon Mint Syrup: Heat until dissolved, ¼ cup honey, ¼ cup water, ¼ cup lemon juice, ¼ cup mint and an optional 1 tbsp minced fresh ginger. Keeps for weeks in the fridge.*
- *Strawberry Syrup: Purée half a punnet of strawberries with ½ cup orange juice and 2 tbsp runny honey. Keeps 1-2 days in the fridge.*
- *Passionfruit Syrup: Combine equal amounts of pulp and sugar in a clean jar. Cover and keep in the fridge; it will keep for months.*

Dark Rich Chocolate Sauce

This shiny chocolate sauce is a perfect partner for chocolate cake or ice cream.

To Prepare: 3 minutes
To Cook: 2 minutes

> *20g unsalted butter*
> *½ cup cream*
> *250g bittersweet chocolate*

In a small saucepan heat the butter and cream until the butter melts. Chop the chocolate into small pieces. Incorporate the chocolate into warmed cream and mix until smooth. If you desire a thinner chocolate sauce, add warm water. Makes about 1½ cups. Keeps for about a week refrigerated.

Variation: Use a large Mars bar in place of the chocolate.

Hot Jaffa Sauce

A wickedly rich sauce wonderful for chocolate cake and ice cream.

To Prepare: 5 minutes
To Cook: 5-10 minutes

>   200g dark chocolate pieces
>   juice and finely grated rind of
>   1 orange
>   2 tbsp butter
>   1 tsp vanilla
>   1 egg yolk
>   1/2 cup cream

Place chocolate pieces in a bowl with the juice and rind, butter and vanilla. Heat in a double boiler until melted but not boiling; or microwave on medium power for 2 minutes and stir well until melted. Take off heat if using a pot. Beat in egg yolk and mix in cream while hot. Mixture firms when chilled. Reheat on 50% power to soften. Keeps for about 2 weeks in the fridge.

Mother's Old Fashioned Chocolate Sauce

Here's a fat-free chocolate sauce that is quick, economical and keeps for ages in the fridge.

To Prepare: 2 minutes
To Cook: 5 minutes

>   1 tbsp cornflour
>   3 heaped tbsp cocoa
>   1 cup of sugar
>   1/2 cup boiling water
>   1 generous tbsp golden syrup
>   1 tsp vanilla essence

Combine all ingredients in a microwave bowl or pot. Microwave for 3-4 minutes, stirring every minute; or boil stirring all the time for 5 minutes. Kept in the fridge, it will last for weeks.

Berry Coulis

Thaw a packet of frozen berries and purée to make this tangy sauce.

To Prepare: 5-10 minutes

>   2 cups frozen berries,
>   eg boysenberries or raspberries
>   2 tbsp icing sugar
>   2 tbsp water or orange juice

Purée together until smooth. If desired, pass through a sieve. Store in the fridge until ready to use. Keeps for 3-4 days.

Butterscotch Sauce

This excellent dessert sauce will keep in the fridge for up to a week. It thickens as it cools, so warm it in a microwave or over a low heat in a pot just to soften before serving.

To Prepare: 5 minutes
To Cook: 5 minutes

>   3/4 cup sugar
>   1/4 cup boiling water
>   50g unsalted butter
>   3/4 cup brown sugar
>   1/2 tsp vanilla essence
>   1/2 cup cream

Place sugar in a pot over gentle heat until it turns a deep gold. Carefully pour over boiling water and stir until smooth. Mix in butter and brown sugar, stirring until mixture is smooth and sugar has dissolved. Stir in vanilla and cream. Remove from heat. Excellent with baked or grilled bananas and ice cream. Keeps in the fridge for about a week.

The Art of Delicious Fruit Salad

You don't need a lot of different fruits to make a wonderful fruit salad, even one or two will do.

- *Choose a range of 2-5 different fruits, selecting for quality and freshness.*
- *Peel and slice attractively into pieces about 3-4cm (not too small).*
- *Spoon over about 1 tsp runny honey per serve (or liqueur, etc) and mix through jam, to provide a marinade that allows the fruit to form its own juices.*
- *Add passionfruit pulp if available, or a little fresh orange juice.*
- *Leave to stand for about 1 hour before serving.*
- *Add fruits that brown easily, such as bananas and pears, just before serving.*

Vanilla Pods

When a human baby is first born, the scent that attracts it to its mothers nipple is the same as that of vanilla. Perfume companies have figured that vanilla is a powerful pheromone, but it is in the kitchen that vanilla's subtly exotic flavour comes to the fore. The seed pods of this tropical climbing orchid are supple and intensely aromatic. Store them in your sugar container. Add whole to hot cream or milk to infuse vanilla flavour. After using rinse, dry and return to the sugar jar — they can be re-used a number of times. For maximum flavour, split the pods and scrape the fine black seeds from them.

THE ART OF DELICIOUS FRUIT SALAD

Fresh fruit is a deliciously refreshing way to end a meal and gives balance, especially after something heavy or rich. Choose seasonal fruits and prepare different flavoured syrups to add variety to your fruit salad repertoire.

- Strawberries, icing sugar and Drambuie
- Sliced oranges with Grand Marnier
- Puréed strawberries with mango slices
- Melon, honey and fresh ginger
- Fresh figs and raspberries
- Pears, passionfruit pulp and honey

- Persimmons, kiwifruit, passionfruit and ginger
- Paw paw and lime juice
- Kiwifruit, feijoas and pears with passionfruit syrup
- Fresh pineapple, sliced kiwifruit, passionfruit pulp and sugar
- Strawberry purée with sliced watermelon

Roasted Fruits Full of Flavour

THE INTENSE FLAVOURS AND TEXTURES PRODUCED BY ROASTING ARE WONDERFUL WITH FRUIT. THIS METHOD WORKS BEST WITH DENSE FRUIT LIKE FEIJOAS, PINEAPPLE, TAMARILLOS, STONE AND PIP FRUITS SUCH AS APPLES AND PEARS.

Roasted Pears in Pink Ginger Syrup

Roasting the pears after they have been poached adds an extra depth of flavour and gives them a better texture. For maximum colour and flavour, poach the pears a day or two before you plan to serve them. While they roast, the poaching liquids are reduced so they become glazy. For a party, serve each pear with a wedge of hot gingerbread brushed with a little heated Drambuie (microwave in a jug for 20-30 seconds) and top with a dollop of crème fraîche. Extra Drambuie can be poured over each serving at the table and then flambéed. It's divine.

To Prepare: 15 minutes

To Cook: 30 minutes to poach and 20-30 minutes roasting

> 2 cups sugar
> 4 cups water
> 20 very thin slices fresh ginger
> 1 cinnamon quill
> 1 cup crème de cassis
> about 3-4 tbsp grenadine or raspberry syrup
> 6-8 just ripe pears, peeled with stems intact

Find a pot that will fit the pears snugly in a single layer standing upright. To make the syrup, heat sugar, water, ginger, cinnamon, crème de cassis and grenadine, stirring until sugar has dissolved. Add pears, arranging so they are all submerged as much as possible in the syrup. Cook gently for about 25-30 minutes, turning often. Pears can be prepared to this point, covered and kept in the fridge for up to 2 days in the syrup (it actually improves them). To serve, pre-heat oven to 180°C, lift pears out of syrup and arrange in a shallow baking dish. Bake for 20 minutes. On top of the stove boil poaching liquid hard until it reduces by half and gets thick and syrupy. Serve each pear with a spoonful of hot syrup and some ginger. Serves 6-8.

Above: Roasted Pears in Pink Ginger Syrup

Opposite: Fresh Fruit Salad of Pears, Feijoas and Kiwifruit with Passionfruit Syrup

Magic Macaroon

The macaroon topping used on the roasted peaches is incredibly versatile.

- *Add 1 tsp crushed cardamom seeds or 1 tsp dry ginger to macaroon mixture, fill into a pre-cooked pastry crust and bake at 160°C for 45 minutes.*
- *Pile macaroon mixture onto fresh halved stone fruit and bake at 160°C for 45-50 minutes.*
- *Leave out berries from macaroon mixture and sprinkle over sliced peaches or apricots in a baking dish. Bake at 160°C for 45 minutes.*
- *Omit berries and form mixture into small cookies. Bake at 160°C for 40-45 minutes.*

Tamarillos

Native to South America, tamarillos fruit over the winter months and are not only delicious but a powerhouse of vitamins as well. Like tomatoes, they slip their skins when pricked and dropped in boiling water for a minute or two. After taking off skins, slice fruit and sprinkle with sugar. They form a wonderful juice and macerated in this way can be kept in the fridge for up to a week.

Peaches with Ginger Crumble

This easy crumble is delicious on top of fresh peaches. It's also nice with apricots, or as a topping for cooked apples.

To Prepare: 5 minutes
To Cook: 20 minutes

> *6 fresh peaches, halved and stones removed*
> *4 crushed gingernuts (or 8 crushed amaretti biscuits)*
> *1 tbsp brown sugar*
> *50g butter*

Place the peach halves, cut side up in a baking dish. Combine the gingernuts, sugar and butter and divide over the top of the peaches. Bake at 180°C for about 20 minutes, until the peaches are semi-soft. Serves 6.

Roasted Peaches with Macaroon Topping

This is one of the yummiest ways to cook juicy summer peaches.

To Prepare: 5 minutes
To Cook: 45-50 minutes

> *6 large ripe peaches, eg Golden Queen*

Macaroon Topping
> *1 cup sugar*
> *1 cup cream*
> *4 cups coarse coconut*
> *1/2 tsp vanilla essence*

Optional: half punnet fresh raspberries

Halve peaches and remove stones. Heat cream and sugar until it boils and sugar has dissolved. Remove from heat and mix in coconut and vanilla. Allow to cool and mix in optional berries. Divide over peaches. Bake at 170°C for 45-50 minutes, until peaches are soft. Serves 6.

Baked Bananas with Maple Syrup and Coconut Cream

Baking bananas gives them a wonderfully rich caramel flavour.

To Prepare: 2 minutes
To Cook: 30 minutes

> *6 bananas*
> *1/2 cup maple syrup*
> *250mls thick coconut cream*
> *juice of 1 lime*
> *1 cup roasted cashews*

Bake bananas at 200°C for 30 minutes or until skins burst. Put onto serving plates. Split open as wide as possible. Pour over a spoonful of coconut cream and maple syrup. Squeeze over lime juice and top with chopped cashews.

Roasted Figs with Raspberries

Savour the fig's fleeting season with this sublimely simple dessert. I first made this after an autumn trip to the Neuilly market, where fat glistening figs and late autumn raspberries were irresistible.

To Prepare: 5 minutes
To Cook: 20 minutes

> *8-12 fresh figs*
> *1/4 cup runny honey*
> *2 bay leaves*
> *4-5 whole star anise*

Garnish: 1 punnet fresh raspberries and crème fraîche

Cut a small cross in the bottom of figs. Place in a baking dish and drizzle over honey. Sprinkle bay leaves and star anise around. Bake at 200°C for 20 minutes until figs are soft and juices are starting to caramelise. Serve with fresh raspberries and crème fraîche. Serves 4.

Slow-baked Apricots with Cardamoms

Rich with the flavours of North Africa, these easy apricots make a wonderful dessert partnered with mascarpone or Greek Yoghurt.○

To Prepare: 5 minutes plus
overnight soaking
To Cook: 1 ½ hours

> *250g dried apricots*
> *2 cups water*
> *½ cup sugar*
> *4 cardamom pods crushed lightly*
> *2 cinnamon quills*

Soak dried apricots in water overnight. Drain liquid into a non-reactive oven proof pan, add sugar and crushed cardamoms and bring to a boil. Add apricots and stir to cover. Cover with a lid and bake at 150°C for 1½ hours. Serve at room temperature. Serves 6-8. These will keep in the fridge for over a week.

Roasted Stonefruits with Berry Compote

All kinds of stonefruits as well as pears and apples take well to roasting in this manner.

To Prepare: 5 minutes
To Cook: 40-45 minutes

> *4-6 fresh ripe stonefruit, eg*
> *peaches, apricots, nectarines or*
> *plums*
> *1 tbsp sugar*
> *½ cup water*
> *1 recipe Berry Compote ○*

Place fruit in a shallow roasting dish with water. Sprinkle with sugar. Bake at 200°C for 40-45 minutes until soft and starting to golden. Heat berry compote with any cooking juices. Serve 1 whole hot fruit per person with hot compote spooned over.

Above: Roasted Stonefruits with Berry Compote

Some Like It Hot

PEOPLE THINK YOU'VE GONE TO SO MUCH TROUBLE WHEN YOU GIVE THEM A HOT PUDDING.

THAT OLD FASHIONED COMFORT DELIVERS SUSTENANCE TO BODY AND SOUL.

Fruit Crumble with Ginger, Cardamom and Cashews

There's crumble and then there's CRUMBLE. Cardamom and ginger with the tropical twist of coconut and cashews are a terrific combination in this easy dessert. Try it also with other seasonal fruits available – tamarillo and apple or rhubarb and strawberry. If using frozen berries such as raspberries or boysenberries which release a lot of liquid, thaw and drain before putting into the baking dish.

To Prepare: 10 minutes

To Cook: 45 minutes

> *2 cups cooked apples or 1 x 550g*
> *can apple slices*
> *1 cup fresh or frozen berries, try a*
> *combination of cherries and*
> *redcurrants, drain if frozen*
> *1/4 cup sugar*

Topping
> *1 cup plain flour*
> *1 cup brown sugar*
> *1 1/2 cups rolled oats*
> *1 1/2 tsp cardamom seeds, crushed*
> *1 tsp ground ginger*
> *1 cup coarse thread coconut*
> *150g butter, melted*

Optional: 1 cup raw cashew nuts

Pre-heat oven to 170°C. Mix fruits with sugar. Spread into a 30cm x 35cm baking dish or roasting dish. Place dry ingredients, spices, coconut and optional nuts in a large bowl and mix to combine. Pour over melted butter and mix through. Spread crumble evenly over top of fruit. Bake for 40-45 minutes until golden. Crumble can be assembled ready to cook and refrigerated for several hours before cooking. Serves 8-10.

Old Fashioned Apple Pie

This pie uses 500g of homemade pastry. If preferred, you can use commercial puff pastry.

To Prepare: 10 minutes

To Cook: 30 minutes

Flaky Butter Crust Pastry
> *250g frozen butter*
> *2 cups plain flour*
> *1 tsp baking powder*
> *1 tbsp castor sugar*
> *pinch of salt*
> *2 tbsp iced water*

Filling
> *about 3 cups of cooked apple,*
> *or 2 x 550g cans apple slices*
> *pinch ground cloves or a few whole*
> *cloves*
> *2-3 tbsp sugar*

Optional: 2 tbsp marmalade

Grate frozen butter into combined dry ingredients, add iced water and mix gently, just until dough forms together, and then chill. Roll out onto baking paper to fit the top of a 23-25cm diameter pie dish. Mix apple with cloves and sugar. Add marmalade if you like. Fill the pie dish. Top with pastry crust, brush with milk or beaten egg and bake at 200°C for 30 minutes until golden. Serves 6-8.

Crushed Cardamom

To crush cardamom seeds, grind whole pods in a mortar and pestle. Discard pods and use the seeds. Crushed cardamom has much more flavour than cardamom powder.

To Fold a Mixture

Folding is the name given to the technique of mixing where ingredients are slowly combined in a scooping motion. Using a large wide spoon or paddle make deep scoops into the mixture, lift and turn to fold the ingredients gently together.

Rhubarb and Raspberry Pie

Nostalgia reigns with this satisfying dessert pie. Grating a third of the pastry over the top gives a great look and texture. However, if preferred, the filling can be sandwiched in pastry more conventionally like a shortcake.

To Prepare: 20 minutes

To Cook: 1 hours plus 30 minutes chilling for pastry

> 1 recipe Crunchy Sweet Pastry (see side panel) or 400g sweet shortcrust pastry

Filling

> 500g rhubarb, chopped
> ¼ cup water
> ½ cup sugar
> 2 tsp finely grated lemon rind
> 250g raspberries (fresh or frozen)
> 2 tsp cornflour

Prepare pastry or use commercial pastry. Press ⅔ of pastry into a 24cm pie dish to cover base and sides. Chill with remaining ⅓ of pastry. While pastry chills, prepare the filling. Place rhubarb, water and sugar in a saucepan and cook over a medium heat for 6-8 minutes, until rhubarb is tender. Cool. When cold, gently fold in lemon rind, raspberries and cornflour mixed with a little water. Spoon filling over pastry base. Grate the remaining ⅓ of pastry over top of filling. Bake at 180°C for 50-60 minutes until golden. Serve warm, sprinkled with icing sugar. Serves 6.

Above: Rhubarb and Raspberry Pie

Crunchy Sweet Pastry

For a crunchy sweet pastry, combine in the bowl of a food processor 2 cups of plain flour, ¼ cup sugar and a pinch of salt. Add 125g of diced unsalted butter at room temperature and 2 lightly beaten eggs. Whizz ingredients together for about 30 seconds, or mix with a fork. Turn onto a lightly floured surface and knead briefly. Chill. Makes enough for a 26cm pie dish.

Creamy Rice Pudding

Here's one for the stove top. Short grain rice is the key to creamy rice pudding. Stirring the rice as it cooks also helps to create a creamy result.

To Prepare: 5 minutes

To Cook: 20 minutes

> 4 cups milk
> 1 cup short grain rice
> 3 tbsp honey or sugar
> finely grated rind of $^1/_2$ a lemon
> generous pinch nutmeg
> 1 tsp vanilla essence
> *Optional:* 2-3 tbsp cream, $^1/_3$ cup sultanas
>   or raisins

Place all the ingredients in a saucepan and stir over a low heat for about 20 minutes, until the mixture is creamy and the rice is cooked through. Serve hot or cold.
To microwave, mix in $1^1/_2$ tbsp cornflour with the milk and place with all other ingredients in a large microwave bowl. Cover tightly and cook at 70% power for 8 minutes, stirring twice. Reduce power to 50% and cook a further 11 minutes, stirring every 3 minutes, until the rice is cooked and creamy. Serve hot or cold. Serves 4.

Fruit Sponge

When we were kids, every evening meal finished with pudding. Light warm fruit sponges like this were among our cold weather favourites. Serve it with custard or lightly whipped cream.

To Prepare: 5 minutes

To Cook: 30 minutes

> about 2-3 cups cooked
>   sweetened fruit
> 2 eggs
> 2 heaped tbsp sugar
> 2 tbsp plain flour
> 1 tsp baking powder

Pre-heat oven to 190°C. Place fruit in a shallow baking dish and put into oven to heat while preparing sponge. Beat the eggs and sugar until very thick and creamy. Add flour and baking powder and fold in lightly. Pour over hot fruit. Bake for 30 minutes until golden.
Serves 4-6.

Ginger and Pineapple Upside-down Cake

Whizzed together in a blender, this makes a great pudding. Vary the fruit used – pears are also nice.

To Prepare: 15 minutes

To Cook: 45 minutes

> 2 cups self-raising flour
> 1 tsp baking soda
> finely grated rind of 1 orange
> 2 eggs
> 1 cup milk
> $^3/_4$ cup brown sugar
> $^1/_3$ cup golden syrup
> $^1/_2$ cup salad oil
> 1 tsp ground ginger
> *Topping*
> 50g butter, melted
> $^1/_2$ cup brown sugar
> 2 tbsp golden syrup
> 225g can pineapple rings, drained
> $^1/_2$ cup chopped glace ginger

Pre-heat oven to 180°C. Place all ingredients for cake batter in a blender or mixer bowl and quickly process until smooth. Melt topping butter with sugar and golden syrup. Spread over the base of a 23cm loose-bottomed cake tin. Arrange pineapple and ginger on top of sugar. Pour over batter. Bake at 180°C for 45 minutes. Serves 6-8.

Crème Anglaise

Beat together 3 egg yolks, 2 tbsp sugar and 1 tbsp cornflour. Heat 2 cups of milk with one vanilla pod or 1 tsp vanilla essence. Whisk in the beaten yolk mixture, stirring over low heat until mixture is thick enough to easily coat the back of a wooden spoon. Lay a piece of buttered paper on the surface to cover and stop a skin forming. Store in the fridge.

Meringue Topping

Beat 2 egg whites to soft peaks using an electric or hand beater. Gradually add $^1/_2$ cup castor sugar until well combined and mixture is shiny and glossy. Use as a topping for dessert pies. Bake at 200°C for about 10 minutes until lightly golden.

Tamarillo Clafoutis

Essentially a light pancake batter baked over fruit, this classic French dessert lends itself well to any kind of tasty fruit.

To Prepare: 10 minutes

To Cook: 25-30 minutes

Batter

> 1/2 *cup plain flour*
>
> *pinch salt*
>
> 1/2 *tsp baking powder*
>
> 1/4 *cup sugar*
>
> *3 eggs*
>
> *1 cup milk*
>
> *1 tsp vanilla essence*

Fruit Filling

> 30g *butter, melted*
>
> *6 peeled and sliced tamarillos*
>
> *1 tbsp sugar*

Beat together the batter ingredients. Preheat a sponge roll tin or small roasting dish with the butter for 5 minutes at 220°C. Peel and slice the tamarillos or other fruit. Arrange in the heated dish and quickly pour over the batter. Sprinkle over 1 tbsp sugar and bake at 220°C for 12-15 minutes, until the clafoutis is puffed, golden and cooked through. To test if cooked, push a skewer into the centre of the clafoutis; if it comes out clean the mixture is cooked. Serve warm or at room temperature. Clafoutis is also delicious made with apples – add 1 tsp cinnamon to the batter mixture. Serves 6.

Variations:

- *In place of tamarillos, use 2 cups pitted cherries(fresh, frozen or bottled)*
- *Use any stone fruit or berry fruit or sliced feijoas*
- *Add 1 tbsp of grated root ginger to the cake batter, especially good with apple or apple and rhubarb.*

Apricot and Orange Soufflés

These easy, foolproof, light as air soufflés involve simply folding a hot fruit purée through stiffly whipped egg whites.

To Prepare: 10 minutes plus overnight soaking

To Cook: 10 minutes

> 150g *dried apricots*
>
> 1/2 *cup white wine*
>
> 1/2 *cup orange juice*
>
> *finely grated rind of 1 orange*
>
> *2 tbsp honey*
>
> *2 egg whites*
>
> *2 tbsp sugar*

Soak apricots overnight in the wine, orange juice and rind and honey. Cook them in their soaking liquid until soft, then purée them in their liquid and add extra sugar if desired to taste. About 10 minutes before serving, heat the purée to almost boiling. Whisk the egg whites stiffly with 2 tbsp sugar. Divide 1/4 of purée between 6 small buttered soufflé dishes. Fold 3/4 of the hot purée into whites with a metal spoon until mixture is well combined. Work quickly. Spoon mixture into dishes, top each with a few slivered almonds and bake at 200°C for 10 minutes or until they are lightly golden and well risen. Serve immediately. Serves 6.

Variations:

- *Prune Soufflés: Use dried pitted prunes in place of apricots.*
- *Raspberry Soufflés: Purée 1 cup raspberries with 1 cup raspberry jam.*

Filo Fruit Parcels

The wonderfully pliable texture of fresh filo pastry means you can fold or scrunch it into any shape you like. Instead of forming neat parcels, try this easy way. Brush or spray a sheet of filo pastry with melted butter or cooking spray oil. Scrunch up to form a nest shape. Spoon about 2 3 tbsp cooked, sweetened fruit into the centre, dust with sugar and bake at 190°C for 12-15 minutes until golden.

Filo Filling Combinations

- *Stewed feijoas and ginger*
- *Cooked apples, cinnamon, cloves and pistachio nuts*
- *Sliced, cooked plum halves with a pinch of 5-spice powder*
- *Canned peach slices with coconuts and mixed spice*

Let Them Eat Cake

PEOPLE WHO DON'T BAKE THINK CAKES ARE HARD WORK. THEY ARE NOT, YOU JUST NEED TO BE ASTUTE ABOUT FOLLOWING THE RECIPE AND MEASURING CAREFULLY. WITH A CAKE IN THE TINS ALL THE WORK IS DONE AND A DELICIOUS DESSERT IS JUST A MATTER OF 'SLICE AND SERVE'.

Above: Orange and Almond Syrup Cake

Orange and Almond Syrup Cake

The syrup cakes of Greece and Turkey are always fine textured and moist thanks to semolina and ground nuts, and a hot syrup poured over once they are cooked.

To Prepare: 10 minutes
To Cook: 30-35 minutes

3/4 cup self-raising flour
1/2 cup semolina
1 cup ground almonds
125g unsalted butter
1 cup castor sugar
finely grated rind of orange,
* no pith*
1 tsp vanilla essence
1 tbsp rum or brandy
3 eggs
60mls orange juice
about 20 blanched toasted almonds

Syrup

1/2 cup water
1/4 cup orange juice
1/2 cup sugar
finely grated rind of 1/2 orange,
* no pith*
1/2 cinnamon quills
3 whole cloves

Pre-heat oven to 180°C. Grease a 23cm cake tin. In a mixing bowl, combine the flour, semolina and almonds. In another bowl, beat together butter and castor sugar until creamy. Beat in eggs one at a time, stir in half the flour mixture then the orange juice, vanilla and rum or brandy. Stir in remaining flour, mixing to evenly combine. Pour mixture into the greased tin, top with almonds and bake for 30-35 minutes until a skewer comes out clean. While the cake cooks, make the syrup. Place all ingredients in a pot and bring to a boil, stirring to dissolve sugar. Simmer 10 minutes. Strain off solids. When the cake comes out of the oven pour the syrup over it evenly. Leave for 5 minutes, before turning out onto a serving plate. Keep in the fridge. Serves 8-10.

French Plum Cake

This great recipe makes two moist fruity dessert cakes or one huge one, which can be cooked in a roasting pan. They freeze well.

To Prepare: 20 minutes
To Cook: 60-65 minutes

> 6-8 fresh plums or other stonefruit
> 3 tbsp sugar
> 300g butter
> 1½ cups sugar
> 3 eggs
> finely grated rind of ½ lemon
> 1 tsp vanilla essence
> 1 cup milk
> 3½ cups high grade flour
> 1 tsp baking powder

Pre-heat oven to 180°C. Slice plums into a basin and sprinkle with 3 tbsp sugar. Toss and leave to sit while preparing cake. Cream together butter and sugar. Add eggs, lemon rind and vanilla essence. Stir in milk, flour and baking powder. Divide batter between two baking paper lined springform tins or a large roasting dish.

Arrange plums on top. Bake at 180°C for 60-65 minutes or until a skewer inserted into the centre of the cake comes out clean. The fruit will sink into the cake as it cooks. Freeze if not using the same day. Use other fruits as available. Each cake serves 6-8 people.

Blueberry & Macadamia Coffee Cake

Unlike many coffee-style cakes, this one keeps well for a few days. You might like to try it with an apricot and walnut topping, or almonds and raspberries.

To Prepare: 20 minutes
To Cook: 60-65 minutes

Topping
> ⅔ cup plain flour
> ½ cup tightly packed brown sugar
> 125g cold butter, chopped
> ½-1 cup macadamia nuts, chopped

Cake
> 125g butter, softened
> ⅔ cup sugar
> 1 egg
> 1 tsp vanilla essence
> 1¾ cups self-raising flour
> ½ cup milk
> 1 punnet blueberries,
>   or blackcurrants

Pre-heat oven to 180°C. Grease a 23cm cake tin. Make topping. Mix flour and brown sugar and rub in butter until mixture resembles fine crumbs. Mix in nuts. Put to one side. To prepare cake, beat together butter and sugar until creamy. Beat in egg and vanilla. Mix in flour and milk and combine evenly. Spread into prepared cake tin and sprinkle over berries and then the topping. Bake for 40-50 minutes until a skewer inserted into the middle comes out clean. Stand 15 minutes before turning out of the tin. Allow to cool before cutting. Serves 8-10.

Cooking Containers for Baking

Different cooking containers will absorb and transmit heat differently resulting in variations in cooking times. Metal is the best conductor of heat (and cold) and tends to bake pies, cakes, batters, etc more quickly than a porcelain or Pyrex surface.

How to Stop Cakes Sticking

Before the arrival of baking paper people used old butter papers to line cake tins to prevent cakes sticking. Whichever you choose, it is worth taking a little extra time to line cake tins before filling. Cut the bottom shape to fit the tin, and use a long strip to line sides. This avoids the need to butter the tin.

How to Blanch and Toast Almonds

Pour boiling water over almonds and leave to cool. Pinch at one end to pop off skins. Then toast in a large oven tray at 180°C for 10-15 minutes until golden.

Almost Fudgy
Chocolate Cake

If you love chocolate cake, then you'll probably eat all of this rich, moist almost fudgy cake. I like it so much that I make double and freeze one. For a party, sandwich cakes with chocolate mousse. You can freeze this too.

To Prepare: 15 minutes
To Cook: 1 hour

> 200g dark chocolate
> 200g butter
> 1/4 cup strong coffee
> 6 eggs
> 1 1/2 cup sugar
> 2 tsp vanilla essence
> 1 cup plain flour
> icing sugar to dust, with shreds of
>   dark chocolate and cocoa
>   powder

Optional: 1 cup raisins

Pre-heat oven to 180°C. Place dark chocolate and butter with coffee over gentle heat until melted, but not too hot. Beat or blend eggs and sugar together until thick, foamy and pale yellow – about 5-7 minutes. Add vanilla. Gradually beat in chocolate mixture. Fold in flour, then add raisins. Pour mixture into 2 greased 20-23cm cake tins and bake at 180°C for about 1 hour. Cool in tin, then turn onto a serving platter and dust with icing sugar, garnish with shreds of dark chocolate and dust with cocoa. Serves 6-8. If desired, sandwich cakes with chocolate mousse and serve, dusted with cocoa. Cakes freeze well, both filled and unfilled.

Surprise Chocolate Cake

Vegetables, whether they be carrots, courgettes or pumpkins, add moisture and some great nutrition to cakes and muffins without any discernible flavour. If there's a vegephobe in your life it's a great way to sneak in the goodies.

To Prepare: 15 minutes
To Cook: 50 minutes

> 3 eggs
> 1 cup brown sugar
> 1/2 cup white sugar
> 1 tsp vanilla essence
> 125g butter, softened
> 1/2 cup plain, unsweetened yoghurt
> 250g peeled, seeded pumpkin,
>   grated
> 250g choc bits or chips
> 2 1/2 cups flour
> 1/4 cup cocoa
> 2 tsp baking soda
> 1 tsp cinnamon
> 1/2 tsp mixed spice

In a food processor or using a beater, mix together the eggs, sugars and vanilla. Add the butter and yoghurt, blending until smooth. Fold in the pumpkin and chocolate bits and combined dry ingredients. Mix gently to combine. Spread into a greased 26cm tin and bake at 180°C for about 50 minutes. Allow to cool before turning out and icing. Serves 8. Keep in the fridge.

Tips for melting chocolate

Chocolate is capricious stuff. It hates water and getting too hot. Heat it gently in the microwave in 30 second bursts or in a bowl over a pot of boiling water. Don't allow it to come into contact with any water or its texture will change and it will seize into clumps.

Chocolate Mousse

A heady mousse to savour on its own or as a filling. Whisk 2 eggs in a bowl over a pot of hot water until frothy; add liqueur. Remove bowl from water and stir eggs into 200g melted chocolate. Cool. Beat 600ml cream to soft peaks. Fold in 1/3 of cream, then the rest. Chill for one hour in the refrigerator. Serves 6-8. You can also add 2-3 tbsp of your favourite liqueur after the cream.

Opposite: Almost Fudgy Chocolate Cake sandwiched with Chocolate Mousse.

Sweet Treats

SOMETIMES AT THE END OF A MEAL ALL YOU FEEL LIKE IS SOME SMALL SWEET MORSEL.

THESE FAVOURITE AFTER DINNER TREATS CAN ALL BE MADE AND STORED.

Above: Chocolate Truffle Fudge Cake

Chocolate Truffle Fudge Cake

A fast track to someone's heart, this fabulous fudgy slice from my friend Louise Brankin is seriously, wickedly divine.

To Prepare: 10 minutes
To Cook: 10 minutes, plus 1 hour setting time

> *125g butter*
> *¼ cup castor sugar*
> *2 tbsp golden syrup*
> *2 tbsp milk*
> *2 tbsp drinking chocolate*
> *1 tbsp cocoa*
> *1 pkt plain sweet biscuits, crushed*
> *1½ cups chocolate cake crumbs or crumbed chocolate sponge*
> *nip of whisky or rum*
> *60g cherries, chopped*
> *⅓ cup raisins*
> *250g dark chocolate melted, for icing*

Heat butter, sugar, milk and syrup. Add drinking chocolate, cocoa and ½ biscuits and mix. Add remaining ingredients and mix. Press into 20cm sandwich tin or flan dish. Melt dark chocolate and spread over to ice. Allow to set. Cut with a sharp hot knife. Store in the fridge in a sealed container. Makes about 30 small pieces.

Spice Trail Biscotti

Biscotti are always double-baked. Slice thinly into biscuits or risk breaking teeth! This excellent recipe contains no added fat and will keep crisp in an airtight container for weeks.

To Prepare: 10 minutes
To Cook: 35-45 minutes

> 500g plain flour
> 350g castor sugar
> pinch salt
> 1 tsp baking powder
> 1 sprig rosemary leaves, roughly chopped
> finely grated rind of 1 orange and 1 lemon
> 1 tsp fennel seeds
> 4 eggs, lightly beaten
> 1/4 tsp vanilla essence
> 75g pistachio nuts

Pre-heat oven to 200°C. Mix flour, castor sugar, salt, baking powder, rosemary, citrus rinds and fennel seeds in a cake mixer bowl. Mix well. Add the eggs, vanilla essence and nuts. Mix to form a sticky dough. Divide into three pieces. Lightly flour the bench and roll each piece into a log 4cm wide. Place on greased baking sheets and bake for approximately 25-30 minutes or until firm and pale gold. Allow to cool slightly.
Cut diagonally into long thin cookies. Lay out on baking trays and return to oven for 10-15 minutes to dry, turning over once. Cool on wire racks. Store in an airtight container. Makes about 60.

Panforte

This dense rich Italian cake will keep for weeks in a sealed container. Serve very thin slices. Great at Christmas.

To Prepare: 15 minutes
To Cook: about 35 minutes

> 1 cup almonds, toasted and very roughly chopped
> 1 cup hazelnuts, toasted, skinned and halved
> 2 1/2 cups (combined amount) of dried fruit, eg mixed peel, raisins and chopped dried figs
> 2/3 cup plain flour
> 2 tbsp cocoa
> 1 tsp cinnamon
> 60g dark chocolate
> 1/2 cup honey
> 1/2 cup sugar
> icing sugar to dust

Combine nuts, peel, raisins and chopped dried figs. Mix through the flour, cocoa and cinnamon. Heat honey and sugar in a saucepan; boil until it reaches 'soft ball' stage. Add chopped chocolate and stir until chocolate is melted and mixture is smooth. Pour into dry ingredients and quickly stir until the whole mix is combined, using a very strong wooden spoon. Press into a well greased or baking paper lined 20cm round cake tin, preferably shallow and with a removable bottom. Bake for approximately 35 minutes in 150°C oven until set. Remove from tin while still warm. When cool, dust liberally with icing sugar. Store in an airtight container.

To Crumb Sponge Cakes or Sponge

Like bread, it is best if cakes or sponges are crumbed when slightly stale. Rub surface of cake to release small crumbs.

'Soft ball' Sugar

When you make toffee, you boil sugar until it forms a hard ball when dropped into cold water. Before this, sugar forms soft balls and at this stage is ideal for panforte. To test the stage sugar is at, drop a small amount into a glass of cold water, wait a few seconds then press between your fingers. If mixture moulds into a soft ball, it is ready.

A great dessert biscuit to serve with coffee, these tasty cookies will keep fresh in an airtight container for weeks.

To Prepare: 10 minutes
To Cook: 30 minutes

> 250g butter
> 125g icing sugar
> 250g high grade flour
> 50g custard powder
> 50g polenta or corn grits, or coarse cornmeal
> 1 tsp crushed cardamom seeds
> finely grated rind of 1 lemon

Cream butter and sugar until fluffy. Add all other ingredients and mix until it forms a ball. Press out onto a piece of baking paper or plastic wrap and chill for about 30 minutes, then roll out to 1.5cm thickness. Use a cutter to cut shapes, eg stars. Place on a greased baking tray and bake in a pre-heated 150°C oven for about 30 minutes or until pale gold. Remove from tray and cool on a baking rack. They will keep fresh for weeks stored in an airtight container. Makes about 30 medium stars.

Chocolate Brownies

These yummy brownies can be varied by adding extra flavours such as peppermint essence, finely grated orange rind, or other nuts such as macadamias, hazelnuts or almonds.

To Prepare: 20 minutes
To Cook: 35 minutes

> 225g butter
> 200g dark chocolate
> 2 cups sugar
> 4 eggs
> $1\frac{1}{4}$ tsp vanilla essence
> $1\frac{1}{2}$ cups plain flour
> $\frac{1}{2}$ cup cocoa, sieved
> $1\frac{1}{2}$ cups walnuts, roughly chopped

Brownie Topping
> 200g melted dark chocolate

Melt butter and chocolate over a low heat. Combine melted chocolate with sugar. Add eggs, one at a time, beating well after each addition. Stir in vanilla essence. Mix in flour, cocoa and walnuts until evenly combined. Pour into a greased 30cm x 24cm baking tin. Bake at 180°C for 35 minutes until set. Cool. Spread over melted chocolate. Allow to set then cut in squares and lift carefully from baking tin. Makes about 30 pieces.

Apricot Coconut Slice

The combination of apricots and coconut in this easy, no-cook slice keeps it from tasting too rich. Other dried fruits can also be used, eg figs or raisins.

To Prepare: 20 minutes plus setting time

> 100g butter
> $\frac{3}{4}$ cup sweetened condensed milk
> 375g plain sweet biscuits, crushed to fine crumbs
> 150g dried apricots, finely chopped
> 1 cup desiccated coconut
> 2 tbsp lemon juice

Icing
> 50g butter
> 3 tbsp boiling water
> 1 tsp lemon juice
> $3\frac{1}{2}$ cups icing sugar

Melt butter and condensed milk. Bring to boil. Simmer for 2 minutes. Remove from heat. Add crushed biscuits, apricots, coconut and lemon juice. Mix well. Press into a 30cm x 24cm baking tin. Refrigerate until set, then ice. Melt butter and mix with boiling water, lemon and icing sugar to a smooth consistency. Spread over base. Cut into pieces and store in a cool place in an airtight container. Makes about 24 slices.

Crumbing Biscuits

You need to be careful when crumbing biscuits in the blender, as they get pasty if over processed. Put biscuits into a clean plastic bag and pulverise with a rolling pin.

Shortbread

You can make melt-in-the-mouth traditional shortbread simply by omitting the polenta, cardamom seeds and lemon rind from the Polenta Cardamom Christmas Star Biscuits recipe. Prepare the same way and cook for 30 minutes.

Chocolate Peppermint Slice

To the Apricot Coconut Slice base mixture of butter, brown sugar, condensed milk and biscuit crumbs, add 1 cup coconut, 1/4 cup cocoa, 1 tsp vanilla essence and 1/2 tsp peppermint essence. Ice with 200g melted dark chocolate.

Berry Compote

This easy mixture makes a great sauce for pavlovas, meringues, ice cream and flavoured mascarpone.

To Prepare: 10 minutes
To Cook: 20 minutes

> *3 cups mixed frozen berries,*
> *eg boysenberries, blueberries*
> *1 cup sugar*
> *1 vanilla pod*
> *2 bay leaves*

Heat all ingredients together in a stainless pot, stirring until sugar is dissolved. Simmer about 15-20 minutes until mixture has reduced and is very slightly syrupy. Lift out vanilla pod and bay leaves. Serve warm, sauce re-heats well. Makes enough for 8-10 servings.

Kish Mish

Dried fruits swollen with the heady flavour of alcohol are a wonderful indulgence. Keep in the fridge and they will last for months.

To Prepare: 5 minutes plus overnight soaking
To Cook: 25 minutes

> *300g dried apricots*
> *300g dried pears*
> *300g dried figs*
> *300g raisins*
> *water to soak*
> *1/2 cup honey*
> *2 cinnamon quills*
> *rind of 1 lemon*
> *2 cups brandy*

Cover the dried fruits with the water and soak overnight. Place in a pot with the liquid, add the honey, cinnamon and lemon rind and simmer slowly about 20 minutes, until the fruit is soft. Allow to cool, then mix in the brandy. Spoon into jars and top up with syrup. Cover with tight lids. Store in the refrigerator. Serve well chilled with whipped cream.
Makes 4 medium jars.

Above: Polenta Cardamom Christmas Star Biscuits

Coffee

Freshly roasted beans make the best coffee. Store them in the fridge or freezer and grind to order. You don't need a fancy machine to make good coffee – the Italian stove-top espresso pots work really well. Use your old plunger machine to froth up the hot milk. And have you ever noticed how no one in Europe seems to suffer from caffeine insomnia? The high roasting temperature of beans for espresso causes more of the caffeine to be burnt off.

Classic Chocolate Chip Cookies

The trick to these buttery cookies is the nuggets of chocolate – created by chopping chocolate roughly. The mixture is very soft; chilling it slightly before shaping makes it easier to work with.

To Prepare: 10 minutes

To Cook: 15-20 minutes

> 500g butter
> 1 cup sugar
> 6 tbsp sweetened condensed milk
> few drops vanilla essence
> 4¹/₂ cups plain flour
> 4 tsp baking powder
> 500g Energy chocolate, hand-chopped into chunks, not too small

Pre-heat oven to 170°C. Beat together the butter and sugar until creamy. Beat in the condensed milk and vanilla essence. Stir in dry ingredients and chopped chocolate. Chill. Roll into large walnut-sized balls. Place on cold, greased oven trays, allowing some room to flatten. Flatten with the palm of your hand. Bake at 170°C for 15-20 minutes until lightly golden. Cool, then remove from trays and store in an airtight container. Makes about 70 biscuits.

Kisses

These are a traditional Christmas favourite but they keep so well, and taste so divine, it's nice to eat them year round.

To Prepare: 5 minutes

To cook: 15 minutes

> 1¹/₂ cups sweetened condensed milk
> 1 cup coconut
> 1 cup each of dates, walnuts and raisins
> ¹/₄ cup preserved ginger
> 5-8 dried figs
> extra coconut for coating

Mince the fruits and nuts and mix with condensed milk and coconut. Shape into small balls, roll in extra coconut, forming into little pyramids. Place on a baking tray and bake at 160°C for about 25 minutes until lightly golden. Stored in an airtight container, they will keep for weeks. Makes about 40 Kisses.

Above: Kisses

Creaming Butter and Sugar

'Creaming' is the name given to the method of beating butter and sugar together, which is often the first step in cake and biscuit making. This incorporates air bubbles into the fat and is the vital step for volume and lightness. The butter needs to be softened so it will become creamy when beaten with sugar. The butter must not be melted.

Chocolate Truffles

These fresh cream truffles make a wonderful after dinner treat or Christmas gift.

To Prepare: 10 minutes

> 200ml cream
> 50g unsalted butter
> 1/4 cup liqueur of your choice
> 450g dark chocolate pieces,
>   preferably Belgian, or white
>   chocolate
> dark or white chocolate or cocoa
>   for dipping

Melt cream and butter then remove it from the heat and allow to cool slightly. Mix in the liqueur and any other flavourings of your choice, then add the broken chocolate and stir until the mixture is smooth. Refrigerate until firm enough to roll into balls. Form into small balls then chill again before dipping into either melted chocolate or rolling in cocoa or ground nuts. Makes 30-36.

Truffle Variations

- **Grand Marnier:** *Use Grand Marnier liqueur and dust with cocoa. Garnish with crystallised orange rind.*
- **Crème de Menthe:** *Use Crème de Menthe liqueur and roll in toasted ground hazelnuts or top with sliced dried fruits.*
- **Baileys Irish Cream:** *Use Baileys and dip into white chocolate, top with half a pistachio nut.*
- **Supreme:** *Use white chocolate for the mixture, add 1/2 cup sultanas and dip into white chocolate. Garnish with a hazelnut.*

Louise Cake

Crisp shortbread topped with jam and a rough coconut meringue that keeps well.

To Prepare: 10 minutes

To Cook: 40 minutes

Base

> 1 3/4 cups white sugar
> 225g butter
> 4 eggs, separated
> 3 cups plain flour
> 2 tsp baking powder
> 1 tsp vanilla essence

Topping

> 1 cup raspberry jam
> 1 cup white sugar
> 1 cup coconut

Pre-heat oven to 160°C. Beat the first quantity of white sugar with butter until creamy. Mix in the egg yolks and then add the flour, baking powder and essence. Press this mixture into 2 medium sponge roll tins lined with baking paper, or into a large, lined roasting pan. Spread raw base with raspberry jam. Using a clean beater, beat egg whites to soft peaks, then beat in second measure of sugar until mix forms a glossy meringue. Fold in coconut and spread over jam base. Bake at 160°C for about 1 hour until crisp and golden. Cut in pieces while warm. Makes 40 pieces. Store in an airtight container.

Walnut Meringue Pie

Prepare base as for Louise Cake, adding 1 tsp almond essence in with vanilla. For topping, beat the 4 egg whites stiffly and beat in 1 1/2 cups brown sugar and 1 cup finely chopped walnuts. Spread over raw base. Decorate with 1/2 cup walnut halves and bake as for Louise Cake.

Below: Louise Cake

Glossary

Al dente – Cook, usually pasta or noodles, until tender but with some resistance.

Baste – Spoon or brush over the surface of cooking meats, fruits and vegetables, either pan juices, glazes, butter or marinades. Its purpose is to keep food moist, add flavour and sometimes develop a glaze.

Batter – A liquid flour mixture used for coating, fritters and pancakes. Usually fried.

Blind baking – Pies with pastry bases are often partially cooked before filling. In order to stop the pastry rising or collapsing at the sides, a cover of tinfoil or baking paper is placed over the top of the pastry shell and weighed down. You can buy baking beans to do this or use rice or dried beans.

Boil hard – Cook over high temperature in water, stock or some other liquid so the mixture boils quickly with lots of bubbles. Often used to reduce and concentrate flavours.

Braise – A slow method of cooking which combines stewing, steaming and roasting in a covered pan. Can be done on the top of the stove or in the oven.

Bruschetta – Lightly grilled slices of rustic Italian country bread, sometimes rubbed with garlic or brushed with olive oil.

Chicken supremes – Chicken breasts with trimmed wing bone attached.

Chop – Cut into small even-sized pieces.

Coat – Cover the outer surface with flour, breadcrumbs or batter to provide protection and flavour.

Crimp – Use your finger and thumb to pinch pastry together to seal pastry and form a fluted edge as well.

Crispy noodles – Deep-fried noodles.

Crush (garlic) – Peel the cloves of garlic, cut them with a wide knife then chop very finely until almost a paste.

Deep-fry – A method where food is fully immersed in hot oil or fat to cook.

Dice – Cut into 1cm cubes.

Drain – Remove surplus liquid either with a sieve or colander or on absorbent paper.

Dredge – Apply a coating of flour or sugar to the surface of food. Most easily done in a bag.

Finely chop – Cut into $\frac{1}{2}$-1cm pieces.

Finely grate – Use the fine edge of a grater or a zesting tool to get fine gratings. Used mostly for parmesan cheese or citrus peel. In the case of citrus peels, take care not to grate past outer skin as the white pith underneath is bitter.

Flavour paste – A paste which can be pesto, olive paste, sun-dried tomato paste, or simply a purée of herbs with a little oil.

Florets – The small tips of broccoli or cauliflower.

Fold – Usually used for light mixtures with stiffly beaten egg whites. Very gently combine mixtures with a large scooping motion, using a big flat spoon.

Glaze – Anything used to give a glossy surface to sweet or savoury foods.

Grate – Rub against a sharp or rough-edged grater to produce medium fine shreds.

Grill – Cooking by direct heat from above or below.

Infuse – What happens to your teabag when you pour hot water over it – the release of flavours in a hot liquid.

Julienne – Fine matchstick strips, most often used for crisp vegetables.

Legumes – Plants that bear seeds in the pod, eg peas, beans, lentils and tamarind.

Lightly fry – Heat a little oil (1 tbsp) in a heavy fry-pan. When it is hot, add food and cook over a high heat, turning often until either wilted, softened or lightly browned.

Macerate – Soaking fruits, biscuit or cake in a flavouring liquid, usually a liqueur or wine.

Marinate – Used to either flavour or tenderize food before cooking. Elements of a marinade usually include a tenderizer in the form of yoghurt, fruit juice or wine, flavours such as herbs and spices, and oil to carry flavours.

Mash – Crush into a fine texture, either by passing through a sieve, or with a fork or a vegetable masher.

Mayonnaise – One of the most versatile of sauces. An emulsion made with egg yolks and oil.

Mince – Chop so finely the ingredients look like a paste.

Palm sugar – A solid sweet sugar cake made from the boiled-down sap of coconut and palmyrah palms. Chop, crush or grate.

Pare – Remove the skin from fruits and vegetables.

Preserve – A means of keeping food for long periods, either by bottling, freezing, smoking or drying.

Purée – Blend, usually by machine, until mixture is fine, smooth and lump free.

Reduce – Boil hard until mixture reduces in volume, to intensify flavour and lightly thicken texture.

Refresh – Drain and cool under cold running water to prevent loss of colour in vegetables after pre-cooking.

Remove pin bones – The line of bones which runs up the middle of a salmon and trout fillet is easily removed by plucking them out individually with tweezers.

Rest – Stand meat or chicken after cooking to allow juices to disperse evenly. The larger the cut the longer it should rest – allow 2-3 minutes for steak and 10-15 minutes for larger roasts.

Scoring – Make shallow cuts in the surface of food to improve its flavour or appearance, or to help it cook quickly.

Searing – Brown meat quickly over a high heat in a little oil before grilling or roasting.

Season – Add salt and pepper to taste. Sea salt is usually coarser than fine salt. It weighs less per spoonful. For everyday cooking use iodised salt to ensure an adequate iodine intake.

Segmented – Usually refers to oranges or other citrus. After removing rind and pith, flesh is cut between the membranes to create small segments.

Separating eggs – Crack egg open by tapping the shell with a knife. Tip yolk from one half of shell to other,

taking care not to break, allowing the white to fall into a clean, dry, glass or china bowl. If using for meringue or where whites need to be stiffly beaten, make sure that no yolk breaks into whites and that there is no fat on your fingers.

Shave – Use a potato peeler to cut fine shavings.

Shred – Cut food into long thin slivers with a very sharp knife or coarse grater.

Shuck – Remove top shell of shellfish, eg oysters.

Simmer – Cook at a very gentle boil – liquid should just bubble a little, not fast. In a very gentle simmer, liquid just quivers on the surface.

Soak dried fruits – Cover dried fruits with water, alcohol or juice and leave for at least 1 hour to plump up. To hurry up the process, microwave for 1-2 minutes, then stand 20-30 minutes.

Springform cake pan – A cake pan with a loose bottom and a side lever to release it.

Sterilise – Necessary when preserving food. Preserving containers must be boiled or heated above 100°C to destroy all living organisms.

Stir-fry – Cook quickly in a wok or pan with a little oil and sometimes a little water, using a spoon or metal spatula to toss food while it cooks.

Stock – Extract from bones of meat, poultry or fish, or from vegetables, usually made by simmering ingredients for a long time in water to extract their essence. An important ingredient in soups and sauces.

Terrine – Originally the name of an earthenware cooking dish, it has come to mean a kind of baked meat cake which is served cold.

Toasting Nuts – Either place on a baking tray and bake at 200°C for 10-12 minutes, or microwave on 100% power for 2-3 minutes per cup, stirring every minute.

Toss – Combine gently in a scooping motion, used in salads to distribute dressing through ingredients evenly.

Weight – Weigh down a dish to condense texture.

Zest – Thin oily outer skin of citrus fruits. In cooking it refers to a thin shaving of orange, lime or lemon peel or the coloured part of the peel.

Index